Focus On OpenView

A Guide to Hewlett-Packard's Network and Systems Management Platform

Focus On OpenView

A Guide to Hewlett-Packard's Network and Systems Management Platform

Nathan J. Muller

Illustrations by:
Linda L. Tyke

Printed in the United States of America.

Trademark Acknowledgments
CA-UNICENTER is a registered trademark of Computer Associates International, Inc.
COMMAND is a registered trademark of ISICAD, Inc.
DECnet, LAT, VAX, and VMS are registered trademarks of Digital Equipment Corporation.
Ethernet is a trademark of Xerox Corporation.
HP and HP OpenView are registered trademarks of Hewlett-Packard Company.
Intel, 386, 486, and Pentium are trademarks of Intel Corporation.
MS-DOS is a registered trademark and Windows is a trademark of Microsoft Corporation.
NetLabs/DiMONS and NetLabs/NerveCenter are trademarks of NetLabs Inc.
NetWare is a trademark of Novell Inc.
OS/2, MVS, and SNA are trademarks of IBM Corporation.
OSF and OSF/Motif are registered trademarks of Open Software Foundation Inc.
SecurePath, Crossbow, Crossbow Plus, SmartLink, Extend24, Extend12, and LightWatch/
    Open are trademarks of Fibermux Corporation.
StationView, StationView/OV, StationView Agent, ServerView, and OpenSNA are trade-
    marks of Peregrine Systems, Inc.
The X Window System is a trademark of Massachusetts Institute of Technology.
UNIX is a registered trademark in the United States and other countries, licensed exclu-
    sively through X/Open Company, Ltd.

All other trademarks are the property of their respective owners.

Library of Congress Cataloging-in-Publication Data

Muller, Nathan J., 1949—
        A guide to Openview : applications for systems and network
        management / by Nathan J. Muller ; illustrations by Linda Lee Tyke.
        p.   cm.
        Includes index.
        ISBN 1-878956-48-5
    1. Computer networks — Management. 2.OpenView I. Title
        TK5105.5.M857 1995
        005.4'3—dc20   94-44372
                                                           CIP

Please address comments and questions to the publisher:
CBM Books
1300 Virginia Drive, Suite #400
Fort Washington, PA 19034
(215) 643-8000 FAX (215) 643-8099

Editor: Andrea J. Zavod
Editorial Coordinator: Debbie Hiller
Typesetting and Design: Patty Wall

To
Jim and Kathy
and their little ones,
Adam and Bethany

Table of Contents

Preface

THE CURRENT MARKET SUCCESS OF HP'S OPENVIEW IS APPARANT BY THE MANY internetworking vendors who use this network management system as the framework for managing bridges, routers and hubs. OpenView is installed on more than 35,000 networks worldwide, and it is expected to eclipse NetView in 1995, making it the premiere network management system. In addition, key portions of OpenView form the basis of the Open Software Foundation's (OSF) Distributed Management Environment (DME).

OPENVIEW IN PERSPECTIVE

Many industry analysts and consultants regard OpenView as one of the most technically advanced and architecturally elegant integrated network management solutions available today. Early on, however, there was a widespread perception that Hewlett-Packard lacked the market presence of the industry giants — AT&T, IBM and Digital Equipment Corp. — and that its accomplishments would be so overshadowed that not many companies would have an opportunity to be exposed to OpenView.

In recent years, the fortunes have turned for these giants. During 1992 and 1993, the management systems of AT&T, IBM and Digital underwent major shifts in market positioning, while another important management system, SunConnect's (now integrated into SunSoft, Inc.) SunNet Manager, rose to industry prominence along with OpenView[1].

Despite its promise, AT&T's Accumaster Integrator did not fare well during its seven-year life span. This forced AT&T to take a new approach. In mid-1994, it announced OneVision, an end-to-end management framework that incorporates HP's OpenView management platform, NetLabs' NerveCenter event correlation technology, and its own BaseWorX application development and runtime software. AT&T evaluated other platforms, including IBM's NetView/6000, but chose OpenView based on market de-

---

[1]In 1994, SunConnect, SunPro, SunSolutions and SunSelect, all formerly part of SunTechnology Enterprises, were integrated into SunSoft, which is now a single software company within Sun Microsystems Inc. SunNet Manager is now a product of SunSoft.

mand, application developer support and openness. By choosing HP's OpenView, AT&T acknowledged that it is the de facto standard platform for network and systems management.

In 1993, IBM announced a major shift in its network management strategy that entailed the replacement of host-based NetView with its AIX NetView/6000 platform, which is assuming the manager-of-managers role held by NetView. This move is intended to expand the scope of NetView from managing SNA networks to managing LANs, while increasing support for industry-leading databases and giving users the ability to scale the platform to handle increasingly larger networks.

Early on, IBM adopted OpenView as the foundation for its RISC-based NetView/6000 platform, until it suddenly decided to switch to the Tivoli Management Environment (TME). TME and OpenView use competing object management technologies. Although IBM decided not to license OpenView 4.0 as the basis for future versions of NetView/6000, it will continue to support the OpenView application programming interfaces (APIs) already in NetView/6000.

Digital has repackaged its DECmcc Director in favor of its Polycenter framework. The two are essentially the same, but Digital's sales have slumped in recent years because of a widespread perception that its products are proprietary. Digital has tried to overcome this reputation by renaming DECmcc to Polycenter, thus conveying a more open image. In 1994, with sales still lagging, Digital took the next step of announcing its intention to migrate Polycenter users to IBM's NetView/6000 platform. The new package is called Polycenter NetView.

When this book was written, it remained to be seen how current users of Digital's Polycenter framework and IBM's NetView/6000 will respond to such dramatic changes, especially because these network management platforms appeared to be stabilizing.

With the Big Three management system providers now struggling with difficulties that include revenue shortfalls from network management products (AT&T and Digital), organizational restructurings and product repositioning strategies (AT&T, Digital and IBM) and perceptual problems among would-be customers (AT&T and Digital), Hewlett-Packard and SunSoft along with IBM, have emerged as key players, in multivendor network management.[2]

---

[2]While Novell is trying to position its NetWare Management System as a platform for multivendor network management, so far it lacks the power and features to manage large, complex multivendor networks.

SunNet Manager is now a leading UNIX-based distributed network management system. It is installed on more than 20,000 networks. The system's protocol-independent, distributed management architecture supports the Simple Network Management Protocol (SNMP) and offers a comprehensive set of tools for automated fault isolation and network monitoring. It also automates management functions and includes a broad set of integrated tools.

Like Hewlett-Packard, SunSoft has a partners program that encourages third-party applications integration with SunNet Manager. In fact, SunSoft built its early lead over HP on strong third-party support. However, OpenView's success is largely because HP surpassed SunSoft in terms of the number of third-party applications available for it. Another reason for the relative decline of SunNet Manager is because SunSoft failed to improve the product's underlying technology, while HP pursued an aggressive upgrade program.

SunSoft is rethinking its approach to network management. Its new strategy calls for SunNet Manager to be deployed at the departmental level, with its new Encompass platform aimed at enterprise-wide management. Encompass is based on Dimons 3G (licensed from NetLabs Inc.), one of the leading distributed object-oriented management platforms currently available. Its request broker technology will enable Encompass to distribute management functions across geographically dispersed consoles, an important capability for global networks.

All of the major management platform providers support SNMP. Although it is the de facto industry standard for multivendor network management, SNMP is not well suited as an enterprise management system. Its reliance on centralized polling, for example, can consume too much internetwork bandwidth. It also is cumbersome to use and is not sufficiently flexible for many users. By comparison, OpenView and competing network management systems conserve bandwidth, go beyond SNMP in feature-richness, and provide sophisticated graphical user interfaces (GUIs) that hide the programs' underlying complexity to simplify useage. Nevertheless, OpenView and competing offerings use SNMP as a domain manager, enabling the SNMP-compliant components of other vendors to be managed on the same network.

Hewlett-Packard's stated goal is for OpenView to become the DOS of the network management realm, becoming so prevalent that every major network management vendor will want to develop products to run on top of it. If OpenView's meteoric success is any indication, this is no idle boast. Aside from the HP environment, there are OpenView network and system management applications for DEC, IBM, Novell, Sun and UNIX environments. In fact, there are more than 170 complementary OpenView-based network and system management solutions available on a variety of platforms, including HP 9000 and HP 3000 business systems and servers, SunOS-based workstations and Microsoft Windows PCs. In addition, OpenView is licensed to Hitachi, Data General, Groupe Bull and IBM.

This book is not meant to imply that HP's OpenView is flawless. Perhaps the most glaring weakness of the platform is its lack of a fully distributed management capability, which is essential for managing large enterprise networks. A distributed management capability would allow the use of multiple local workstations, which would filter gathered data before sending only the critical information to the central console. Whereas today's large enterprise networks may consist of tens of thousands of nodes, currently OpenView can manage only 4,000 network nodes. The only way to manage larger networks is to run multiple copies of OpenView, which cannot communicate with each other. OpenView also lacks a common data repository which, among other things, would permit third-party applications to be more tightly integrated with the platform and allow network administrators to view several variety of network types on a single map.

Despite these serious limitations, OpenView has proven itself to be a popular and reliable management platform. But networks have grown in size and sophistication since the platform was designed in the 1980s. In 1994, Hewlett-Packard outlined its next generation of OpenView which promises to remedy these deficiencies.

SOLUTION CATEGORIES

A strategic asset of OpenView is the HP OpenView Solution Partners Program, which encourages third-party development of complementary management applications. The various network and system management products described in this book are categorized by Hewlett-Packard according to their level of HP involvement:

- **HP OpenView Premier Solution:** Solutions in this category have achieved the highest level of integration with the HP OpenView platform in key application areas.

- **HP OpenView Certified Solution:** Applications in this category have passed qualification testing by HP for one or more levels of integration with HP OpenView, providing customers with an added measure of confidence regarding interoperability.

- **HP OpenView OEM:** These companies resell HP OpenView products bundled with their value-added management applications, generally under their own name. This combination of HP OpenView and OEM applications provides turnkey solutions for their customers. Complete support for the turnkey solution is provided by the original equipment manufacturer (OEM).

- **HP OpenView Solution:** This category of products provides HP OpenView complementary functionality. Solutions in this category typically only make use of the OpenView GUI.

There also is the category of HP OpenView Systems Integrator. Firms in this category provide HP OpenView system and network management integration, consulting and custom software services.

GOALS

This book has three goals:

- To introduce OpenView as a network management platform and explain its most important technical features.

- To explain the various components of OpenView and their functions.

- To discuss important applications available from Hewlett-Packard and third-party developers, thereby providing a sense of OpenView's depth and breadth as a platform for network and systems management.

This book also covers many practical issues confronted by network and systems managers on a daily basis. Professionals who are new to these fields will gain insight into day-to-day operations, especially as they relate to:

- Alarm and fault management.

- Automated operations.

- Capacity planning.

- Configuration management.

- Inventory management.

- Management reporting.

- Performance management.

- Security management.

This book is particularly valuable to those who need a central source of introductory information on OpenView. It also will be helpful for those who have progressed in planning or implementing network management systems and need further input into their decision-making processes.

The book is written to be understood by anyone with a basic knowledge of UNIX and Simple Network Management Protocol (SNMP). The content is written in sufficient detail to properly orient network technicians, managers and administrators to the OpenView platform as well as to some of the the key network and system applications that can be integrated with it. This book also provides useful information for consultants, systems integrators and applications developers who need a concise reference on one of today's most popular and reliable network management platforms.

The information contained in this book, especially as it relates to specific vendors and products, is believed to be accurate at the time it was written and is, of course, subject to change with continued advancements in technology and shifts in market forces. The mention of specific products and vendors is for illustration purposes only and does not constitute or imply an endorsement of any kind by the author or the publisher.

— Nathan J. Muller

Acknowledgments

I want to acknowledge the following people and organizations for their valuable assistance in preparing this book:

Yogesh Gupta and Michael Kornspan at Computer Associates International, Inc.

John Elliott, Eric Olinger and Laura Jordan at Peregrine Systems, Inc.

Kelly Emo, Robert Kraekel, John Petrera, Karen Cunningham and Belinda Yung-Rubke at Hewlett-Packard Co.

Wendy Campanela and Paddy Jane Farrell at ADC Fibermux Corp.

Francine Plaza at NetLabs, Inc.

Bruce Anderson, George Christensen, Tammy Fennell and Lori Wahl at ISICAD, Inc.

Janet Burnett at Remedy Corp.

Jill Huntington-Lee of Brandywine Network Associates.

The OpenView Framework

HP's OpenView is a framework within which a portfolio of system and network applications reside to address all of the management activities defined by the International Organization for Standardization (ISO) and expanded by Hewlett-Packard. Within this framework, HP addresses these key management areas:

- **Fault management:** identifies, classifies and reports problems; analyzes network faults for causes; and furnishes a resolution by directing operators or initiating automatic restorals of faulty components.

- **Configuration management:** collects and stores information about circuits, hardware and software on the network; enables or disables network components; and distributes network information and systems application software.

- **Security management:** tracks information flow within network nodes and across network links; and identifies sources of network misuse and unauthorized access.

- **Accounting management:** charges cost centers for network access and controls levels of usage; and furnishes usage information to help prepare communications budgets and to justify network expansion.

- **Performance management:** helps to monitor network usage and tune network and application components.

- **Operations management:** provides the tools necessary for ensuring system integrity and an optimum grade of service.

- **Storage management:** provides the tools necessary for ensuring file backup and archiving as well as the seamless movement of files from backup to archive and back to the system when needed.

In OpenView, Hewlett-Packard provides a flexible, open platform for integrating multivendor systems and network management capabilities. The HP OpenView architecture offers a model for incorporating object-oriented management applications based on international standards such as the OSF/Motif graphical user interface, Simple Network Management Protocol (SNMP), TCP/IP, Common Management Information Protocol (CMIP) over TCP/IP (CMOT), and CMIP over OSI.

As part of HP's multivendor approach to network management, it also has extended management functionality to IBM SNA and Novell NetWare environments. Through the OpenView Solution Partners Program, management functionality is extended to these and other environments.

Hewlett-Packard's OpenView strategy is designed to integrate all systems and network management capabilities across all devices within the network. It addresses various user requirements, ranging from standalone element managers to customizable integrated network management systems. It is a hardware-independent management platform that incorporates the best features of existing standards, surpassing them in the realm of the user interface. OpenView's user interface, data management and communications services furnish users with consistent functions using shared data.

SYSTEM MANAGEMENT

OpenView provides many applications for system management tasks, including products for:

- **Backup/Recovery:** for central backup of networked environments, unattended operation and high-speed recovery.

- **Hierarchical storage management:** for efficient management of large amounts of on-line data across magnetic and optical storage media.

- **Performance management:** for the collection and analysis of performance data used to calculate future resource requirements.

- **Output spooling:** for central administration of the distributed spooling environment, including control of form and font handling, security and paper jam recovery.

- **Software distribution and installation:** for central network-wide software distribution and installation.

These management applications facilitate central monitoring and control of multiple systems, which can be located at the central site or distributed among remote sites.

NETWORK MANAGEMENT

OpenView supplies the ability to fully integrate LAN and WAN multivendor environments under central control. The application portfolio includes products that perform:

- **Management of network elements:** Various products provide configuration, monitoring and control for bridges, routers, hubs, terminal servers, switches and packet assembler-disassemblers (PADs). HP devices are supported as are the devices of other vendors that use standardized management protocols, such as the Simple Network Management Protocol (SNMP).

- **Distributed LAN management through probes:** Through a variety of monitors and analyzers, link level network messages are collected, node statistics generated, and the protocols of different network layers decoded to aid problem resolution.

- **Management of multivendor Transmission Control Protocol/ Internet Protocol (TCP/IP) networks:** HP provides centralized fault, configuration and performance management for a network of TCP/IP nodes. Network resources are discovered, mapped and monitored automatically. Events, trends and statistics can be collected and displayed. Threshold-based alerts can cause a corresponding symbol on the map to be highlighted.

OPENVIEW COMPONENTS

The OpenView framework provides an infrastructure for the management of computing environments, from single LANs to global WANs. It allows management activities to be structured, from centralized to distributed, according to specific organizational or user needs.

There are four major components of HP's OpenView framework (Figure 1-1):

- User Interface Presentation Services.

- Distributed Communications Infrastructure.

- Data Store Management.

- Communication Protocols.

PRESENTATION SERVICES

HP has placed significant emphasis on standardizing the user interface, which is handled by the User Interface Presentation Services component of OpenView. OpenView Windows OSF/Motif, based on X Windows, provides a consistent graphical user interface (GUI) across network management applications. From a single display, a network administrator can view a graphical representation of network components and their interrelationships, make configuration changes, run diagnostics and gather performance statistics.

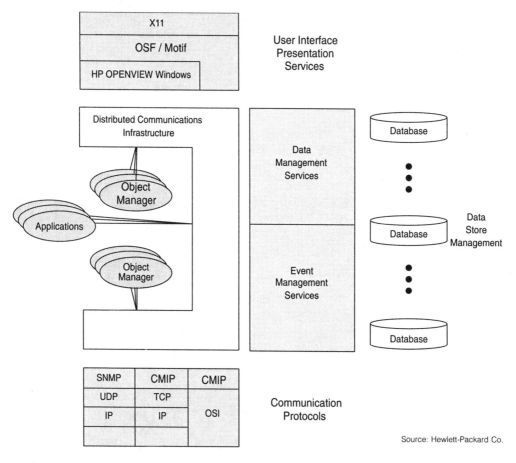

Source: Hewlett-Packard Co.

Figure 1-1: Hewlett-Packard's OpenView

X Windows: The X Window System, version 11 (also known as X11) was developed at the Massachusetts Institute of Technology (MIT) and is now an American National Standards Institute (ANSI) standard. It was developed as a platform on which various user interfaces can be implemented. The particulars of a user interface are determined by the X clients running on the system. X clients are programs that use X Windows to display information and receive input; OSF/Motif is one such client. X11 separates window functions into two parts: the application program and the display station. The two parts communicate through network protocols such as TCP/IP. The X11 implementation also allows multiple operators to share a common map display running off the same network management server.

Motif: Developed by the Open Software Foundation (OSF) in 1989, Motif provides a complete set of tools to help developers create applications that run in the X environment. Motif is comprised of a libraries of graphical objects, such as buttons and menus; a windowing manager that allows programmers and users to control the style and size of the windows that appear on-screen; and a style guide to help programmers with interface design.

OpenView Windows: The OpenView Windows developer's kit provides software templates that allow network administrators to create basic routines for menu-handling, data entry, windows management and other routine tasks. The developer's kit includes programming tools that aid in resource optimization and application concurrence testing.

New object classes or extensions to existing object classes are defined using the kit's metadata compiler. Object classes, attributes, actions and events are defined using templates that can be compiled into ISO ASN.1 notation, as is executed within the OSI management standards.

The development kit also includes on-line help software that allows administrators to create on-line help for each new application. The help function handles indexing, querying and hypertext access.

OVDraw is the run-time component of OpenView Windows that provides a facility for creating and editing maps and icons. The icons represent various network devices and are linked on the map using subnet symbols. There can be multiple, independent maps, each with several layers. This multilevel display capability helps organize and manage the many devices on an internet.

DISTRIBUTED COMMUNICATIONS INFRASTRUCTURE

As its name implies, the Distributed Communications Infrastructure makes it possible for management applications to access the services of OpenView across a network, without needing to know where the service components are located. The communications infrastructure consists of a Postmaster, Local Registration Files, and the OpenView Communications Infrastructure API (OVc API).

Postmaster: The Postmaster provides basic message routing services between network management components. It operates as a table-based, object-oriented message router. The routing table is the focus of the Postmaster's functionality and is itself a managed object. Given a message — perhaps from an application — addressed to a specific managed object, the Postmaster searches for the managed object's name in the routing table to find the information necessary to deliver it. The fields in the Postmaster's routing table provide the managed object name, the communication profile number and profile-specific data. The information needed to perform the name-to-address translation can be retrieved from a directory service.

Local Registration Files: Local Registration Files maintain the identity and location of objects and corresponding object managers in the network. When an application request is made, the Postmaster uses address information in the Local Registration Files to automatically route the request to the correct network address.

OVc API: The OVc API is the means by which access is provided to the communications protocols, management services, and object managers which reside in the network management server, including those used in conjunction with SNMP, CMIP and CMOT.

EVENT MANAGEMENT AND DATA MANAGEMENT SERVICES
Access to Event Management and Data Management services and communications protocols is provided by the communications infrastructure in the network management server. Event Management services gather and forward such events as node failures and application changes, while Data Management services allow information about network elements to be stored in a common location.

Event Management Services: Event Management services provides a central point to generate, receive and log network events such as component failures, object state changes and security violations. This facility routes these events to management applications and historical logs. It also stores events in an event log for future reference or historical analysis of critical parameters, device performance, network traffic and resource use.

The OpenView Event Sieve Agent collects and reports events. It runs on all nodes to route and deliver events to management applications. On the managed node, the sieve agent forwards event reports from the generating node to the sieve agent on the management station. On the management station, the sieve agent delivers incoming event reports to any management applications or agents that have registered for the event.

Applications can request receipt of specific events by registering one or more Event Sieves. An event sieve is an object used by the Event Sieve Agent to associate applications with the events in which they have interest. An event sieve also may be used to forward events from a managed node to the management station. In this case, the event sieve identifies the destination for the event report.

Event Sieve Managers determine which other server nodes should receive copies of particular events, and they also route events to registered applications. The routing of events across servers is controlled by a distribution list, which is a simple ASCII file edited manually by operations administrators.

Data Management Services: Data Management Services organizes data access to protect the application developer needing to know the details of data storage, eliminating the requirement for a data storage subsystem. Instead, data is stored in a common, shared data store. Data Management Services implements a common, shared data store for all applications and management services on the server. Access to stored data is through a set of application programming interfaces (APIs) that protect developers from dependence on the actual physical structure of the database. The server's Data Manager stores and retrieves all data in object form (i.e., as instances of defined object classes). The APIs in the network management server provide the set of service elements defined by the CMIS standard (Figure 1-2).

A key feature of Data Management Services is *metadata*, a database representation of all MIB[1] information which enables applications to dynamically adapt to and use new objects. The metadata compiler — available in the developer's kit — integrates information about each new object into the MIB.

This object-oriented programmability makes it possible to manipulate information about objects. In this scheme, network elements are described as *objects*, even if they are not managed using the OSI protocols. Modules, called object managers, translate between the object-oriented procedures within OpenView and whatever mechanisms the real element uses to send and receive management data.

---

[1] The management information base (MIB) is the collection of management information that can be accessed through SNMP. The SNMP agent contains the intelligence required to access the various MIB values.

References to stored data can use the scoping and filtering mechanisms defined in CMIS that allow for the selection of multiple object instances in a single reference. By designing its API to conform to CMIS, HP enables applications to retrieve information from the network or the database using the same syntax.

The actual database delivered with the server is specially engineered to meet the performance requirements of real-time network management. HP provides a facility for exporting data from the database to an SQL-compatible database management system (DBMS).

DATA STORE MANAGEMENT

Data Store Management provides database and event management services through interfaces to standards-based database management systems where information such as topological, event and problem resolution data, is stored. SQL provides the means to create reports and track historical data.

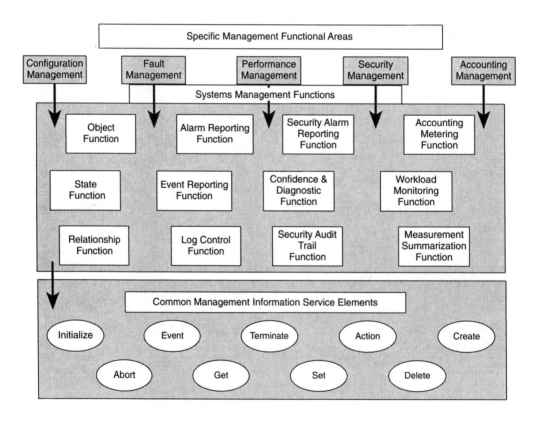

Figure 1-2: Common Management Information Service Elements

The actual repository for systems and network management information is the Ingres database management system (DBMS). HP is extending OpenView to include other databases, starting with Oracle's Oracle 7 database and following with Informix and Sybase. In the future, HP will offer database-independent repository technology based on Microsoft's Open Data Base Connectivity (ODBC) standard.

COMMUNICATIONS PROTOCOLS

The Communications Protocols component of OpenView implements OSI and TCP/IP management protocols between the network management server and managed objects. Management applications programs access these common services through a set of APIs implemented by the Distributed Communications Infrastructure.

HP's implementation of SNMP includes enhancements, such as automatic retry of requests that time out and access to aggregate objects without performing repeated get requests.

MANAGEMENT SOLUTIONS

Hewlett-Packard offers two development platforms: one is based on SNMP; the other embraces OSI-based CMIP and CMOT, as well as SNMP. Both platforms consist of a developer's kit and run-time program, which run on HP 9000 Series 300, 400, 600, 700 and 800 systems, SunOS and Solaris systems.

SNMP MANAGEMENT PRODUCTS

SNMP specifies a structure for formatting messages and for transmitting information between reporting devices and data-collection programs. As such, it supports transaction-based queries such as get, put and set. The SNMP devices are polled for performance-related information, which is passed to the network management server. Alarms also are passed to the server. There, the gathered information can be viewed by the network management station to pinpoint problems on the network or stored for later analysis.

SNMP is a flexible network management protocol that can be used to manage virtually any object. An *object* is an abstraction of the real resource being managed: hardware, software, or a logical association such as a connection or virtual circuit. A functional definition of an object is held in a management information base (MIB).

There are three MIB formats: SNMP MIB I and MIB II, which are IETF standards; and private or extended MIBs, also referred to as enterprise-specific MIBs or proprietary MIBs, which are defined by vendors for use with their own products.

Issued in 1990 the first MIB, MIB I, is primarily concerned with Internet Protocol (IP) routing variables used for interconnecting different networks. There are 110 objects that form the core of the standard SNMP MIB.

The latest generation, MIB II, in addition to IP, is designed to provide real-time protocol management for devices that use External Gateway Protocol (EGP), Internet Control Message Protocol (ICMP) and Transmission Control Protocol (TCP). There are 165 objects that form the core of MIB II.

The type and number of objects always is expanding. The MIBs extend SNMP capabilities to a variety of media and network devices, marking a shift from Ethernets and TCP/IP wide area networks to all media types used on LANs and WANs. Many vendors want to add value to their products by making them more manageable, so they create private extensions to the standard MIB, which may include 200 or more additional objects.

The MIBs determine the alarm and reporting characteristics of each device on the network. Under SNMP, for example, each network element must be equipped with an agent that can monitor the device (called an object), collect performance data, and send requested information to the network management station.

The part of the management protocol that sits on the managed element — the agent — has the basic duty of keeping certain information (usually counters, such as the number of bad packets during a specific period) as defined in the MIB. It then responds to requests for that information from the management side of the protocol. The agent also can respond to a certain set of commands from the management station, also as defined in the MIB.

HP's SNMP management products consist of the OpenView SNMP Developer's Kit and the OpenView SNMP Platform. Both are used for building and running applications that manage TCP/IP networks. HP's Network Node Manager is one such application. It provides fault, configuration and performance management of multivendor TCP/IP networks.

Developer's Kit: The Developer's Kit includes the header files and libraries necessary to develop applications using the HP OpenView SNMP APIs. (The Developer's Kit includes the SNMP Platform and the API libraries.) The kit supports two major APIs: the Direct SNMP API and the HP OpenView Windows API.

The Direct SNMP API provides access to the protocol stack to perform management operations on SNMP devices. It includes programmatic access to the HP OpenView trap dispatcher so that applications can receive and process traps (events) sent to the network management station.

The OpenView Windows API provides programmatic access to OpenView Windows for interacting with the network map, drawing and modifying application-specific submaps, and registering applications in a menu bar.

SNMP Platform: The OpenView SNMP Platform contains the executable files needed to run OpenView applications developed by HP or third-parties with the SNMP Developer's Kit. It includes OpenView Windows, automatic IP node discovery and map creation, the SNMP run-time library, trap handling, and a MIB loader and MIB browser — both accessible by end users.

Both the Developer's Kit and Platform can, as an option, contain the run-time version of the Ingres SQL relational database, which is used to store topology information gathered by the SNMP Platform.

Figure 1-3 summarizes the HP OpenView SNMP Management products. Figure 1-4 summarizes the functional interrelationship of Network Node Manager with the SNMP Developer's Kit and SNMP Platform.

DISTRIBUTED MANAGEMENT PRODUCTS

OpenView Distributed Management products (the Developer's Kit and Platform) represent the next generation of OpenView Network Management Server products that initially were released in mid-1990. Distributed Management products offer updated versions of Network Management Server components, including the Communications Infrastructure and its related components: metadata, object registration and event management services.

The Distributed Management products provide an application development and run-time environment for creating network and system management solutions. In addition to SNMP, CMIP and CMOT are supported to extend the range of Distributed Management products into the OSI environment. Other OpenView applications, including Network Node Manager, can operate on the Distributed Management Platform.

Like SNMP, CMIP is an object-oriented management protocol that keeps a database of objects, each with an ability to represent an actual network device, such as a workstation, bridge or router. The database also defines the relationships among the objects. Network management software, in turn, uses the data stored in the CMIP database to monitor network performance.

SNMP operates over the User Datagram Protocol/Internet Protocol (UDP/IP), so its agents require only a four-layer protocol stack to support network management. In contrast, CMIP agents — software that resides on each network element to be managed — must use OSI's full seven-layer protocol stack, which requires more memory than most network devices have to spare. A typical CMIP agent requires 400 kbytes or more of memory, whereas an SNMP agent needs between 20 kbytes and 60 kbytes.

Being datagram-based, SNMP is a connectionless protocol. Because a path is always available, a session does not need to be established before information can be sent to the network management station. CMIP, on the other hand, is a connection-based protocol; that is, the agent and manager must establish a connection before passing information, ensuring its safe arrival at the network management station. This method entails a higher overhead burden on both the agent and network management system.

CMOT is merely CMIP running over TCP/IP. CMOT is the CMIP protocol that interfaces to applications built on Common Management Information Services (CMIS). The only difference is that CMIP has been modified to run on top of TCP and UDP transports. The modifications involve writing a minimal presentation layer and eliminating the session

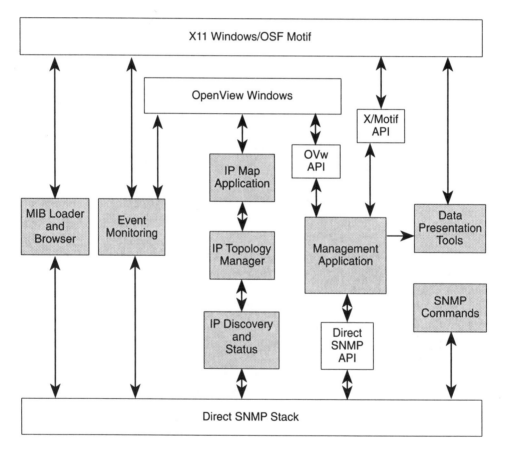

Source: Hewlett-Packard Co.

Figure 1-3: *HP OpenView SNMP Platform*

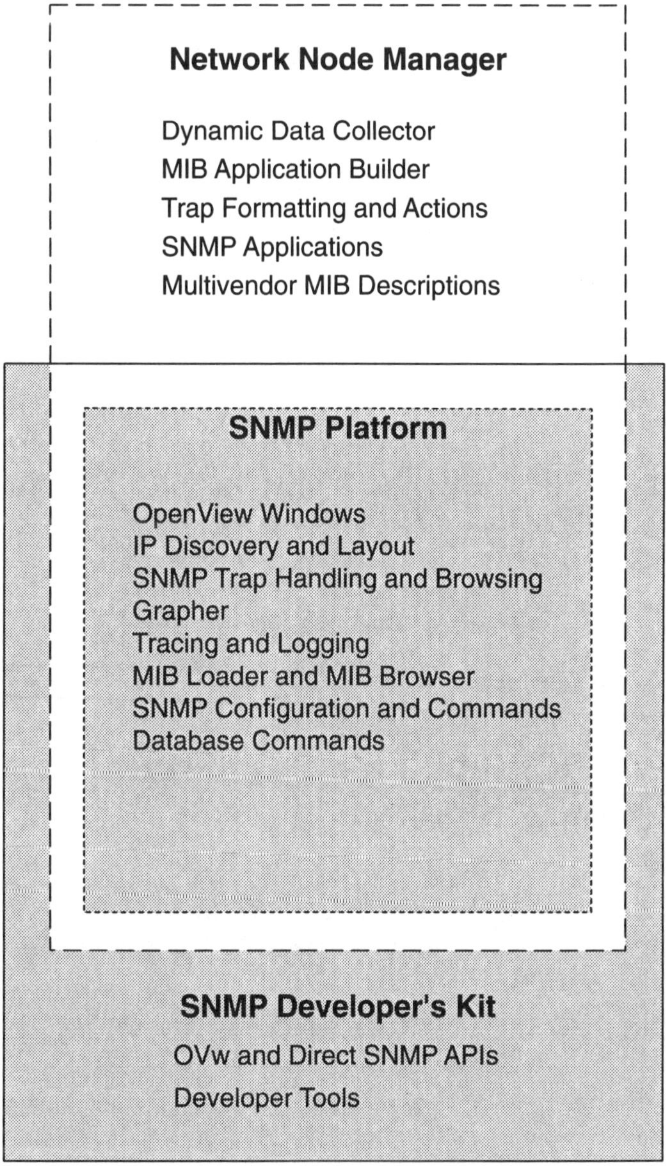

Network Node Manager

Dynamic Data Collector
MIB Application Builder
Trap Formatting and Actions
SNMP Applications
Multivendor MIB Descriptions

SNMP Platform

OpenView Windows
IP Discovery and Layout
SNMP Trap Handling and Browsing
Grapher
Tracing and Logging
MIB Loader and MIB Browser
SNMP Configuration and Commands
Database Commands

SNMP Developer's Kit

OVw and Direct SNMP APIs

Developer Tools

Source: Hewlett-Packard Co.

Figure 1-4: Functional Interrelationship: Network Node Manager, SNMP Developer's Kit and SNMP Platform

layer, neither of which is explicitly supported in the TCP/IP architecture. The full protocol is implemented on both management stations and managed elements, and requires only 60 kbytes to 120 kbytes of memory.

Originally, CMOT was envisioned as the transition between SNMP and CMIP, making some of the greater functionality of OSI network management applications available on TCP/IP. However, it has not worked out that way. SNMP has proved to be a popular management protocol and, consequently, few vendors support CMOT. Early in the development of OpenView, HP made the decision to support CMOT because there were no CMIP objects out there to be managed and CMOT looked promising at the time.

Developer's Kit: The Distributed Management Developer's Kit provides a standards-based environment for object definition, management protocol access and applications programming. It provides all header files and libraries needed to create OpenView applications. The corresponding Distributed Management Platform, a run-time copy of which is included in the Developer's Kit to facilitate applications testing, then can be used to manage a diverse set of objects and protocols.

The Developer's Kit contains all the APIs provided in the SNMP Developer's Kit (OpenView Windows and Direct SNMP APIs), plus the X/Open Management Protocol (XMP) and related X/Open Object Manipulation (XOM) APIs. The XMP API provides programmatic access to both SNMP and CMIS services, and provides access to Event Management Services that filter, route and log events.

These tools include an XMP package generator and an XOM code generator that allow developers to run object definitions through the package and code generators, which build the code automatically. These tools hide the complexity of the APIs.

The Developer's Kit can be used to write manager and agent applications, including proxy agents used for managing non-SNMP devices.

A contribution file also is provided with the Developer's Kit, which includes a public domain ASN.1 compiler, utility routines, hypertext help system, and fully functional and reusable sample applications for maximizing programmer productivity.

Distributed Management Platform: In addition to support for OSI-based CMIP and CMOT objects, the Distributed Management Platform discovers and manages IP-addressable, SNMP MIB II, and user-defined SNMP devices. These features are provided by the OpenView SNMP Platform, which is fully contained within the OpenView Distributed Management Platform (Figure 1-5).

This means that the platform can run applications written using the SNMP Developer's Kit, such as Network Node Manager. (Figure 1-6 illustrates the relationship of components in the Distributed Management Platform.) In fact, the Distributed Management Platform can run all of the processes available in the SNMP Platform, including OpenView Windows and the IP discovery, mapping and monitoring routines. The Distributed Management Platform provides further run-time support for applications based on XMP, allowing consolidated access to SNMP, CMOT and CMIP protocols.

Both the Developer's Kit and Platform can contain the optional Ingres SQL relational database, which is a repository of selected OpenView information.

Also optional for the Developer's Kit and Platform is the CMIP stack. This option requires the presence of the full OSI stack, which is offered separately through the HP OSI Transport Services (OTS) product. This requirement makes the CMIP option available only on HP-UX (HP's version of UNIX) systems.

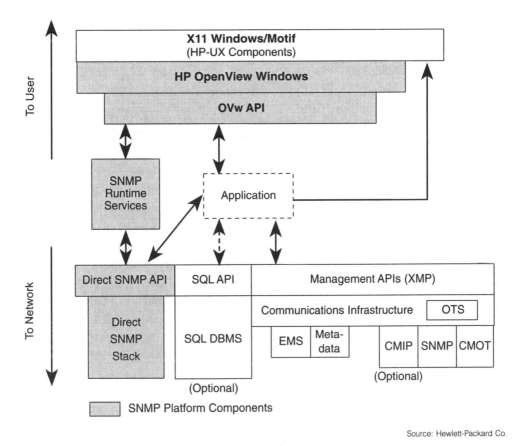

Source: Hewlett-Packard Co.

Figure 1-5: HP OpenView Distributed Management Platform

CMIP is the OSI protocol for the interchange of CMIS service requests such as get, set, create and event (see Figure 1-2). CMIP specifies the protocol and CMIS defines the services. As noted, CMIS service requests and responses also can be transported in an IP environment, by the Distributed Management Platform, using the CMOT protocol. In addition to CMIP, other key Distributed Management services have been enhanced to further support ISO specifications for addressing and events.

The HP OpenView Distributed Management Platform with the CMIP option conforms, in varying degrees, to both the OMNIPoint 1 specification and the U.S. Government Network Management Profile (GNMP). HP's conformance with the OMNIPoint 1 Management Communications category is the key to OpenView's interoperability with other conformant management applications.

DME COMPLIANCE

Hewlett-Packard plans to bring OpenView into full compliance with the Distributed Management Environment (DME) as the Open Software Foundation formalizes the specification and makes DME framework components available. DME has been in development since 1991 and originally was intended to be an industry standard for network management that combined the best technologies from many vendors. The idea was that vendors would license the technology from OSF and use it in their products, which — because of a common base — would all be compatible.

From the users perspective, the purpose of the DME initiative was to create standards to allow network administrators to pool tools and applications from different network management systems providers and allow them to operate on many different platforms.

The object orientation of DME was intended to allow application developers to write a consistent set of functions and APIs. Network nodes and code are rolled into objects that developers can use to write the application code. The objects shield the application developer from needing to know where and how data is stored among different platforms, for example. Because objects consist of self-contained code, they are reusable elsewhere. This quickens application development and contributes to consistency.

The HP OpenView Distributed Management product technologies were selected by OSF for DME. The Communications Infrastructure and related metadata services are core components of the DME network management option. Network map components of the DME Management User Interface were drawn from HP OpenView Windows. The XMP API, co-developed by HP and Groupe Bull, is the standard network management API in the DME development environment.

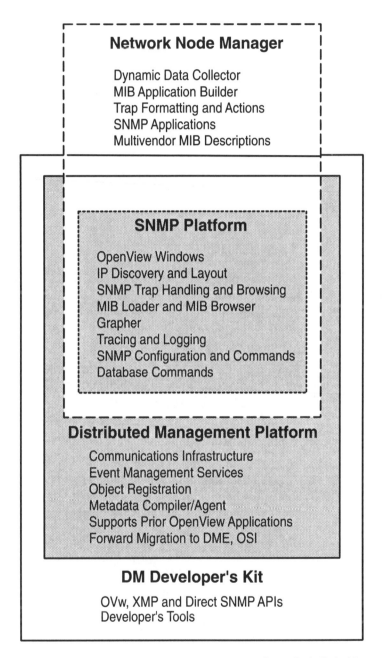

Network Node Manager

Dynamic Data Collector
MIB Application Builder
Trap Formatting and Actions
SNMP Applications
Multivendor MIB Descriptions

SNMP Platform

OpenView Windows
IP Discovery and Layout
SNMP Trap Handling and Browsing
MIB Loader and MIB Browser
Grapher
Tracing and Logging
SNMP Configuration and Commands
Database Commands

Distributed Management Platform

Communications Infrastructure
Event Management Services
Object Registration
Metadata Compiler/Agent
Supports Prior OpenView Applications
Forward Migration to DME, OSI

DM Developer's Kit

OVw, XMP and Direct SNMP APIs
Developer's Tools

Source: Hewlett-Packard Co.

Figure 1-6: *Functional Relationship: Network Node Manager, SNMP Platform, Distributed Management Platform and DM Developer's Kit*

As a technology provider and one of DME's integrators, HP is well positioned to provide early DME-compliant products. This was demonstrated in 1992 with the release of HP OpenView Interconnect Lite, a network management application based on the defined portions of DME. HP OpenView Interconnect Lite implements the DME's user interface specification, which provides a consistent approach for interacting with different vendors' management applications. The program manages interconnected Ethernet and Token Ring LANs from an HP-UX 700 Series workstation or a SunOS workstation. The software discovers, maps and monitors any LAN device that has an IP address. The application also monitors and controls HP products and provides fault isolation, fault management and router configuration.

The introduction of OpenView Distributed Management Platform Version 4.0 in January 1994 marked the first appearance of the DME's Network Management Option (NMO) in product form.

The NMO is one of three main DME components that also includes Distributed Services and the Object Management Framework (OMF). The NMO is the CMIP and SNMP part of the DME. Distributed Services include software distribution, printing, event management, license management and PC services and they can be run on any LAN-attached computer. The OMF includes the management request broker, which is an object-oriented request broker that simplifies development and use of network and systems management applications.

HP expects to offer more than DME in its Distributed Management Platform. In addition to SNMP Version 2, the platform will provide expanded support of OSI, including evolving ITU-TSS[2] X.700 systems management functions, and selected OMNIPoint and Network Management Forum standards. This added management functionality, not supported by DME, is essential for a complete enterprise management solution.

Although release of the final DME specification has been delayed several times and vendor interest seems to be waning, the exercise has led to some beneficial industry consolidation, such as IBM's decision to base its NetView/6000 first on HP's OpenView and then on Tivoli's TME, and Digital's decision to use IBM's NetView/6000 as its network management platform. Many industry analysts also credit the quick success of OpenView to DME. Having incorporated the technology that DME selected, HP answered many user reservations about the continued viability of the enterprise manager concept.

---

[2] The International Telecommunications Union-Telecommunications Standardization Sector (ITU-TSS) is the successor to the Consultative Committee for International Telegraphy and Telephony (CCITT).

OPENVIEW BENEFITS

OpenView offers several key benefits for users, application developers and third-party vendors:

- OpenView provides a framework for integrating multivendor systems and network management software.

- OpenView's task-oriented approach allows users to select management applications based on their needs. The applications enable users to build a modular, scalable network management system and integrate applications from multiple vendors.

- HP provides tools for integrating existing applications with new technologies with minimal reprogramming.

- HP provides a family of interoperable development platforms that provide a smooth path to DME. This allows application developers to focus on their specific differentiators and time-to-market.

- HP uses object-oriented technology, helping application developers to attain shorter development cycles.

- The architecture and the products within the OpenView family employ both SNMP and CMIP. By using both protocols, users gain a considerable amount of flexibility in implementing standards.

OPENVIEW WEAKNESSES

Perhaps the most glaring weakness of the OpenView platform is the absence of a true distributed management capability. Currently, OpenView does not provide a way for other workstations to handle local management tasks or the capability to filter management data so only the most critical information is sent to the central management console. Both are essential for managing large enterprise networks. Although it is possible to run multiple copies of OpenView to manage large networks, they cannot communicate with each other. At this writing, a new version of the OpenView platform is being updated to include distributed discovery, event notification and problem management. It also will let local management systems intelligently filter information before sending it to a central console.

When OpenView supports SNMP2, it will be able to take advantage of its integral security features. Under the new distributed architecture, however, OpenView will be able to use SNMP2 agents to distribute polling information to other management workstations on the network. This will enable OpenView to send agents across tens of thousands of nodes — an increase from its current limit of 4,000.

Another weakness of OpenView is its lack of a common data repository. The current platform requires third-party applications to acquire their own topology and configuration information and event handling data. This is an inefficient process that consumes an inordinate amount of system and network resources. The new OpenView platform will add a common data repository that will allow topology, configuration and event handling information to be stored in one place and be accessible to third-party applications. Instead of using HP's existing proprietary flatfile database, the repository's data schema specifies an information structure that third-party system and network management application developers can use to read and write from the database. This permits a tighter integration between applications and the management platform. Among other advantages, this will allow network administrators to view a variety of network types — including DECnet, SNA and NetWare — on a single map.

THE HP OPENVIEW ARCHITECTURE IS DERIVED FROM THE OSI MANAGEMENT framework and optimized to include TCP/IP networks. Object-oriented concepts and technology are fundamental to OpenView. The architecture reduces the multidimensional management problem to a single dimension by using a common object model for describing all resources to be managed.

In OpenView, HP has developed a hardware-independent platform that incorporates the best features of existing standards and enhances them in the realm of the user interface. The platform can reside on powerful yet relatively inexpensive UNIX (i.e., HP-UX) workstations without requiring a single host in the form of a minicomputer or mainframe. In addition, HP continues to steer OpenView development toward full DME compliance.

Even with its obvious limitations, OpenView has become a popular and reliable platform for network and systems management. With the next release of OpenView, which makes it a true distributed platform with a common data repository, OpenView stands a good chance of continuing as the platform of choice for the rest of this decade and beyond.

CHAPTER

2

OpenView for Windows

HP OPENVIEW FOR WINDOWS IS A NETWORK AND SYSTEM MANAGEMENT software platform that offers multivendor and multinetwork operating system management from a Microsoft Windows-based PC. It features an enhanced graphical user interface (GUI) that supports Windows style guidelines, a status and toolbar for quick access to frequently used commands, and simplified application registration.

The platform's autodiscovery and layout capabilities find all Internet Protocol (IP) and Internet Packet Exchange (IPX) devices on the network and arrange them hierarchically on the network map. It also supports the simultaneous display of multiple network submaps, allowing network administrators to view different portions of the network at the same time.

OpenView for Windows includes an SNMP Manager that allows network administrators to develop simple SNMP management applications that can be launched directly from the network map's pull-down menu. These applications can browse, poll and graph management information base (MIB) variables. The SNMP Manager includes a library of precompiled MIBs, with which other MIBs that are not in the library, can be generated.

While HP OpenView UNIX products, such as Network Node Manager, are designed to manage enterprise networks of more than 1,000 nodes, HP OpenView for Windows is designed for smaller networks from site networks to workgroups. Although they cannot communicate with each other directly, the two platforms can be used side-by-side to manage the complete corporate network, from the enterprise down to the local workgroup (Figure 2-1).

The platform's open applications programming interfaces (APIs) have allowed software developers to build powerful end-user management applications. These applications allow network administrators to create a network topology map and monitor network events and alarms.

Until mid-1994, OpenView for Windows was sold exclusively through HP's OEM partners as an applications platform for managing hubs, routers and PC LANs. A hub manufacturer, for example, might purchase the OpenView for Windows Development Kit to develop a user-friendly GUI for its own management application, and then sell the entire package. Now OpenView for Windows is being offered as a standalone product available through resellers and integrators. Eventually, it will be offered directly to customers as a shrink-wrapped product.

Currently, the closest competiton to OpenView for Windows is Novell's NetWare Management System (NMS). However, NMS is designed primarily to manage networks running the NetWare operating system and works only on networks that use Novell's IPX transport protocol. OpenView for Windows can be used for managing IP networks as well as those running IPX.

In supporting both IP and IPX protocols simultaneously, OpenView for Windows provides SNMP management of NetWare and TCP/IP networks. In addition, because SNMP services support the Windows Sockets interface, OpenView for Windows will function with any WinSock-compliant protocol stack.

The Windows and UNIX versions of OpenView have a similar interface and a common feature set. This consistency between platforms reduces training costs and increases the productivity of network administrators by allowing them to switch easily between Windows-based and UNIX-based OpenView applications. In fact, with the Workgroup Node Manager application, information can be passed between the Windows- and

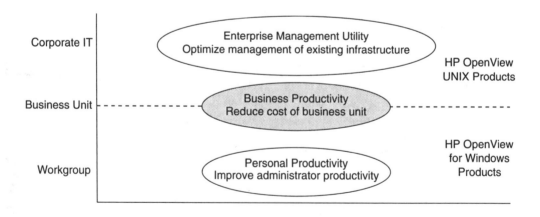

Source: Hewlett-Packard Co.

Figure 2-1: Management Segmentation

UNIX-based OpenView platforms. This means, for example, that OpenView for Windows nodes can forward alarms to OpenView for UNIX nodes, allowing network managers to set up distributed Windows-based management systems to handle local departments that report to a central Windows- or UNIX-based OpenView server. This information sharing permits the use of inexpensive Windows-based management stations that also are easier to use than UNIX, enabling people with less technical background to use them.

Eventually, HP will offer a common database across Windows, UNIX and NT environments, allowing information about network devices and topologies to pass seamlessly from workgroup to enterprise management systems.

DEVELOPMENT ENVIRONMENT

HP OpenView for Windows applications are created using the HP OpenView for Windows Developer's Kit. The HP OpenView for Windows Application Programming Interface (API) contains library routines enabling applications to integrate with HP OpenView for Windows (Figure 2-2). The event-driven API library is based on Microsoft Windows 3.1 programming concepts.

WINDOWS API LIBRARY
The HP OpenView for Windows API library provides a robust, comprehensive facility for presenting network and system management information and map manipulation. The functions provided in the API library range from changing the label of a symbol on the map, to creating a submap and populating it with symbols, to verifying user modifications to the map.

For an application to use the HP OpenView for Windows API library, it must be registered with HP OpenView for Windows in the OVWIN.INI file. This provides the information necessary for HP OpenView for Windows to invoke and manage the application process.

OpenView for Windows also includes a 32-bit API for developing Windows 4.0 and Windows NT-based OpenView applications.

APPLICATIONS BUILDER
The applications builder, Visual OpenView, is a toolkit for creating graphical OpenView applications — backplane diagrams, system performance graphs, and other device characteristics — using Microsoft's Visual Basic language.

APPLICATION INTEGRATION

There are several elements that should be considered when integrating applications with OpenView for Windows. Style consistency within applications is important to ensure that users familiar with one HP OpenView for Windows application can leverage this knowledge and spend considerably less time learning another HP OpenView for Windows application.

HP OpenView for Windows provides user interface style guidelines to follow during the application design. Developers also are encouraged to follow the Microsoft Windows style guidelines.

Within OpenView for Windows are various function categories including:

Session: controls the application's relationship to HP OpenView for Windows. A session starts when HP OpenView for Windows is run. All registered applications are launched automatically.

Registration: registers commands and messages for a particular symbol type. Allows HP OpenView for Windows to cross-reference an application to its symbol(s).

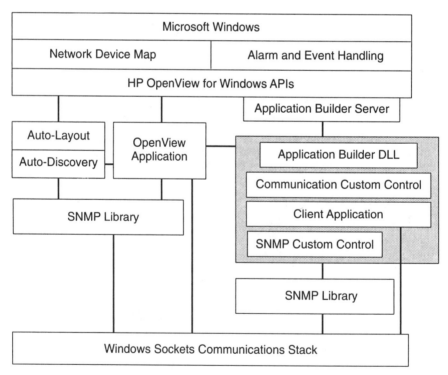

Source: Hewlett-Packard Co.

Figure 2-2: HP OpenView for Windows Architecture

24

Menu: controls HP OpenView for Windows menus. The application can register for default HP OpenView for Windows menus or add its own menu items to the HP OpenView for Windows menu bar.

Map: allows an application to get information from a map. A complete set of APIs allows the developer to get information and manipulate the network map.

Data File: reads and updates data files storing application-dependent symbol information. Provides APIs to interrogate the data file of a network map.

Clipboard: supports clipboard manipulation functions — cut, copy and paste — through the clipboard APIs of HP OpenView for Windows.

Print: provides programmatic printing of a map file.

Status: supplies functions for changing and receiving the status information of objects. This includes programmatic access to event information stored in the event database, as well as symbol status information.

SNMP: provides a full set of SNMP APIs supporting Windows sockets. This allows developers to perform get and set commands on an SNMP device, as well as process SNMP traps over IP and IPX.

Other: provides miscellaneous Windows function calls.

HP OpenView for Windows provides an integrated environment for displaying information from several different applications at the same time. This occurs by combining device and status information from each application.

HP OpenView for Windows must know the name of each application that it will be launching at start-up time. All applications registered with HP OpenView for Windows run in the background. This allows HP OpenView for Windows to control the passing of Windows messages to applications. It is through these messages that information such as alarm events is sent from the application to HP OpenView for Windows. In turn, HP OpenView for Windows passes information such as menu commands, user selection of icons, and other process information to the application.

When an application is started, menu information is passed to HP OpenView for Windows. HP OpenView for Windows displays one combined menu bar integrating menu items from each application. This gives the operator a fully integrated view of all applications. When the operator selects an icon, HP OpenView for Windows activates those menu items used by the application. When a menu item is selected, that information is passed to the appropriate application for processing.

Also, at start-up time, HP OpenView for Windows reads the names and types of icons used by a particular application. These are displayed in the network map. This allows HP OpenView for Windows to display the status of an object as defined by the application. When an object is selected, HP OpenView for Windows passes this information to the correct application for processing.

The developer provides information for HP OpenView for Windows in two .INI files. One is the OVWIN.INI file, which contains the names of the application executables for launching at start-up time. The other is an optional application specific .INI file that is needed if developer-defined object symbols are used.

GRAPHICAL MAP

HP OpenView for Windows displays and manages a graphical map of the network (Figure 2-3). The network is displayed as a collection of device icons and connections on a hierarchical map. HP OpenView for Windows provides tools to enable the administrator to create and edit the graphical map. Access to map editing can be restricted by passwords.

The graphical map consists of symbols that are graphical representations of an object, such as a hub or bridge. Objects displayed on the map can be represented by multiple symbols. Symbols can be lines or icons and they have attributes such as symbol type, label and status.

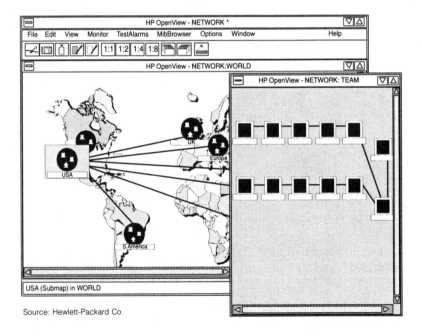

Figure 2-3: HP OpenView for Windows Network Map

HP OpenView for Windows map files can have multiple submap windows. Separate submap windows are useful for distinguishing different management regions or for different presentations of the same management region. Submaps typically are organized in a hierarchy, showing the relationship between different segments of the network. Administrators navigate submaps by using the mouse to select individual submaps or the GoTo submap symbols.

The submaps can be created automatically by the HP OpenView for Windows autodiscovery and layout components or by the network administrator. HP OpenView for Windows applications also can create submaps.

HP OpenView for Windows uses a solid color pattern as the default submap background. The background for any submap can be changed to provide a better physical representation of the network. Administrators can add bit maps and TIFF backgrounds that represent different locations such as buildings and floor plans.

EVENT MANAGER

In HP OpenView for Windows, an event is an unsolicited notification from an HP OpenView application that the status of an object has changed and should be updated as defined by that application. An event that indicates a change in the operational state of a device is called an alarm.

Events are sent to HP OpenView for Windows by each HP OpenView application process running in the background. The alarm manager performs alarm filtering, sorting and history reporting. Device icons change color to one of 10 alarm states to indicate alarm severity, giving network managers a way to prioritize incoming alarms and events. The alarms can be configured to page externally to a remote location, play an audible sound file, or send an electronic mail (e-mail) notification. These alarms are stored in a Paradox database.

When an HP OpenView application wants to update the status of an object, it uses the OVAlarmEvent API to pass the object name, error, new status level and other information. HP OpenView for Windows then will change the background color of the object icon, post the status information in the Alarm window, and ring the system bell. New events are displayed in a color-coded Alarm Log window (Figure 2-4) as current events until they are cleared by the network administrator. Once cleared, an event is placed into a Paradox database for later reporting. To prevent HP OpenView for Windows from using too much disk space caused by a large number of history database entries, the administrator can configure HP OpenView for Windows to delete events older than a specified number of days.

HP OpenView for Windows has several configuration options that allow the administrator to customize the operation of HP OpenView for Windows when events occur. The administrator can configure a different sound file for each status level. These sound files can be configured to repeat sounds once, every *x* minutes, or not play them at all. The administrator also can configure the passing of event messages to other applications for paging or send messages to another location using an e-mail application.

AUTO-DISCOVERY

The discovery process for both IP and IPX networks is controlled by the Discovery Manager, which runs as a background process. When devices are discovered, the Discovery Manager adds them to the discovery database.

The discovery process is extensible by developers. Developers can create their own discovery process to discover any non-IP and non-IPX devices. The Discovery Manger will run the developer-created discovery process and add any non-IP and non-IPX devices into the discovery database.

IP DISCOVERY
The IP discovery process begins by accessing a default gateway router. It finds additional routers by using the router's next-hop table. When a router

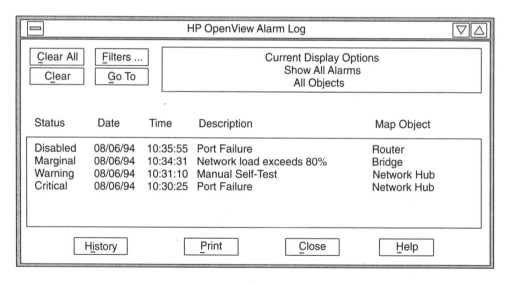

Source: Hewlett-Packard Co.

Figure 2-4: HP OpenView Alarm Log Window

has been identified, the IP discovery process identifies all devices located in the router's Address Resolution Protocol (ARP) cache. The IP discovery process then sends an SNMP request to the identified devices to get the device's system object identification so it can determine what type of device it is. The Discovery Manager limits the scope of the IP discovery process. The IP discovery process will only discover devices on subnets that are specified to the Discovery Manager.

IPX DISCOVERY

The IPX discovery process begins by identifying a NetWare Server. It finds additional servers by using the server's next-hop table. The IPX discovery process then identifies all devices connected to the server using the NetWare Diagnostic Services. The IPX discovery process then sends an SNMP request to the identified devices to get the device's system object identification so it can determine the type of device. The IPX discovery process can identify all IPX devices on a network. The IPX discovery process also can be limited to only discover devices on subnets that are specified to the Discovery Manager or to only discover devices a specific number of hops between NetWare servers.

LAYOUT

When all the devices have been discovered, the layout function will create a graphical map of the discovered devices in the discovery database automatically. Layout creates a router topology map of IP devices and a server topology map of IPX devices. Layout will update the graphical map with newly discovered devices each time it is run.

The Layout function is run manually from a menu item. Layout maps can be supplemented by adding additional submaps with bit map backgrounds to create different views of the network, such as physical buildings or floor plans.

SNMP COMMUNICATIONS

After the network has been discovered and mapped, OpenView for Windows' SNMP Manager can be used to define and execute SNMP queries. Queried data can be displayed in either table or graph format. The graphing capabilities are particularly helpful when querying continuously changing information, such as packet statistics.

To provide communications to SNMP devices, HP OpenView for Windows includes a set of SNMP APIs that can be called by any HP OpenView for Windows application. The SNMP APIs allow any HP OpenView for Windows application to communicate with and receive traps from any device that has an SNMP agent.

The HP OpenView for Windows SNMP supports concurrent use of TCP/IP and IPX protocols, allowing HP OpenView for Windows to simultaneously manage SNMP devices on both TCP/IP and Novell NetWare networks. For TCP/IP networks, the HP OpenView for Windows SNMP will support any Windows Sockets compliant communications stack. For IPX networks, the HP OpenView for Windows SNMP will support either the standard IPX or ODI versions of NetWare.

SNMP MANAGER

HP OpenView for Windows has an SNMP Manager usable by the developers and network administrators. The SNMP Manager allows a developer or network administrator to get and set SNMP information collected by a device on the network. The SNMP Manager displays standard ASN.1 notation information. Information contained in the device's MIB can be selected for display in either tabular or graphical formats.

To create an SNMP query, the network administrator selects the device from the network map. If that device's MIB has been compiled, the SNMP Manager will display the MIB variables and ASN.1 description in the query selection window.

The network administrator then selects the item or items whose values are to be retrieved and viewed. When a query has been defined, the SNMP Manager gets all the selected information. Queries can contain one or more items for display in a query window. Multiple query windows can be displayed at the same time for comparing information from different devices.

When the information has been retrieved, the user can change the information accessed by selecting and editing the field information. When the user has finished editing the information, the SNMP Manager will send all the information to the device at one time. This allows the SNMP Manager to change at one time those items having multiple parameters that must be set at the same time. This block set feature also helps to minimize network traffic by sending groups of data. An integrated polling feature allows for gathering and displaying trend information in a graph. When a query has been defined, it can be saved for later execution. The SNMP Manager can save multiple queries for execution by selecting the query from a selection window (Figure 2-5).

The SNMP Manager includes a library of standard and private MIBs. It also includes a MIB compiler so that additional ASN.1 MIBs can be added. The MIB compiler is based on the compiler used in the UNIX version of HP OpenView, so MIBs used with this version can be used as is in the HP OpenView for Windows SNMP Manager.

OPENVIEW FOR WINDOWS APPLICATIONS

A variety of applications from HP and third-party vendors are available for OpenView for Windows. A brief description of some of these applications will illustrate the functions that are available from this platform.

INTERCONNECT MANAGER (Roseville)

HP OpenView Interconnect Manager/Windows is an SNMP-based workgroup-level manager that encompasses bridges and routers for the management of connected workgroups consisting of hundreds of nodes. It is a superset of Workgroup Manager/Windows, which manages hubs and attached LAN devices including printers, PCs and workstations. Workgroup Manager is upgradeable to Interconnect Manager, allowing more sophisticated management functions while maintaining a familiar management environment.

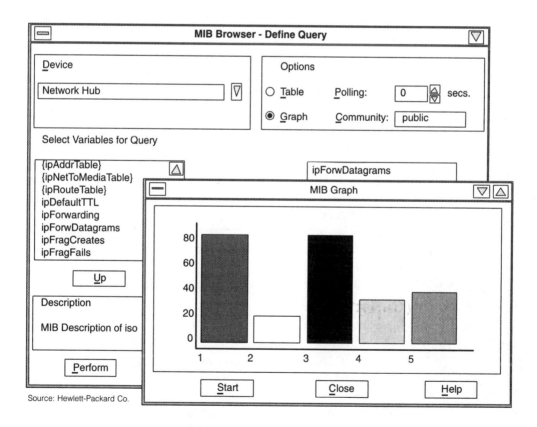

Figure 2-5: Query Definition Window

Both products offer autodiscovery of IP and IPX nodes and lay them in a hierarchical map that accurately represents the network topology. This map is the basis for graphical monitoring and control of HP network devices, as well as the monitoring of multivendor devices down to PCs and printers. For HP EtherTwist hubs, the graphic representation provides control over all hub ports. Performance thresholds for EtherTwist hubs can be set to trigger alarms when needed. The administrator can set *action on events*, such as paging a technician or sending an audio alert when specified events occur.

For HP printers and plotters equipped with SNMP agents, as provided by HP's JetDirect networking cards, the network administrator can be notified of specific printer events, such as paper out, paper jammed and toner low.

Both products also offer a MIB browser, which lets the network administrator browse MIBs from HP and other vendors, as well as a facility for graphing standard MIB-II counters and HP private MIB extensions. In addition, security screens are available for setting network security at a network or device level.

Interconnect Manager exceeds Workgroup Manager's function of monitoring and controlling hubs to provide monitoring and controlling of bridges as well. This includes setting bridge operating modes, spanning tree parameters and wildcard filters. Remote configuration of routers is also performed, through a Telnet connection.

Interconnect Manager uses HP's Embedded Advanced Sampling Environment (EASE) for real-time management functions. This traffic-sampling technology allows network traffic to be monitored and assessed without requiring network analyzers. Instead of capturing and analyzing all packets, a sampling of approximately 0.025 percent of all data packets is performed. This sampling rate is enough to reveal potential trouble spots on the network. Statistics are output in the form of pie charts, bar graphs or time-series charts. This information also can be sent to other management tools for capacity planning and performance tuning.

System Manager (Cupertino)

HP OpenView System Manager is a distributed application that allows operators to monitor and control networked HP 3000 minicomputers from a central management console using a graphical network map (Figure 2-6). System Manager runs on up to five HP OpenView Workstations, an HP OpenView console, and one or more Managed Nodes. A single OpenView console supports up to 64 managed nodes. The main application resides on the HP OpenView console, which is an HP 3000 minicomputer running the MPE/iX operating system. The HP OpenView Workstation provides a user interface to the management node's functionality and uses HP OpenView for Windows.

Management by exception frees operators from monitoring every system console message. Instead, operators are notified only of the problems they really are interested in through the OpenView for Windows network map. The types of problems tracked are defined by the operating departments, eliminating unnecessary notifications.

Systems on the map change color to reflect their current status. Operating system commands or command scripts can respond automatically to events, which reduces the amount of events requiring operator attention. The operator can decide whether the events that took care of themselves with automated responses should appear in the event log. The operator can choose to see everything that happened, when intervention was not required, or those that needed operator attention.

For trouble tracking purposes, System Manager has a message annotation feature. After reviewing an event message, the message annotation feature allows operators to append the message with a note describing any

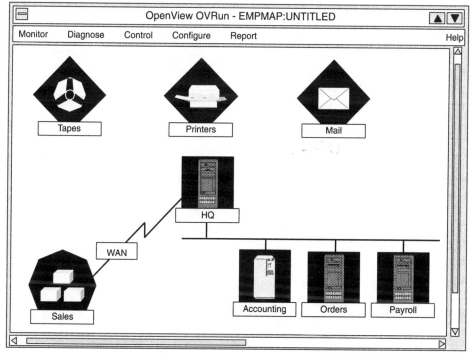

Source: Hewlett-Packard Co.

Figure 2-6: OpenView System Manager Network Map

additional information about that message. This feature is useful in multishift operations when the problem resolution process carries over from one shift to the next and further explanation is required.

From the central console, the operator can exercise system control, including shutdown and restart of all managed HP 3000s. Operators also can centrally monitor and control HP-supplied, user-written or third-party applications that run on the HP 3000. Applications generate a status and send that status to the OpenView console's graphical network map. Operators also can monitor the status of operating systems, all subsystems and job streams.

Messages can be categorized based on groups represented by predefined icons on the screen. This allows all disk-related events to be viewed under the disk icon, for example, or all printer-related events under the printer icon. The icons can be put on one central console, or they can be distributed across multiple consoles. Icons and events can be viewed as they relate to each system, or viewed at a higher overall network level.

For more information, System Manager allows operators to view a summary of outstanding system events as well as their associated console messages. At the first level of detail, System Manager summarizes how many events of a particular severity occurred on each system. For further details, operators may selectively review actual console messages either by system or by event severity.

For long-term problem detection, System Manager logs all console messages in a database residing on the controlling HP OpenView console node. Operations staff can generate customized reports from this log for selective trend analysis.

NetServer Assistant (NSD)

HP NetServer Assistant comes bundled with HP's NetServer LM Series of network servers and is optional with the NetServer LE Series. It offers tools for remote management, problem identification and resolution, configuration management, storage capacity planning, and a centralized launch interface. These tools are used to maintain high availability levels for mission-critical information.

With the subsystem diagnostic function, the operator can test the server's disk subsystem remotely, as well as test the error checking and correction memory status display. Thresholds can be set for disk capacity, and when the threshold is exceeded, an alarm notifies the operator. Using the in-band storage capacity planning function, the operator can view disk-capacity graphs and the dates on which usage increased. This information can be used to aid future disk-expansion decisions.

In addition to providing details about a server's EISA configuration, NetServer Assistant's server information menu choice also lists facts about the NetServer communications ports, BIOS revision, system memory data and processor speed. Novell's SYSCON, PCONSOLE and RCONSOLE utilities can be run directly from NetServer Assistant.

By installing the supplied host portion of Symantec's pcAnywhere package on the file server and attaching a modem, the operator can gain dial-up access to NetServer systems. HP also includes a copy of DiagSoft's QAPlus, which also can be run remotely to test basic PC hardware.

As a companion to NetServer Assistant, HP's optional Remote Assistant provides extra levels of hardware monitoring and control. A self-contained subsystem, the EISA board includes a CPU, modem and battery. Its out-of-band management capability is implemented through a dialup modem connection, which provides complete remote console control. Remote Assistant is able to dial a pager and alert the administrator about a variety of problems, such as a temperature or voltage threshold that was exceeded, or network operating system faults.

Remote Assistant's EISA board also lets the operator power down the server and perform warm or cold boots. The ability to view the entire boot process from memory is a key feature of Remote Assistant.

As part of NetServer Assistant's fault management capabilities, a *ping* feature probes the connection path, indicating whether it is functional.

NetServer Assistant provides no monitoring of the network operating system itself, since its focus is the server. HP offers its OpenView PC Client Manager for that purpose.

PC CLIENT MANAGER
HP OpenView PC Client Manager is a suite of applications that provides a broad view of Novell NetWare clients and the NOS (Figure 2-7). PC Client Manager accomplishes PC client management through the following feature set:

- **Real Time Network Monitoring:** provides real-time insight into what is happening on the network with respect to the clients.

- **Fault Detection and Problem Isolation:** provides error statistics with specific information concerning the error and the offending clients or server. This information is sent to the network manager when errors happen, and before the cascading effect of these errors can be felt on the network. In addition, an alert history is kept so that events that occurred in the same period of time as the alert can be analyzed to determine the root cause of the problem.

- **Hardware Inventory Management:** task is reduced to running reports that provide summary information about all of the hardware.

- **Visual Mapping of the Network:** allows the network manager to see all the nodes on the network, as well as their relationship to each other.

- **Configuration Management:** eases the burden of systems administration by facilitating the addition or deletion of users and the changing of groups, permissions and security.

- **Remote Console:** used to monitor multiple networks from a remote location. This feature provides real-time status updates on the day-to-day operation of each of the client networks.

- **Memory and Disk Utilization:** provides the status of available memory and disk space on the network.

- **Monitor Data Traffic:** enables monitoring of the data traffic on the network in real time.

- **Locate New PCs (clients) on the Network:** automatically with the visual mapping feature.

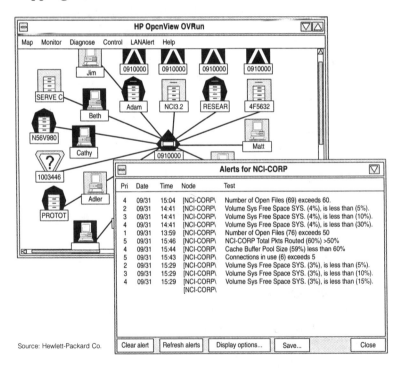

Figure 2-7: OpenView PC Client Manager

- **Alerts or changes:** report on hardware, configuration file, drivers, data traffic and system status.

- **Custom Paging on Network Failures:** provides a way of automatically alerting field personnel about network failures and problems requiring their attention. Definition of what constitutes a failure or priority on a given problem can be determined, and configured to page when a significant problem has occurred.

The PC Client Manager product family consists a single Management Server, File Server Agents and Node Agents on NetWare file servers, Consoles on DOS or Windows PCs and DOS-based Gateways.

Agents: Agents collect, monitor and maintain all the critical data about the LAN. The architecture provides two types of agents: File Server Agents that perform data management functions for NetWare file servers, and Node Agents that perform functions for other LAN nodes.

Together, File Server Agents and Node Agents provide the data required to manage the entire network. Both agent types are implemented as NetWare VAPs or NLMs. This enables continuous running of network management on the network without operator involvement.

File Server Agents are installed on each file server on a network. The File Server Agents are implemented as NLMs under NetWare v3.11+ and as VAPs under v2.12+. Each File Server Agent collects and manages a Btrieve database of server statistics.

File Server Agents also monitor events based on defined or default values and thresholds. When an event or the crossing of a threshold occurs, the File Server Agent logs the event locally and signals the Management Server that an event has occurred. Statistics collection and monitoring occur on-line and in real time with server operation. The network is used only to signal alerts on an exception basis. This significantly reduces the impact of system management on network traffic.

Node Agents are installed on one or more NetWare file servers on a network. The Node Agents are implemented as NLMs under NetWare v3.11 and as VAPs under v2.12. The Node Agent also includes a DOS executable module during login, which gathers hardware and software inventory and configuration information. At initial start-up, Node Agents begin an autodiscovery process to build a network configuration database. When this database has been built and its baseline values established, Node Agents compare subsequently collected configuration data against this baseline. Any variation results in an alert logged locally and passed to the Management Server.

Additionally, Node Agents poll clients, routers, bridges and gateways on their local segment of the network to ensure that nodes remain properly configured and attached. Anomalies result in alerts. Node Agents perform their functions locally on the network on which they execute. The network is used to signal alerts and to perform periodic polling and connectivity tests to network nodes only within the domain defined by the network administrator. As with File Server Agents, exception-only reporting and local polling minimize network traffic.

Consoles: The Console is a DOS or Windows application that can be accessed from any client on the internetwork. Consoles provide the user interface to product functions and data. Through Consoles, agents and alerts are configured, alerts are displayed, and statistics are displayed or printed. Multiple Consoles may be active or no Console may be active. Monitoring and statistics collection are not tied to the presence of an active Console, nor does the product architecture define or require a designated master console.

Consoles are non-dedicated and run on any client on the LAN. Console for Windows runs under Microsoft's Windows 3.1 and provides a user-friendly environment that allows an administrator to monitor that network while running other Windows programs.

Gateways: Gateways are DOS-based programs that provide access into and out of the management environment on NetWare networks. Gateways provide the means for controlling NetWare from HP OpenView for Windows. They also allow remote access to Console functions. In addition, notification of alert conditions can be sent from the network to the client and to paging devices through these gateways.

Management Server: The Management Server is installed on a NetWare File Server. There is one Management Server per network, which is implemented as an NLM under NetWare v3.11 and as a VAP under v2.12. The Management Server controls and coordinates communication and data transfer from all product components. It processes alerts from File Server Agents and Node Agents by logging them to an alert database and forwarding an alert to a Console. Or, the alert may be signaled to a telephone paging device.

The Management Server acts as the central bank for all alert information by:

- Collecting event information from Agents on other file servers.

- Forwarding these alerts to Consoles that are Clients on the network.

- Forwarding alerts to Gateways that send alerts to a pager or remote management site.

LATTISNET MANAGER FOR DOS

SynOptics Communications offers LattisNet Manager for DOS for its System 2000 and System 3000 hubs. LattisNet Manager for DOS works under HP OpenView for Windows.[1] It is an SNMP-based management system for medium to large mixed Ethernet and token ring networks.

LattisNet Manager obtains information through routers and bridges, enabling the data to be reviewed, evaluated and comparatively analyzed at the network management station. Physical- and MAC-layer information, gathered by SNMP agents in non-modular hubs or LattisNet network management modules located throughout the network, is displayed in graphical form at the management station. Specific fault, configuration and performance data can be retrieved and individual station connections can be controlled from any remote location.

A DOS-based LattisNet Manager station, equipped with the appropriate third-party MIB extensions, can manage other SNMP-compatible devices on the network. A compiler provides support for third-party MIBs, allowing the management station to perform management tasks on any compatible devices. Full SNMP compatibility also enables SynOptics devices (or agents) to be managed from other SNMP-compatible management stations in a multivendor environment.

LattisNet Manager for DOS also uses the standardized Telnet and Ping applications for managing compatible devices that do not yet support SNMP. The Telnet application allows multiple sessions to be established simultaneously, on the same screen, to manage and configure third-party devices. The Ping application allows network managers to perform rudimentary connection testing on remote network devices.

A static global view mapping feature, based on HP's OpenView for Windows, allows network managers to create an object-oriented map of the network topology manually. Using icons representing managed and unmanaged devices on the network, managers can create a detailed map that reflects the network's actual physical configuration. Graphic backdrops such as buildings, floor plans or blueprints can be scanned in to customize the map.

---

[1]The company's UNIX-based management system, Optivity, is integrated into the UNIX version of OpenView. SynOptics merged with Wellfleet Communications in 1994 to become Bay Networks.

Nested beneath this static global map are a series of dynamic network views created by LattisNet Manager:

- **Flat Network Views:** provide a system-generated map of Ethernet or token ring segments connected by bridges and bounded by routers to help the network manager understand the physical relationship between bridged segments. Flat network views also report on the state of Spanning Tree environments, including a real-time display showing active and standby bridges.

- **Segment Network Views:** show the logical relationship between hubs in an Ethernet or token ring segment bounded by bridges. Hub icons are displayed in a hierarchical (Ethernet) or logical ring (token ring) configuration. Links between hubs are reported, indicating the media used as well as the slot and port location of the connection. The maps are automatically compiled and updated in real time.

- **Expanded Views:** offers a real-time representation of a selected hub, including installed modules and active LED indicators. Individual connections can be enabled, disabled or partitioned for a set amount of time.

LattisNet Manager also provides Show Nodes and Find Nodes features. Show Node provides a list of all stations or nodes attached to a selected segment or hub. These lists, created in real time based on MAC addresses or alias names, enable the network manager to identify network resources for baselining, fault recovery and network planning. The Find Nodes feature enables network managers to locate individual stations or nodes anywhere on the network. End stations can be identified by MAC address or assigned aliases, enabling user problems to be located, verified and corrected from the management station.

In addition, an Allowed Nodes function offers network access control. To control access to the network, the network manager creates and updates a list of allowed nodes. Any station not on the list will be removed automatically from the system, ensuring that only specific, approved users can access the network.

LattisNet Manager for DOS supports the usual error and status thresholds and logging features. Thresholds for performance, collisions and errors detect potential problems, alert the network manager and initiate immediate, automated corrective actions.

INTERNETWORK MANAGEMENT SYSTEM

CrossComm Corp.'s Internetwork Management System (IMS) manages LAN-based networks — specifically, the company's ILAN bridges — enabling operators to configure and administer the network, manage devices, gather statistics, and diagnose and solve problems.

The IMS resides on a single PC. From the OpenView for Windows screen, any ILAN bridge can be remotely configured, network performance statistics and real-time alarms gathered, and topology map displayed. Moreover, problems on the enterprise network can be isolated quickly using CrossComm's ExperTest, a diagnostic tool that allows a segment-by-segment connectivity test to be performed for determining the exact location of a problem.

For example, a remote ILAN can be instructed to test the connection integrity between itself and a questionable server. Then the ILAN can test the connection between the IMS and the remote ILAN, completing the network test. With ExperTest, any segment of the network can be tested without extra equipment and without dispatching technicians to remote locations.

IMS also provides a variety of network statistics (Figure 2-8). When the network statistics window is opened, the operator can log network statistics to a spreadsheet or graphics program for further manipulation and/or display.

ACTION REQUEST SYSTEM

Remedy Corp.'s helpdesk solution, Action Request System, is a client-server application that automates and manages the resolution of problems and support requests for PC and UNIX networks. It is integrated with OpenView for Windows, as well as the UNIX version of OpenView. This integration allows network administrators to easily confirm the status of open trouble tickets on network or system devices managed by OpenView for Windows. The operator selects a device from the OpenView topology map and then selects a menu item that immediately retrieves the trouble ticket information on that item (Figure 2-9).

The Action Request System offers customizable views and workflow processes and builds an experience database to aid problem resolution. End users can submit service requests using fill-in screens. Other features of the Action Request System include support of leading SQL databases, automatic problem submission, automatic delegation and escalation, proactive notification through a desktop beeper, and fully documented APIs to facilitate integration with other equipment and applications.

A related application is Remedy's Health Profiler, which is also integrated with OpenView for Windows. It is a performance monitoring, reporting and baselining application that charts the health metrics of network and systems equipment and applications. It facilitates the creation of *dashboards* that present statistical and performance information for equipment and processes in a networked environment.

Profiles of statistical behavior can be developed as baselines and analyzed for trends. Any information available through the management platform can be represented in user-defined dashboards, which consist of meters, charts, icons, fields and action buttons. Both real time and historical information can be displayed, with the Remedy Health Profiler providing an efficient way of collecting useful history. Information also can be output in user-defined tabular report formats on an automated or manual basis.

WEAKNESSES OF OPENVIEW FOR WINDOWS

Although OpenView for Windows is sufficiently robust to provide distinct advantages, it provides a limited number of features. It covers the basics with auto-discovery, a network-layout utility for generating network maps, and a MIB browser for monitoring SNMP devices.

It also falls short in third-party applications integration. Not only does much of the management functionality depend on third-party applications,

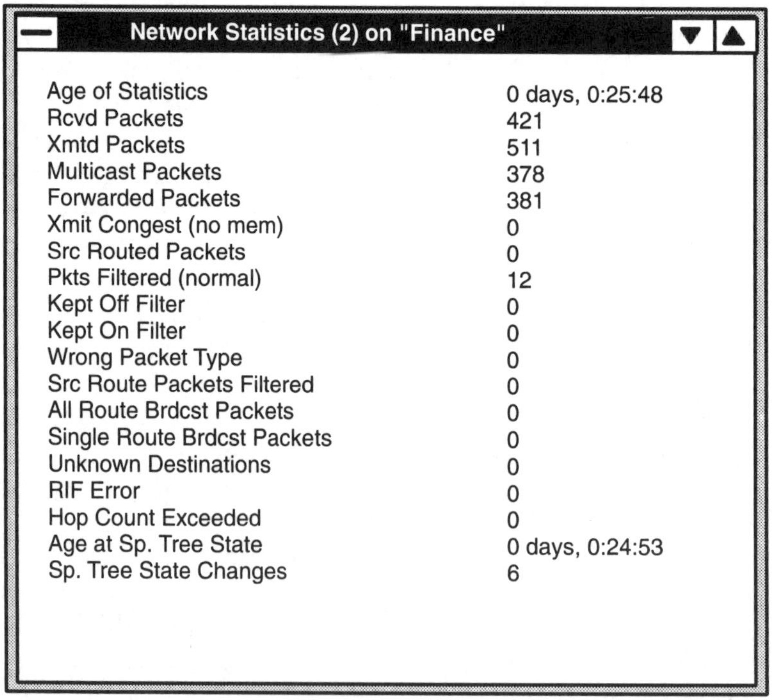 Network Statistics (2) on "Finance"	
Age of Statistics	0 days, 0:25:48
Rcvd Packets	421
Xmtd Packets	511
Multicast Packets	378
Forwarded Packets	381
Xmit Congest (no mem)	0
Src Routed Packets	0
Pkts Filtered (normal)	12
Kept Off Filter	0
Kept On Filter	0
Wrong Packet Type	0
Src Route Packets Filtered	0
All Route Brdcst Packets	0
Single Route Brdcst Packets	0
Unknown Destinations	0
RIF Error	0
Hop Count Exceeded	0
Age at Sp. Tree State	0 days, 0:24:53
Sp. Tree State Changes	6

Source: CrossComm Corp.

Figure 2-8: IMS Network Statistics Window

but many of those applications only can be launched from OpenView for Windows, eliminating the possibility of data sharing.

Even when applications are well integrated with OpenView for Windows, they may not be able to share the same management console. While many applications use IPX, others may want a specific IP stack, while still others might use a proprietary packet driver rather than a standard protocol suite. With applications scattered among several management consoles, the advantages of the platform are diminished appreciably.

Because OpenView for Windows discovers only devices that use IP and IPX, it does not support any other protocol unless a third-party application is added. This will be a problem if the network relies on NetBIOS.

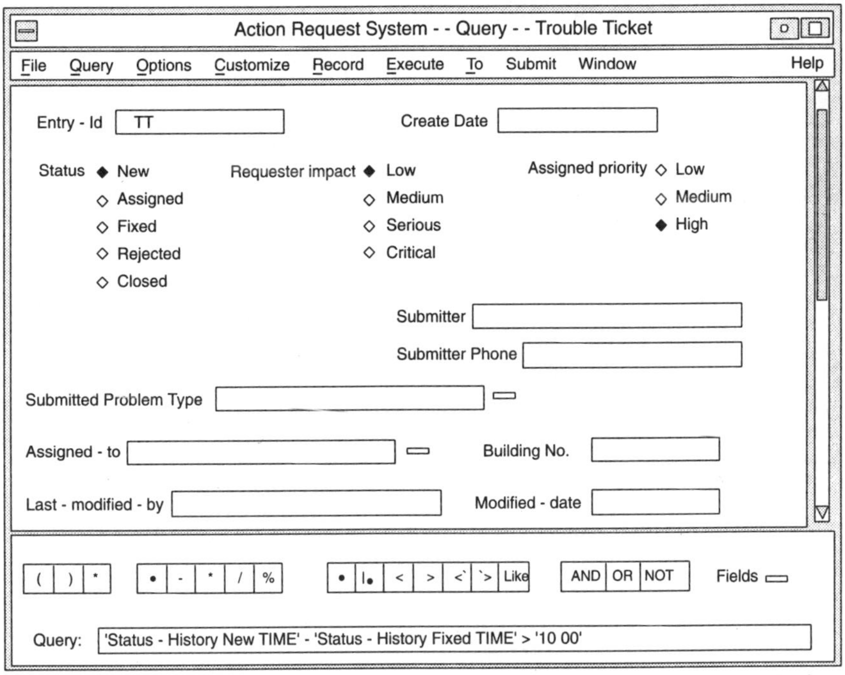

Source: Remedy Corp.

Figure 2-9: ARS Trouble Ticket Window

HP PLANS TO SUPPORT WINDOWS NT AS A PLATFORM FOR NETWORK AND system management in two releases. In early 1995, HP will deliver an OpenView for Windows NT management product for Intel-based PCs that leverages and is a natural migration of the current OpenView for Windows product. Later the same year, HP will deliver a single distributed enterprise network OpenView architecture for Windows, Windows NT and

UNIX. The result will be a common scalable architecture that can be implemented on the user's operating system of choice.

Windows NT already includes an SNMP software agent that provides management information to OpenView. An OpenView management station can communicate with these agents to obtain an integrated, overall view of the SNMP nodes on the network. These agents expand the problem-management process capabilities of HP OpenView OperationsCenter into the Windows NT environment.

HP already has implemented standard communication links between OpenView for Windows and UNIX-based OpenView products through its Workgroup Node Manager application. These links allow event-forwarding and passing of alarm conditions between OpenView for Windows and UNIX-based OpenView consoles.

CHAPTER

3

Network Node Manager

HP OPENVIEW NETWORK NODE MANAGER (NNM) IS A SIMPLE NETWORK Management Protocol (SNMP)-based application that runs under the OSF/Motif-based OpenView Windows graphical user interface (GUI). It uses the standard SNMP manager-agent communications architecture to simplify fault, configuration and performance management functions on multivendor TCP/IP networks. Other applications and shell scripts can be added to NNM and accessed from the OpenView Windows menu bar to provide an integrated management solution.

NNM manages network devices that are Internet Protocol (IP) addressable and run SNMP. These devices include HP 9000s, HP 3000s, PCs and many other devices from HP and alternative vendors. NNM runs on the HP 9000 series of computers and is also available for the IBM RS/6000 and Sun SPARCstation.

AUTOMATIC DISCOVERY

NNM's automatic discovery capability finds and identifies all IP nodes (i.e., devices) on the TCP/IP network, including those of other vendors that support SNMP. Based on discovered information, NNM automatically draws the required topology maps.

Nodes that cannot be discovered automatically can be represented in two ways: first, by manually adding custom or standard icons to the appropriate map views; second, by using HP's SNMP-based application programming interfaces (APIs) for building map applications without manually modifying the configuration to accommodate non-SNMP devices.

NNM also identifies IP devices over any wide-area network (WAN) links it encounters. Network administrators, therefore, do not have to know about serial WAN connections and explicitly request discovery of devices at remote locations.

The network map is updated automatically when the status of any device changes. Device status is displayed via color changes to the map. Any changes to the network map are carried through to the relevant submaps.

The current network map can be saved for comparison against future topologies.

TROUBLESHOOTING TOOLS

Tools to simplify troubleshooting are integrated into the network map. The operator can point and click on a problem node and quickly perform the following tests:

IP test: verifies the physical connectivity of local and remote networks, using the Ping protocol.

TCP test: performs a TCP connection.

SNMP test: checks a node to determine whether it has an SNMP agent running.

To enhance the problem resolution, the operator can quickly access essential configuration information by selecting nodes from the map and choosing menu items. This capability also aids inventory tracking, allowing the operator to obtain and edit descriptions of node-specific information like location, owner, and type, as well as free-form comments such as serial number or asset number.

EVENT REPORTING

Network Node Manager automatically detects and reports the following types of events:

- Occurrences of exceeded threshold limits.

- Changes in network topology.

- Occurrences of errors.

- Changes in an object's status.

- Changes in a node's configuration.

- Occurrences of application alerts.

Events are displayed in a color-coded event window according to importance. Event messages can indicate the severity of the problem, enabling the console operator to distinguish between the failure of a large database server, for example, and less important nodes. Administrators also can filter information based on different views of the network.

TASK-ORIENTED OPERATIONS

Several task-oriented operational steps for using NNM are provided. These include loading MIBs, viewing MIB values, setting MIB values, collecting MIB data, defining thresholds, defining event actions, viewing historical trends, building MIB applications, taking IP Map snapshots and managing MIBs.

Loading MIBs: To manage a device (or agent) on the network, it must run SNMP. If the device has an enterprise-specific management information base (MIB), it must be loaded into the MIB database. NNM comes with certain MIBs already loaded, including MIB II and HP-UX. NNM also provides a tool to load multivendor enterprise-specific MIBs and newly released standard MIBs.

Viewing MIB Values: MIB values can be viewed for a selected node by entering the MIB object ID to call up a specific MIB object whose MIB values can then be queried. Alternatively, the desired MIB object can be selected by moving the MIB tree up or down.

Setting MIB Values: MIB values can be changed after querying the object or can be modified directly, without first querying the object. When the new value for the object is entered, the SNMP set command activates the change.

Collecting MIB Data: MIB data is collected from network nodes at regular, specified polling intervals and saved to disk. The collected data can then be put into graph form to summarize performance over time. Using the combined capabilities of the data collector and the flexible graphing capabilities in Network Node Manager, the operator can gather information, run analyses and create graphs for identification of normal use of resources in the environment. Real-time graphs can be generated to compare current performance against the baseline profile to speed problem isolation and resolution.

Defining Thresholds: Event thresholds can be defined for MIB objects (e.g., when disk usage on a particular device exceeds a limit.) Thresholds on any MIB variable can be set so that deviations in important statistics such as throughput and error rates can be detected before problems arise.

Defining Event Actions: NNM also allows the operator to select the notification method used when a threshold is exceeded. Actions taken at the time of receipt of an event also can be defined. The operator can decide what text and MIB variables are represented in the network event message, as well as identify a program or shell script to be executed when the event is received.

Viewing Historical Trends: Historical MIB information about the MIB objects can be collected and then stored for trend analysis. Historical information can be saved to a file and printed in ASCII format, displayed in a graph, or exported to a spreadsheet for offline planning and reporting.

Building MIB Applications: New MIB applications can be built for Internet-standard and enterprise-specific MIBs without programming. The objects of new MIB applications then can be monitored through the various menu bar selections.

Taking IP Map Snapshots: A snapshot defines the state of the network at a particular moment. When a snapshot is created, it can be opened and displayed. Objects can be selected in the snapshot. The selection list for a snapshot has the same function as a selection list for a map. However, because the snapshot is a read-only file, the snapshot cannot be edited or restored, and it cannot replace the map.

Managing MIBs: NNM can manage new enterprise-specific MIB objects as well as standard MIB objects. Enterprise-specific MIBs are extensions of standard MIBs that have been developed by vendors for use with their products, while standard MIBs define objects that are common to most network devices.[1]

When a new MIB module is loaded into the management station, any of the MIB objects defined in that module can be managed. The operator can get and set the values of MIB objects using the Browse MIB operation. The Browse MIB operation also can be used to find out what the instance is of a MIB object on a device.[2]

THE IP MAP

The IP Map application starts automatically with OpenView Windows. There are two background processes that occur in the IP Map application to discover and update the map: Network Monitor (netmon) and IP Topology Manager (topm).

Network Monitor discovers resources on the network. IP Topology Manager continually accesses semantic information about IP networks, segments, nodes and interfaces stored in the map database. As informa-

---

[1] New standard MIBs continue to be developed by the Internet community. The intent is to consolidate common management information from enterprise MIBs into standard definitions, yielding consistent access to the management information across multivendor equipment.

[2] An object is defined in terms of attributes it possesses, operations performed on it, notifications it issues, and relationships with other managed objects. Each managed object is an instance of a managed-object class. All object instances that share the same elements are members of the same class. The individual object instances may differ in the values of their attributes. An object only needs to be defined once, and the definition can be reused many times for each instance of the object type.

tion in the map changes, and as events take place with systems or connections in the network, IP Map updates the network map.

OpenView Windows creates a Root submap (Figure 3-1) that NNM uses as the foundation for building hierarchies of submaps. Symbols in the Root submap are used to open submaps that provide a top-level view of a specific application, such as an IP Internet or an OSI network.

IP Map initially creates this submap hierarchy:

- Internet submap.

- Network submaps.

- Segment submaps.

- Node submaps.

The hierarchy of submaps can be reorganized and expanded. The Internet submap can be partitioned and symbols added to show additional network locations. A hierarchy of partitioned Internet submaps can be created as many levels deep as needed. The lower levels of the network map can be expanded by creating additional network, segment and node objects. Connections can be added between objects.

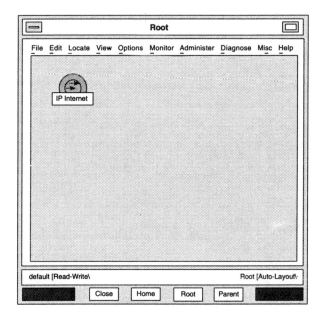

Source: Hewlett-Packard Co.

Figure 3-1: *Root Submap*
The Internet symbol graphically represents all IP-addressable objects in the network. Double clicking on this symbol provides access to the hierarchy of submaps that furnish various views of the network.

Viewing Configurations

NNM provides access to information about network and system configurations through menu selections. The operator can view a description of objects that IP Map manages, such as an internet, network, segment, node or interface. For each node selected, the information is displayed in its own dialog box. Because the information comes from the NNM database, the descriptions are as current as the last SNMP poll.

Internet Object: When the IP Internet object symbol on the root submap is selected for viewing, IP Map provides the following attribute information:

- Number of IP network on the internet.

- Number of segments on the internet.

- Number of nodes contained within the internet.

- Number of interfaces contained within the internet.

- Number of gateways/routers on the internet.

- Status or error messages.

A sample NNM screen showing IP Internet attribute information is shown in Figure 3-2.

Network Object: When a network object is selected for viewing, NNM provides the following information:

- Network name, as it appears on the map.

- Network IP address.

- Subnet mask associated with the network number.

- IP status of the network.

- Number of segments on the network.

- Number of nodes contained within the network.

A sample NNM screen showing attribute information for a network object is provided in Figure 3-3.

Segment Object: When a segment object is selected for viewing, NNM provides the following information:

- IP status of the segment.

- Number of nodes on the segment.

- Status or error messages.

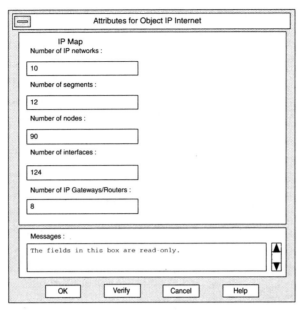

Source: Hewlett-Packard Co.

Figure 3-2: *IP Internet Description*

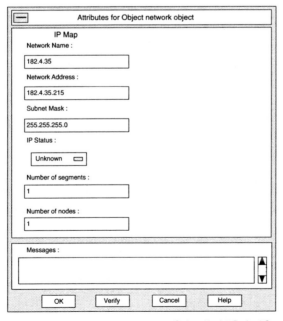

Source: Hewlett-Packard Co.

Figure 3-3: *Network Description*

A sample NNM screen showing attribute information for a segment object is provided in Figure 3-4.

Node Object: When a node object is selected for viewing, NNM provides the following information:

- Host name that was assigned upon creation of the node.

- IP status of the node.

- Information and status about each IP interface on the node.

- System description, as returned by the SNMP agent.

- System location and system contact.

- System object ID of the node, indicating SNMP support.

- Status or error messages.

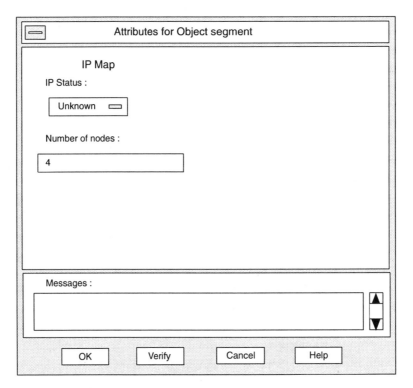

Source: Hewlett-Packard Co.

Figure 3-4: *Segment Description*

A sample NNM screen showing attribute information for a node object is shown in Figure 3-5.

Interface Object: When an interface object is selected for viewing, NNM provides the following information:

- IP address of the interface.

- Subnet mask.

- Link-level address (physical address).

- Interface type.

- IP status.

- Status or error messages.

A sample NNM screen showing attribute information for an interface object is provided in Figure 3-6.

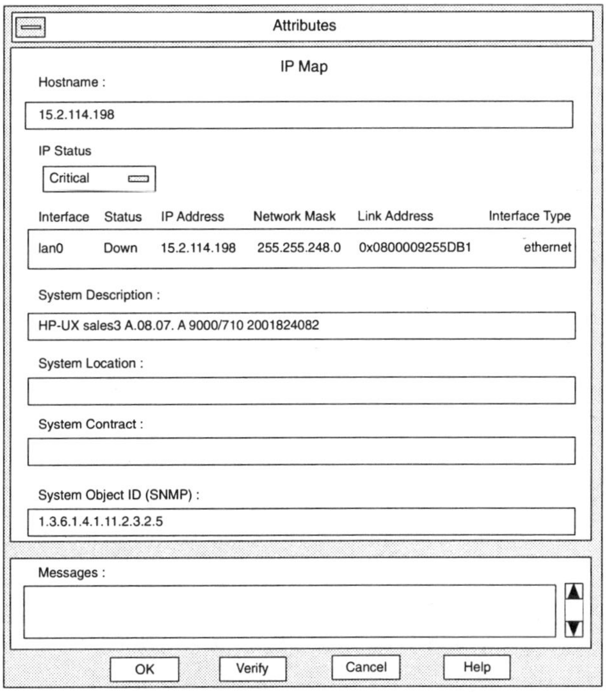

Source: Hewlett-Packard Co.

Figure 3-5: Node Description

Network Addresses: The operator can view SNMP-supported nodes for associated network addresses without looking through configuration files. This information is real-time data taken from the node, rather than static information taken from the NNM database. For each node selected, the following information is provided:

- Interface index.

- Interface name.

- IP address.

- Network mask.

- Network address.

- Link-level address (physical address).

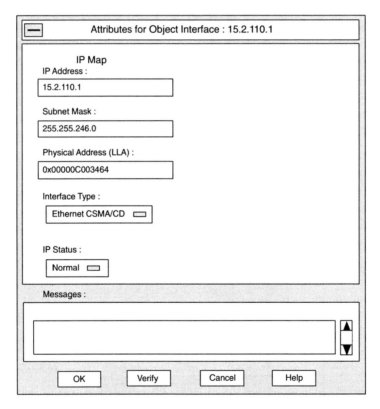

Source: Hewlett-Packard Co.

Figure 3-6: Interface Description

As an example, the displayed information takes the following form:

```
Index  Interface  IP Address  Network Mask  Network Address  Link Address
5      lan1       127.1.0.2   255.255.0.0   127.1.0.0        0x010002044444
4      lan2       127.1.0.3   255.255.0.0   127.1.0.0        0x010002033333
```

Traffic Routes: Viewing the traffic routes table information for a remote SNMP node can be useful in determining more efficient routes on the network, assessing the need for explicit routes, and diagnosing connectivity problems.

For each destination node with which the selected node communicates, the following information is provided:

- Destination name.

- Name of gateway (router) between the selected and destination node.

- Type of route (e.g., directly connected to a LAN, through a remote gateway, or route currently not available).

- Name of the interface used to reach the destination.

This information is displayed in the following format:

```
Destination     Gateway                Type       Interface
------------------------------------------------------------------
default         gateway1.grp.org.com   remote     lan1
127.1.0.111     sys1.grp.org.com       direct     lan1
127.3.0.222     sys1.grp.org.com       direct     lan0
localhost       localhost              direct     lo0
```

Address Translation Table: The Address Translation Table for a remote SNMP node can be viewed using the Address Resolution Protocol (ARP) cache. This information can be useful for diagnosing connectivity problems because it can tell if two nodes are using a different address for a third node. The information displayed is real-time data taken from the selected SNMP node, rather than static information taken from the database.

For the selected node, the following information is displayed:

- Node name or IP address.

- Link-level address (physical address) associated with the node name.

- Interface name (of the selected node) associated with the node and the physical address.

Information from the address translation table is displayed in the following format:

```
Node                    Link Address           Interface
- - - - - - - - - - - - - - - - - - - - - - - - - - - - - - - - - - - - - - - -
127.1.66.32             0x01000205720          lan1
deptac.grp.org.com      0x01000204422          lan2
deptsa.grp.org.com      0x01000201313          lan2
```

Node Services: The IP networking services for which a remote SNMP node is listening can be viewed. This information is useful to determine what configured services a node is currently running. The information displayed is real-time data taken from the selected node, rather than static information taken from the database.

For the selected node, the following information is displayed:

- Service protocol: either Transmission Control Protocol (TCP) or User Datagram Protocol (UDP).

- Port to which the service is bound.

- Service for which the node is listening (for example, smtp, telnet, ftp or nfs); if no service is listed, the service is either unavailable or unknown.

This information is displayed in the following format:

```
Protocol       Port                  Service
- - - - - - - - - - - - - - - - - - - - - - - - - - - - - - - - - - - - - - - -
tcp            512                   ftp
tcp            10                    telnet
tcp            333                   portmap
tcp            20                    smtp
udp            200                   snmpd
udp            203                   syslog
```

Disk Space: The available file system disk space on a specified node can be viewed. The displayed information is real-time data from the node, rather than static information from the database. Because this information is generated by an HP enterprise-specific MIB, it is only available from an HP 9000, Sun SPARCstation or IBM RS/6000 workstation running OpenView SNMP agent software.

For the selected node, the following information about each file system on the selected node is displayed:

- File system name.

- Total amount of disk space, in kilobytes.

- Number of kilobytes used.

- Number of kilobytes available.

- Percent of total capacity in use.

- Directory name on which disk is mounted.

Disk space information is displayed in the following format:

```
Filesystem      kbytes   used     avail  capacity  Mounted on
- - - - - - - - - - - - - - - - - - - - - - - - - - - - - - - - - - - - - - - - - - - - - - - - - -
/dev/dsk/0s0    442227   249880   187676   57%     /
/dev/dsk/0s1    543036   70370    437225   13%     /backup1
/dev/dsk/0s2    377067   307555   287676   82%     /backup2
/dev/dsk/0s3    439998   248720   186878   57%     /sales/net
```

CONTROLLING NETWORK AND SYSTEM CONFIGURATIONS

NNM provides access to systems for administration purposes through the System Administration Manager (SAM) tool, which is available only on HP 9000 systems, or a terminal emulator that is used to access other systems.

If the selected node is an HP 9000 system and it has the SAM application installed, the following information may be viewed or modified:

- User accounts.

- Group memberships.

- File systems.

- Disk space.

- Printer status.

- Print requests.

- Networking services.

- Kernel configurations.

If the selected node is not an HP 9000 system, it can be accessed with the terminal emulator using an appropriate virtual terminal protocol. NNM supports the following virtual terminal protocols:

- **Telnet (hpterm):** provides log-on to a remote UNIX or non-UNIX system from an HP 9000 management station.

- **Telnet (xterm):** provides log-on to a remote UNIX or non-UNIX system from an HP 9000, Sun SPARCstation or IBM RS/6000 management station.

- **Vt3k (hp3000):** provides log-on to a remote HP 3000 system from an HP 9000 management station.

The network and system configuration utilities of other vendors may be integrated into NNM by the administrator and accessed via NNM's menu bar.

Monitoring the Network

When the network has been discovered and laid out by IP Map, the operator can monitor the state of the network by:

- Looking at maps for color alerts.

- Looking at maps for new nodes.

- Creating special submaps for monitoring status.

- Checking the events notification window for changes.

- Establishing baselines for normal network performance.

- Building an application to monitor trends.

- Setting up thresholds for monitored MIB values.

- Fine-tuning threshold monitoring.

- Setting up event-triggered actions.

The last five steps can be used in combination to proactively monitor the network.

Looking at maps for color alerts: NNM allows the operator to easily identify objects exhibiting an abnormal condition, without looking at every object on the network map. A color alert on a symbol indicates that some part of that object is experiencing a problem. The color of the object indicates the severity of the problem. For example, yellow indicates a marginal problem, while red indicates a critical problem.

As noted, the status indications of objects are propagated through to all related submaps, from each child object to the parent object. To isolate a fault on the network, the operator merely follows color alerts by opening child submaps of objects that contain a color alert until the specific parent object that is not functioning is reached.

Looking at maps for new nodes: Although IP Map automatically discovers new IP-addressable nodes, sometimes it does not know where to place the symbol for that node. This happens when a gateway (hub), for example, does not have the ability to tell IP Map where a node should be placed.

In these cases, IP Map places the symbols of newly discovered nodes in the default Segment submap, which acts as a holding area. The operator checks the default Segment submap periodically for new nodes that may have been discovered. The operator then can move newly discovered objects from the holding area to a specific location using the drag-and-drop technique.

Creating special submaps for monitoring status: The operator can create submaps that are logically, rather than physically, organized. For example, it may be necessary to have a submap that contains all of the gateways for a particular location to facilitate specialized monitoring. To do this, the operator copies objects from other submaps into the newly created map using the cut-and-paste operations accessed from the OpenView Windows menu bar. A background graphic can be added to the new submap. (Sample graphics are supplied with OpenView Windows.) The special submap can then be opened from its own symbol in the Internet submap.

Checking the Events Notification Window for Changes: Whenever a change occurs on the network, an event is generated. This happens, for example, when a new node is added, when a node becomes inoperable, or when a threshold is exceeded. Through various NNM internal processes, the event is sent to a predefined category in the Events notification window (Figure 3-7), which provides notice when new events occur. This window has buttons that correspond to the various event categories. When a button changes color, it is an indication that an event has occurred.

The types of events that are sent by SNMP nodes and displayed in the Events notification window are:

- **Threshold Events:** indicate that a threshold has been exceeded.

- **Network Topology Events:** indicate that an object or interface has been added or deleted.

- **Error Events:** indicate that an inconsistent or unexpected behavior has occurred.

- **Status Events:** indicate that an object or interface has changed up or down, or that an object or interface has started or stopped responding to ICMP echo requests.[3]

- **Node Configuration Events:** indicate that a node's configuration has changed.

- **Application Alert Events:** indicate that an OpenView Windows application has generated an alarm or alert.

- **All Events:** lists all of the above events and other events in one dialog box.

To view an event, the operator clicks on the corresponding button, which is colored white. A dialog box appears that lists all unacknowledged events in that category. For each event listed, specific information is provided, including the date and time of occurrence, and the address of the node on which the event occurred. The operator can then view the node and invoke appropriate operations from the menu bar to further diagnose and correct the problem. After viewing events, the operator can acknowledge selected events or all events, so they do not reappear the next time the dialog box is opened. Acknowledging all events clears the corresponding event button.

Establishing baselines for normal network performance: A baseline for normal network performance is useful for monitoring the extent of deviation, which can act as an early warning of impending problems. To establish a baseline, a selected system(s) must be monitored during the course of one or two weeks. A gateway, for example, might be selected for monitoring because it has a heavy traffic load and is critical to the network.

Two NNM tools are used for baseline performance monitoring: the MIB Browser and the Data Collector.

Using the MIB Browser, the operator can review the MIB tree to determine what information to monitor on a system. On a gateway, for example, this information can include inbound octets, outbound octets, input errors and output errors.

---

[3] The Internet Control Message Protocol (ICMP) is used by the Internet Protocol (IP) to transmit error and control messages. One message is the "echo request," which is used to test whether a destination is reachable. In Internet terminology, this is called "pinging." The echo request message also keeps track of the time it takes to get a reply so that average delay time on a line can be determined for comparison with the delay threshold of the application. For example, a host-based application may time out if the line delay is too long.

Next, a data collection operation is created on each selected MIB object. The setup procedure entails selecting the interfaces to be monitored on each system, setting the collection mode — in this case, no threshold — and the polling interval.

Building an application to monitor trends: Through menu selections, an application can be built that will display the collected information as a table, form or graph, which also will be output to a printer. With the application, data can be monitored for any period of time. Two weeks is usually ample time to provide the data needed for trend analysis. In graph form, the resolution of the collected data can be changed to get a better view of the trend being represented. For example, it may be difficult to pick out the trend in data collected over a 24-hour period at five-minute intervals because of the sheer number of points shown on the graph. By changing the time interval represented on the graph to only four hours, it is easier to identify trends and choose appropriate thresholds.

Setting up thresholds for monitored MIB values: After analyzing the trends, a threshold can be set for each MIB object. This allows an event to be generated and sent to the Events notification window whenever the threshold is exceeded.

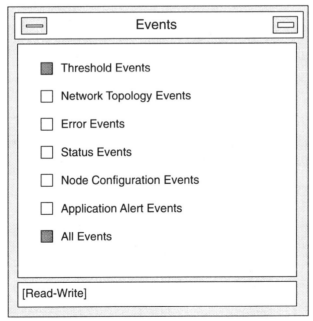

Source: Hewlett-Packard Co.

Figure 3-7: *Events Notification Window*

Setting up a threshold starts with selecting the MIB object and the collection mode. In this case, a collection mode is selected that allows data collection to continue even as events are generated when a threshold is exceeded. Next, the polling interval and trap identification (ID) are set. Data collection can be customized by assigning a trap ID consisting of an odd number between 1001 and 1999. This enables special event notifications to be set up on specific data collections. The even numbers between 1002 and 2000 are reserved for the respective rearm trap IDs, which are generated automatically.

For example, if a gateway is being monitored for inbound octets and outbound octets, setting the thresholds to 50 and the rearms to 10, means that an event will be generated when the number of octets exceeds 50 during a given polling interval. A rearm event will be generated if the value drops below 10 percent of 50, or five, at a subsequent polling interval. Another threshold event will not be generated until the rearm event occurs and the collected value again exceeds the threshold value. This process is depicted in Figure 3-8.

By periodically checking the Events notification window, the operator can determine if a threshold has been exceeded. If so, appropriate action can be taken to resolve the problem. If it is discovered that a problem doesn't exist, it may be that the selected threshold value does not provide

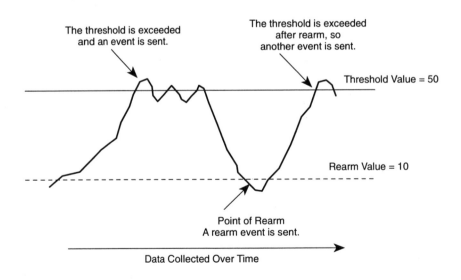

The threshold is exceeded and an event is sent.

The threshold is exceeded after rearm, so another event is sent.

Threshold Value = 50

Rearm Value = 10

Point of Rearm
A rearm event is sent.

Data Collected Over Time

Source: Hewlett-Packard Co.

Figure 3-8: The Effect of Rearm on Event Notification

the granularity necessary for fault diagnosis. In this case, some fine-tuning is necessary.

Fine-tuning threshold monitoring: The threshold value may have to be monitored for a period of time to ensure that it is an appropriate selection. If several threshold events occur daily without any loss in network performance, the threshold and rearm values should be reset to yield more useful information.

Setting up event-triggered actions: When threshold settings are stable, an action can be specified to occur when threshold values are exceeded. Setting up an action can range from having a message appear in a pop-up window to having a hand-held beeper provide notice of an alert. An action can be set up that invokes a script that automates fault recovery. Actions also can be set up for rearm events.

NETWORK NODE MANAGER IS POPULAR AMONG SYSTEM ADMINISTRATORS who have moved away from mainframes completely. HP OpenView Network Node Manager was designed to meet the needs of a variety of users. Helpdesk staff can use the up-to-date maps to understand the current status and health of the network. Technicians can use NNM's tools to quickly isolate and correct problems. Administrators can take advantage of NNM's network and system configuration capabilities to minimize the time spent in routine management activities. NNM offers planners more flexibility and control in collecting and analyzing performance information for the entire network.

HP's nearest competitor is IBM, which also is positioning its NetView/6000 for the widest range of network users possible. Both NetView Distribution Manager (DM) and OpenView Network Node Manager support HP-UX, SunOS, Solaris, DOS and Windows.

With the next major release of the OpenView platform in 1996, network managers also will be able to divide management tasks among distributed consoles located across the enterprise using a new version of the Network Node Manager. And using SNMP2 agents, Network Node Manager will be able to distribute the polling information to other workstations on the network. This will enable OpenView to send agents across tens of thousands of nodes — up from its current limit of 4,000.

CHAPTER

4

OperationsCenter

TO KEEP DISTRIBUTED COMPUTING RESOURCES AVAILABLE IN MULTIVENDOR environments, maintain the productivity of operations staff and contain operating costs, the management application must:

- Prepare and deliver management information to a central location.

- Present only the relevant, significant information.

- Execute management tasks from the central location.

- Automate responses to events.

- Offer problem-resolution guidance.

- Provide the means for historical analysis.

HP's OpenView OperationsCenter is an example of this kind of management application. It provides central operations and problem management of multivendor distributed systems (Figure 4-1). The management solution increases the availability of computing resources, decreases the time to resolve problems and, in the process, helps to reduce the cost of managing the client-server environment.

OperationsCenter extends the OpenView platform beyond Simple Network Management Protocol (SNMP) to the management of workstations. Within a computing environment managed by OperationsCenter, a specific system is selected as the central management station. The management station performs activities such as receiving and presenting management information, initiating actions and activating the agents. All other systems in the environment: connected by either LAN or WAN to the management station: are managed nodes.

An intelligent agent on each managed node collects and processes management information about CPU use, disk space, I/O and other system operations. OperationsCenter monitors values originating from sources such as system or application log files, SNMP traps, or any customized monitoring application. Using filters and thresholds, only requested information is collected from the various management agents and passed on to OperationsCenter using remote procedure calls (RPCs). In monitoring key system (and application) variables against threshold values, OperationsCenter can provide an early warning of developing problems.

At this writing, the agent software works with the following platforms: AT&T Systems 3000, SunSoft Solaris 2.3, IBM RISC/6000, Sun Microsystems SPARCstation, BULL HN Information Systems DPX/20 and HP 9000 and 3000 Series systems.

OperationsCenter processes and consolidates the collected information for presentation at a central management station. This reduces unnecessary network overhead and minimizes processing at the central management station. Upon receiving retrieved the information, OperationsCenter immediately can initiate corrective actions and provide individual guidance for problem identification and further problem resolution.

OperationsCenter responds to events in several ways: automatically, without operator intervention; with predefined actions that are initiated by the operator, or with on-screen displays of event-specific help text and instructions.

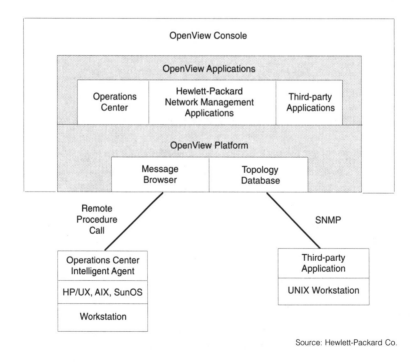

Source: Hewlett-Packard Co.

Figure 4-1: *HP OpenView OperationsCenter*

66

OperationsCenter also can forward events into a trouble ticket system for in-depth problem-resolution tracking.

All management information and associated records are stored in a central repository for future analysis and audit. The historical data allows the generation of event-specific help texts and the automation of certain problem resolution processes.

Administrators can create multiple, individual management workspaces tailored to match the skills and responsibilities of operations staff members. For example, an operator in charge of system backups and performance monitoring only will receive events from these applications or services and only will be given access to those functions required to manage backup and monitor performance.

OperationsCenter also can receive and display alerts and messages from IBM's SNA, Novell's NetWare and Digital's DECnet. Each has graphical map and event collection capabilities under OpenView and can be represented with its own icon in OperationsCenter. A different operator can be assigned to each environment. The maps and events of each environment are consolidated into OperationCenter's Message Browser database, a log of active and inactive system events.

OPERATIONSCENTER STRUCTURE

Two important elements of OperationsCenter's architecture are managed nodes and the management server. The managed nodes are controlled by the management server. The system running the OperationsCenter application is designated as the management server. By default, the management server is also a managed node. Figure 4-2 shows this structure.

Managed nodes are systems that OperationsCenter monitors and controls. OperationsCenter has the following types of managed nodes:

Controlled: All management and monitoring capabilities can be applied to controlled nodes.

Monitored: Management information is collected and forwarded to the management server, but corrective actions cannot be started. Monitored nodes are useful for restricting access to the node for security purposes.

Message allowed: No agent software is loaded, but messages are accepted by OperationsCenter. Intelligent network devices such as peripherals or nodes belonging to remote networks can be message-allowed nodes.

Unmanaged: No agent processes are started. Incoming messages from these nodes are ignored.

The *management server* runs the OperationsCenter application. It is here that the entire software is stored, including the complete current configuration. There is one management server per OperationsCenter in-stallation. The management server's basic tasks include:

- Collecting data from managed nodes.

- Re-grouping messages.

- Calling the appropriate agent to start actions (local automatic actions are started on the managed node) and initiate sessions on managed nodes.

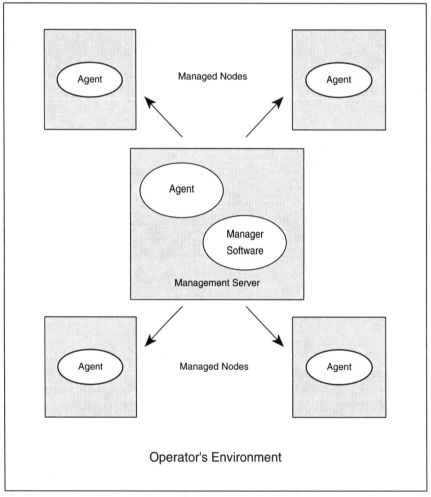

Source: Hewlett-Packard Co.

Figure 4-2: OperationsCenter Architecture

- Controlling the datastore for messages, actions and configuration information.

- Forwarding messages to display stations.

- Installing OperationsCenter agent software on managed nodes.

- Intercepting SNMP traps.

SOFTWARE COMPONENTS

OperationsCenter's software consists of two basic components: agent and manager.

HP's intelligent agent software is located on the managed nodes and is primarily responsible for collecting and forwarding information, monitoring parameters, generating messages, and starting and controlling actions.

The basic capabilities of intelligent agent software include:

- **Message interception:** Logfile, console (MPE/iX), and OperationsCenter interface messages are intercepted on the managed node.

- **Message filtering:** Messages are compared to conditions and arranged into groups. Filters can accept or suppress messages.

- **Message logging:** Messages can be locally logged, or they can be optionally logged on the management server.

- **Message buffering:** If the management server is not reachable, messages are retained in a storage buffer until the management server can receive them.

- **Action execution:** Actions can be started locally or remotely.

- **Threshold monitoring:** Performance values are monitored at specified intervals, and messages can be generated when performance varies from predefined limits.

- **Self monitoring:** OperationsCenter can monitor its own processes.

Intelligent agents are capable of tracking a large number of parameters. They not only inform operators of potential problems, but can correct them in predefined ways automatically.

The management software is located on the management server and communicates with, controls and directs the agents. The agents are accessible through the management software, which provides the graphical user interface.

USER ROLES

OperationsCenter supports the roles of both administrator and operator. The administrator is primarily responsible for installing and configuring the OperationsCenter software and for establishing the initial operating policies and procedures.

The administrator also has the responsibilty to:

- Maintain the software.

- Change the configuration to add or change operators, nodes and messages.

- Collect and analyzing historical data.

- Define management processes and security policies.

Operators monitor and maintain the managed systems and objects. They work with OperationsCenter almost continuously, monitoring status changes and performing tasks and actions as required, including reviewing and managing messages; starting corrective actions; and starting applications, scripts and programs.

Each operator has a task-oriented management environment with a customized view and set of tools. The view is defined by the administrator and includes only those managed nodes and messages for which the operator is responsible. The administrator decides what tools the operator needs to maintain the assigned nodes and perform the required tasks.

CENTRAL CONTROL

Managing status information and resolving problems requires the operator to have control over defined environments and direct access to systems from a central management station. As mentioned, each OperationsCenter operator has control over a specific set of systems or nodes.

After collecting information about a problem, the operator selects the application or tool that helps solve the problem. For this, the Application Desktop is used. It is similar to a toolbox: operators select the proper tool for the task.

The operator can access the problem system directly through a virtual console and begin corrective actions. A direct physical console connection also can be configured. Or, using OperationCenter's Broadcast Command capability, the operator can select one or more nodes and issue a single command that is completed on each of the selected systems.

CENTRAL MONITORING

Central monitoring of the environment provides realtime and proactive problem solution measures. OperationsCenter offers a variety of monitoring techniques:

- **Threshold monitoring:** For each critical variable selected, acceptable limits of performance, called thresholds, are defined. These thresholds can be minimum or maximum values. A threshold can be configured to issue warning messages before a process exceeds its limits. A polling interval for each threshold also can be defined.

- **System-alive monitoring:** This checks that each managed node is operating.

- **Self monitoring:** This monitors its own operations and verifies that all of its elements are properly operating.

OperationsCenter uses events, messages and actions to observe and control status, formulate and provide information, and respond to and correct problems.

EVENTS

An event is a change in status, a particular occurrence, or an incident within the computing environment. An event occurs on an object. Typically, an event represents either a change in status or a violation of a threshold. For example, the status of a printer changes when the paper tray empties. Or, a threshold is violated when CPU-load exceeds acceptable limits. Each of these occurrences is an event. A message can be generated for each event.

Although many events represent problems that must be corrected, but not all events are problems. For example, when a user logs on or off a system, the status of the system changes, and an event occurs. However, this event requires no action on the part of an operator.

MESSAGES

Messages are structured pieces of information created by events. OperationsCenter intercepts and collects messages to learn of events. Messages can be any length, from a few bits to a complete text description of the event.

OperationsCenter intercepts messages from the following sources:

- **Logfiles:** OperationsCenter encapsulates logfiles of applications and systems, extracts message information and checks their status.

- **SNMP traps:** OperationsCenter intercepts traps.

- **MPE/iX consoles:** OperationsCenter intercepts messages sent to the MPE/iX console.

- **OperationsCenter message interface:** These messages are generated by an OperationsCenter-specific command or application programming interface (API).

- **Monitored objects:** Threshold levels for monitored objects can be set up. When measured values of monitored objects exceed configured threshold levels, OperationsCenter can generate appropriate messages.

After intercepting a message, OperationsCenter can completely restructure it; for example, to present the message to the operator in an understandable format, or to change the severity of the event. Messages that report problems require actions to resolve the problem.

ACTIONS

An action is a response to an event. If the event creating the message represents a problem, an action must be started to correct it. However, actions also are used to perform daily tasks, such as starting an application every day on the same nodes. An action can be a shell script, program, command, application start, or any other type of response.

The two categories of actions within OperationsCenter are message-bound actions and self-started actions. Message-bound actions are preconfigured by the OperationsCenter administrator as responses to specific messages. There are two types of message-bound actions:

- **Automatic:** This action begins automatically when the message is received.

- **Operator initiated:** The operator reviews the message, then starts the action.

Self-started actions are started by an operator, usually as part of a routine task; for example, starting an application every day. They are not related to a specific incoming message. The operator chooses from a set of available tools and completes procedures.

PROBLEM RESOLUTION

In OperationsCenter, operators have access to the resources needed to resolve various problems. OperationsCenter provides the following:

- **Automatic actions:** implement corrective responses immediately on receipt of the message without operator intervention.

- **Operator initiated actions:** the operator reviews the message and then starts the corrective action.

- **Specific problem-resolution instructions:** information displayed in the Message Details window assists the operator to resolve the problem.

- **History logs of message annotations:** used to help track resolution techniques used in previous or similar occurrences of the problem.

- **Application Desktop:** to start applications, broadcasts commands to multiple systems, or opens a virtual (or physical) console directly on the affected systems and begin corrective actions.

DAILY TASKS

The daily tasks that an operator can perform using OperationsCenter, include:

- Reviewing the environment.

- Managing the environment.

- Examining message attributes.

- Browsing messages.

- Reviewing message details.

- Using the History Message Browser.

- Solving problems.

- Evaluating an action's results.

- Using the Application Desktop.

- Annotating and acknowledging messages.

- Generating reports.

REVIEWING THE ENVIRONMENT
The working environment contains the following primary windows:

- Managed Nodes.

- Message Groups.

- Message Browser.

- Application Desktop.

Each window presents unique information, customized to match the specific environment and responsibilities of the operator. Each of these windows opens every time the operator logs in to OperationsCenter.

Managed Nodes: This window contains a symbol for each node or group of nodes for which the operator is responsible. The operator can use the window to check the status of each node and select nodes on which a specific task must be performed.

Node symbols are displayed in colors corresponding to the highest severity level of any message received from the node. For example, if a node symbol turns red, the node has at least one open critical message. After critical messages have been acknowledged, the node symbol changes color to indicate the highest severity level of any remaining messages.

Symbols in this window can be compound, which means they can represent layers. For example, all nodes located in a single building or function can be grouped together and represented by a single symbol. Double-clicking on a compound symbol opens a submap detailing the individual nodes of the group. In the example in Figure 4-3, double-clicking on Sales opens a submap displaying the nodes of the sales group.

Message Groups: OperationsCenter uses message groups to bring together management information about similar or related managed objects and to provide status information on an aggregate level. Messages are organized into groups to simplify message handling and managing and to facilitate the operator's work in a task-oriented method. For example, one operator can be responsible for all backups, regardless of the system. All messages related to backups are then grouped for this operator and displayed in the Message Group window.

Similar to the Managed Nodes window, the color of a particular symbol represents the current status. A change in the color of a symbol on the Message Group's window indicates a change in status within the operator's environment.

Message Browser: The Message Browser window (Figure 4-4) provides a unique view of the messages received at the operator's display station. OperationsCenter collects messages from the operator's managed nodes and delivers them to the display station.

This window can be used to review and manage messages and to direct problem management activities. Incoming messages are displayed with preconfigured attributes and with status information. The operator can look at all the details about a single message and initiate an action to resolve the event that triggered a message, or OperationsCenter can perform an action automatically. The operator can prepare message reports, and OperationsCenter's annotation facility provides the means to document actions and read through actions already performed.

Finally, the operator can use the Message Browser window to acknowledge messages for which actions have been completed. When a message has been acknowledged, it is removed from the Message Browser and put in the history database. The operator can use the History Message Browser window to view these messages and unacknowledge them.

Application Desktop: The Application Desktop window (Figure 4-5) displays icons for all applications and custom programs registered with OperationsCenter. Clicking on an icon activates the desired action. This working environment can be configured to match the skills and responsibilities of the individual operator, in terms of management information supplied and capabilities granted. OperationsCenter's internal notification service makes operators aware of critical events by changing the color of the affected icons according to the OpenView color coding scheme. In addition, external notification services: such as a pager, warning light, or telephone call initiation: can be activated through a command interface.

Like the Managed Nodes window, the Application Desktop might be structured hierarchically with compound symbols, each of which represents a group of applications. Double-clicking on such a symbol opens a second-level desktop containing the applications assigned to that group.

Tools also can be displayed as compound symbols. For example, Backup Tools can be the symbol in the first level, and **tar**, **dd** and **cpio** can be the tools represented on the second level.

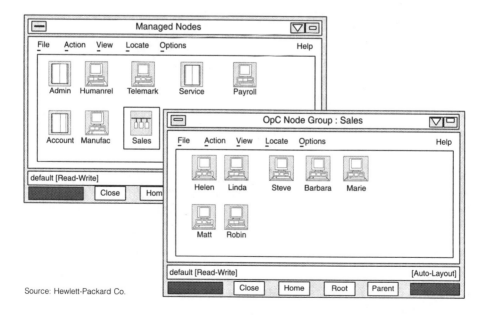

Source: Hewlett-Packard Co.

Figure 4-3: Opening a Hierarchical Node Group Submap

MANAGING THE ENVIRONMENT

The primary daily OperationsCenter tasks are:

- To keep the environment operational.

- To receive notification about changes in status and about events.

- To manage messages.

With OperationsCenter, the operator can provide higher service levels and reduce the time spent doing simple, repetitive tasks. Messages allow the operator to observe the activities of managed nodes, permitting problems to be detected at early stages of development, so that corrective actions can be taken before they become critical and impact end users. Keeping that in mind, the operator can select from multiple tools, information sources, and problem-solving techniques. The operator also can maintain a complete history database for all resolved problems.

Resolving Problems: Problem resolution and message management are closely related. A system of messages allows the operator to fully understand problems and develop solutions.

The major areas of problem resolution are illustrated in Figure 4-6 and are briefly described as follows:

Notifying: The operator detects the problem within the user interface or via external notification services.

Investigating: The operator examines the problem, determines where and what has occurred, and develops a plan to resolve it.

Solving: The operator corrects the problem. Although automatic actions do not require operator intervention, the operator chooses when and where to start other actions. After finishing the actions, they are reviewed to determine if they have indeed solved the problem.

Documenting: The operator closes the problem, records the actions performed and measures the resulting values, and moves the message to the history database.

Notifying and Investigating: The operator uses the Message Browser, the Managed Nodes and the Message Groups windows to detect problems, review messages and node status, and direct problem management activities. These windows notify the operator about what has happened and where the problems are occurring.

The Message Browser window is the first source that can be used to become aware of a problem. The window shows the operator what has happened, how serious it is, and if there are actions configured to respond to the problem.

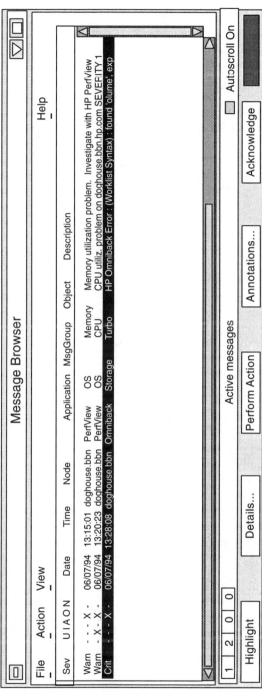

Figure 4-4: Message Browser Window

Locating the Problem: The operator quickly can locate the problem by clicking on the message in the Browser and choosing the Highlight button. As shown in Figure 4-7, the Managed Nodes and Message Groups windows open, or are moved forward in the display, and the names of the node and message group appear with highlighted text.

EXAMINING MESSAGE ATTRIBUTES

The Message Browser window's key information is contained in the message buffer, the section of the window displaying incoming messages. Each line of the message buffer displays a single message and its attributes. For example, the operator can quickly learn the following by reading the message attributes:

- Message severity.

- Configuring actions.

- Available instructions.

- Available annotations.

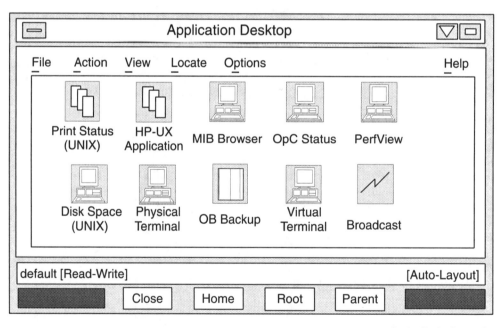

Source: Hewlett-Packard Co.

Figure 4-5: Application Desktop Window

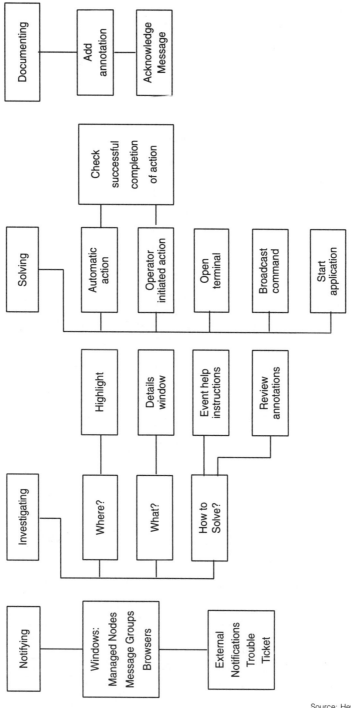

Figure 4-6: Components of Problem Resolution

Source: Hewlett-Packard Co.

The attributes appear across the Browser Headline. The message displays a value beneath each attribute. A dash indicates that the message does not have a value matching the attribute. For example, a dash beneath the *A* indicates that no automatic action has been configured for the message (Figure 4-8).

BROWSING MESSAGES

The first column in the Browser Headline is Sev., which informs the operator of the relative importance and status of the message. Figure 4-9 shows some typical severity flags.

The OperationsCenter administrator assigns a severity level to a message based on its importance in the environment assigned to a particular operator. OperationsCenter's severity levels are:

Crit: Critical indicates a service-affecting condition has occurred and immediate corrective action is required.

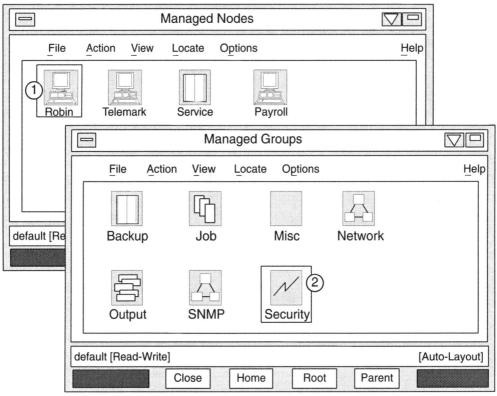

Source: Hewlett-Packard Co.

Figure 4-7: Managed Node and Message Group

Warn: Warning indicates a potential or impending service-affecting fault. Action should be taken to further diagnose and correct the problem and prevent it from becoming a more serious fault.

Norm: Normal indicates expected message output; for example, when a process starts or completes, or other status information.

?: Unknown indicates that the severity level cannot be determined.

As shown in Figure 4-8, other message attributes in the Browser Headline are:

U: Unmatched messages do not match any of the filters defined for a message source. Filters are conditions that configure OperationsCenter to accept or suppress messages. These messages require special attention because they can represent problems for which no preconfigured action exists.

H: Help instructions aid in the resolution of the problem. If available, these instructions are displayed in the Message Details window.

A: Automatic action indicates that an automatic action has been configured for the message and gives the status of the action. The value of the attribute indicates if the action was successful (S), has failed (F), or is running (R).

O: Operator initiated action indicates that an operator initiated action has been configured for the message and gives the status of the action. The action can be started by the operator after reviewing the message. The value of the attribute indicates if an action is available (X), was successful (S), has failed (F), or is running (R).

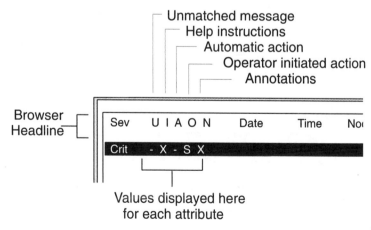

Source: Hewlett-Packard Co.

Figure 4-8: Message Attributes and Values

N: Annotations indicates if annotations exist for the message. The operator can review annotations for procedures used to resolve similar problems by using the History Browser window.

Date: Specifies the date the message was received on the OperationsCenter management server.

Time: Specifies the time the message was received on the OperationsCenter management server.

Node: Specifies the node that issued the message.

Application: Specifies the application that was affected by or detected the message.

MsgGroup: Specifies the message's message group.

Object: Specifies the object which was affected by, detected, or caused the message. This can be, for example, a printer which sent a message when it stopped accepting requests, or a backup device that sent a message when a backup stopped.

Description: Displays the text of the message. The message's original text can be reviewed in the Original Message window, accessible from the Message Details window.

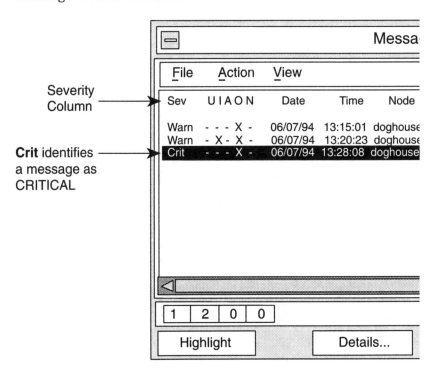

Source: Hewlett-Packard Co.

Figure 4-9: Severity Column and Severity Flags

82

REVIEWING MESSAGE DETAILS

The Message Details window contains the full details of a message (Figure 4-10). The operator can use this window to perform many investigating tasks.

The Message Details window is divided into the following sections:

Attributes: This section is used to review the full description of the message, including:

- Node and application.

- Message group.

- Object.

- Source of the message (SNMP trap, logfile, console, interface).

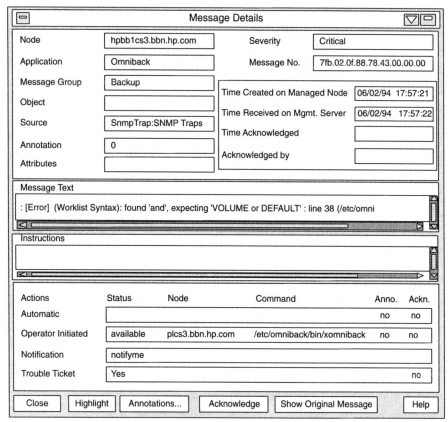

Source: Hewlett-Packard Co.

Figure 4-10: Reviewing Message Details

- Annotations, if any.

- Attributes.

- Severity of the message.

- Message number.

- When message was sent, received, acknowledged.

- Message text.

Instructions: Are directions from the OperationsCenter administrator to help the operator resolve the problem. Not all messages have instructions.

Actions: Show the automatic and operator initiated actions which were configured for a message and where the action will be started. Automatic annotations and acknowledgements are indicated, as are external notification and trouble ticket configurations.

Pushbuttons: Are used to complete the following tasks:

- Highlight: To locate the source of the message.

- Annotations: To create or review existing message annotations.

- Acknowledge: To move the message to the history database after the operator is finished working with it.

- Show Original Message: To review the original text of the message. (Compares the message text as displayed in the Message Details window with the original message text.)

Scanning Policy: When the operator scans the Message Browser window for incoming messages, the following priorities and policies can make the process more effective.

Severity: Severity flags can be used to search for messages that represent problems. Color-coded severity levels speed this process.

Actions: Messages can be searched for which operator initiated actions must be started.

Failures: Messages can be searched for which automatic or operator initiated actions have failed.

Procedures: Messages can be searched that do not have a configured action but that require a response from the operator to correct a problem.

Priorities: As part of the scanning policy, if the operator wants node status to be the first priority, the Managed Nodes window can be used in conjunction with the Message Browser. A node's symbol changes color, reflecting the highest severity level of a message issued on that node. These colors also correspond with the colors used in the Sev. column of the Message Browser window. For example, if the operator notices that a node's symbol has changed to red (critical), the Message Browser window can be scanned for messages with a Crit flag.

The operator can use the Message Browser Layout window, shown in Figure 4-11, to select message attributes to reflect a personal scanning policy.

Severity Levels: The operator can see how many messages of each severity level are in the Message Browser by checking the color bar beneath the message buffer. The total number of messages for each severity level appears in the corresponding color bar. For example, 8 in the red section of the bar indicates that there are eight Crit messages in the message buffer. Adjacent to the bar is a view identifier which specifies the type of messages displayed (Figure 4-12).

VIEW BROWSER

The View Browser window is the operator's customized presentation of messages. While the Message Browser window displays every message belonging to the operator's assigned managed nodes and message groups, the View Browser window displays only the messages the operator wants

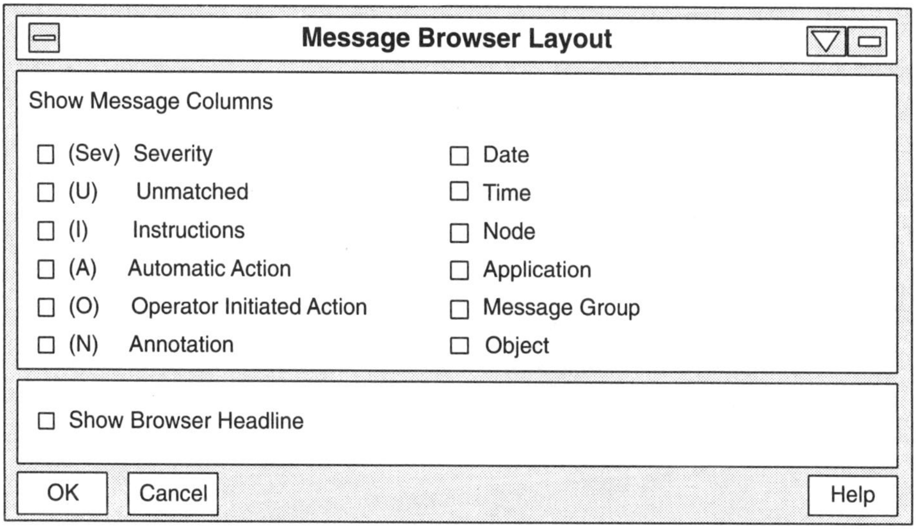

Source: Hewlett-Packard Co

Figure 4-11: Defining a Layout to Match the Scanning Policy

to see. The operator can tailor the view so that only the most important messages are displayed. This enables the operator to concentrate on messages that need swift attention, instead of becoming distracted with a much larger number of routine messages.

The operator can set up simple or complex filters (Figure 4-13) to specify which messages are displayed. Incoming messages can be filtered to display only a subset of messages. For example, if the operator is interested only in messages with warning or critical severity levels, messages can be filtered so that those with unknown and normal severity are not displayed. Messages can also be filtered for display by day or time period.

HISTORY MESSAGE BROWSER

The History Message Browser window displays all acknowledged messages: all messages on which the operator has completed work or which already were sent to the history database by OperationsCenter.

The History Browser window is used as a resource for solving problems. For example, if the operator is not sure about how to perform an action for a message, the history data for occurrences of the same or similar message can be reviewed. By reviewing previous solutions to problems, the operator can develop a plan to solve current problems.

The Browser View window is used to define a set of view filters to open the History Message Browser. A sort filter arranges the messages in the most effective order (Figure 4-14).

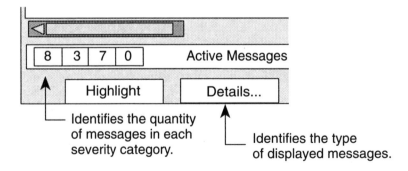

Source: Hewlett-Packard Co.

Figure 4-12: Reviewing the Number and Type of Messages

PROBLEM SOLVING

When the operator is notified of a problem and it has been investigated, the next step is to solve it. For this, multiple tools are available, including:

- Automatic actions.

- Operator initiated actions.

- Operator instructions.

- Applications.

- Broadcast command.

- Terminal or console access.

Automatic Actions: The OperationsCenter administrator can configure automatic actions for many messages. These actions are started when the event is detected. A message's automatic action can be reviewed by opening the Message Details window.

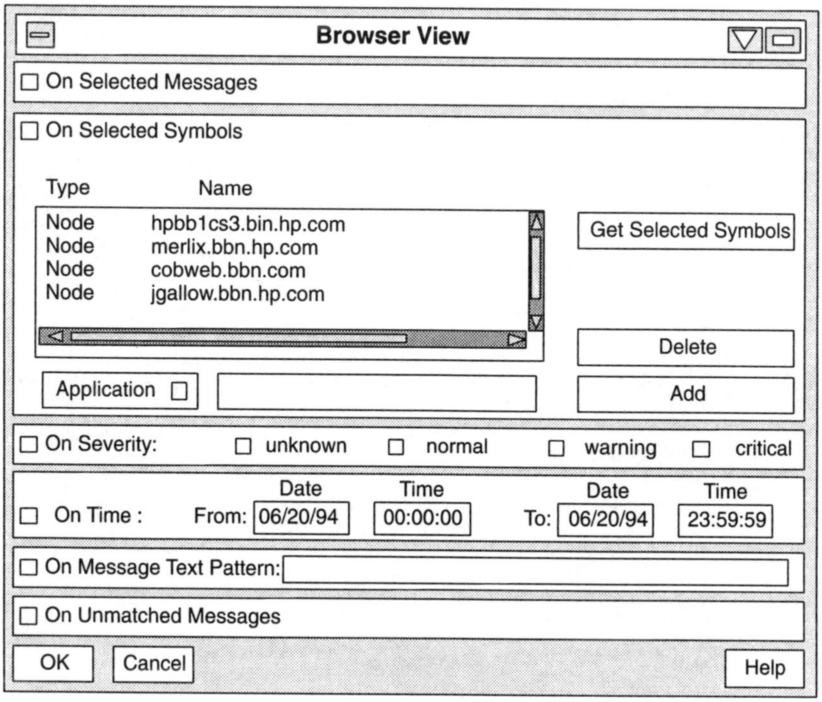

Source: Hewlett-Packard Co.

Figure 4-13: Defining Messages for Viewing

After an action has completed, the operator can review the results to ensure that the problem has been corrected. If the OperationsCenter administrator has configured automatic annotations for the message, these too can be reviewed along with the results of an automatic action by reading the message's annotations. The action's **stdout** and **stderr** are logged as annotations with the message.

The OperationsCenter administrator can evaluate the effectiveness of actions by reviewing annotations and determining if additional or different automatic actions should be configured.

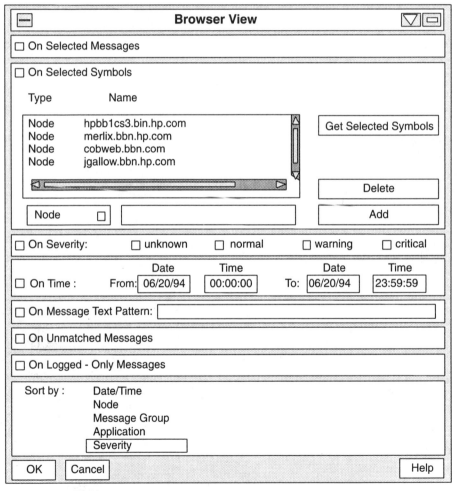

Source: Hewlett-Packard Co.

Figure 4-14: Filter Setup for the History Browser Window

Operator Initiated Actions: The OperationsCenter administrator configures operator initiated actions for messages for which automatic actions might be inappropriate. For example, an automatic action that removes core files from a development environment could result in the loss of necessary data. Or, actions or programs requiring too much CPU should not be started without first evaluating system load factors and requirements. For these types of actions, an operator's intervention and control are necessary.

The operator can review the action by opening the Message Details window and start the action by clicking on the message and choosing the Perform Action button.

After an action is complete, the operator can review the results to ensure that the problem has been corrected. If the OperationsCenter administrator has configured automatic annotations for the message, the results of an operator initiated action can be reviewed by reading the message's annotations. The action's **stdout** and **stderr** are logged as annotations with the message.

The OperationsCenter administrator evaluates the effectiveness of actions by reviewing annotations and determining if additional or different operator initiated actions should be configured.

Operator Instructions: The OperationsCenter administrator can provide written instructions for a message to help the operator solve the problem. As shown in Figure 4-8, an *X* in the *I* attribute column of the Browser window's headline indicates that the message has instructions. The operator reviews the instructions by selecting the message and clicking on the Details button. All instructions for a message are displayed in the Message Details window.

Applications: The operator can start applications from the Application Desktop to resolve unsuccessful automatic or operator initiated actions or messages for which an action has not been configured. However, starting an application to resolve a problem requires that the operator have a thorough understanding of the event and message.

Command Broadcasts: The operator can start corrective actions simultaneously on multiple nodes by broadcasting a command. This entails specifying the command for broadcast and selecting the nodes within the operator's environment on which the command is to be started.

This capability also can be used to investigate problems. For example, it can be used to broadcast the **Ops -ef** command to a node to check the number of current processes. The results of broadcasting a command are displayed in the Broadcast Output window (Figure 4-15).

The operator can start actions directly on problem nodes by opening a terminal window. Using a terminal window, the operator can further investigate a problem, issue commands, scripts or start applications.

EVALUATING AN ACTION'S RESULTS

To maintain a current and accurate overview of the computing environment, the operator must know the status and results of actions. An action's status is the availability and state of the action, and it concerns two issues: whether an action has been configured for the message, or whether the action has been completed successfully.

An action's result is problem resolution, and it concerns the issue of whether the action resolved the problem.

Reviewing action availability is part of the initial investigation of problems. The operator reviews the Message Browser and Details windows to determine the availability of automatic or operator initiated actions. The value beneath the message attribute in the Browser Headline displays the availability and state of the action. Figure 4-16 shows the state of an automatic action that failed and one that was completed successfully.

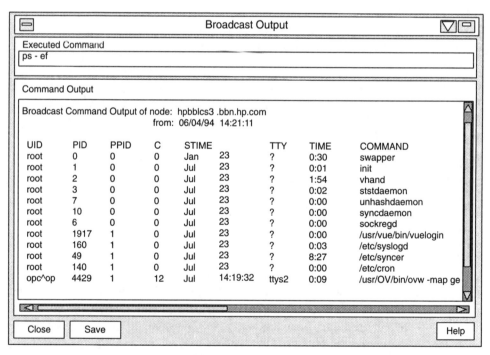

Source: Hewlett-Packard Co.

*Figure 4-15: Reviewing Output of the **ps -ef** Command*

Evaluating action results is part of solving problems. Actions might not always be successful in resolving a problem. A successfully completed action does not always mean that the problem has been solved. The action state in the Browser window does not tell the operator the result of an action. The operator can check an action's result in two ways:

• Review the message's annotations: OperationsCenter automatically writes the action's **stdout** and **stderr** as annotations for all automatic and operator initiated actions.

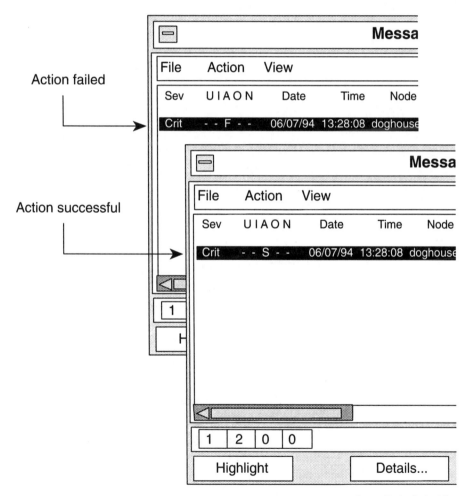

Source: Hewlett-Packard Co.

Figure 4-16: *Status of Automatic Actions*

• Broadcast a script or command, from the Broadcast Command window, to review the Status of the object. In the Broadcast Output window, the results can be reviewed to determine whether the state of the object has changed.

The symbols in this example represent the following capabilities:
Disk Space: Starts the **bdf** command to report the number of free disk blocks on selected nodes.
Print Status: Starts **lp** status to check the **lp** status information.
Processes: Starts **ps -f** to report process status on selected nodes.
Broadcast: Opens the Broadcast Command window when a command to broadcast to multiple nodes is specified.
Physical Terminal: Opens a physical terminal connection to the selected nodes.
Virtual Terminal: Opens a virtual terminal on the selected nodes.
MIB Browser: Starts the OpenView MIB Browser application with which MIB values on selected nodes can be checked and graphed.

APPLICATION DESKTOP

Applications are scripts or programs that have been integrated into OperationsCenter. The OperationsCenter administrator first examines the operator's environment, then determines which applications are needed to maintain it. Each application has predefined startup attributes, including a list of managed nodes on which the application can be started.

Applications also can be programs or services running in the environment; for example, the UNIX **lp** print spooler program. The operator is typically responsible for controlling the status of the **lp** spooler and its peripherals. To maintain the print services, the operator responds to messages issued by the **lp** spooler and sends controlling commands, such as enable. To control programs within the environment, the operator must have access to the correct commands and the user login capabilities.

The operator can change many of the start-up attributes of an application by using the Customized Application Call window. For example, the operator can change nodes on which an application is started, the user name, or the call parameters.

Broadcasting from the Desktop: When the operator broadcasts a command, it is issued once and sent to multiple nodes. The operator can perform global tasks quickly and easily by selecting the nodes in the Managed Nodes window, opening the Broadcast Command window by double-clicking on the broadcast symbol in the Application Desktop, specifying the command to be sent, and then broadcasting it to each of the nodes selected. The output of any broadcasted command is displayed in a window and can be output to a file.

Terminal Sessions: There are two kinds of terminal sessions that can be opened from the Application Desktop to access managed nodes within the environment: virtual terminal and physical terminal.

The operator specifies a node in the Managed Nodes window and double-clicks on the virtual terminal symbol in the Application Desktop. When a terminal window opens on the display station, it can be used by the operator to issue commands or review status. Without leaving the display station, the operator can access any node within the environment, perform tasks and controls, and implement corrective actions.

A physical terminal requires a direct connection with the node. If the LAN is down and a physical connection exists between the display station and a node, the operator can open a physical terminal on the node. Or, if the node restricts execution of certain commands to the system console, the operator can open a physical terminal.

ANNOTATING AND ACKNOWLEDGING MESSAGES

Message annotations can be used to record how a problem was resolved. Acknowledging the message moves it from the current work area and stores it in a history database.

Annotating Messages: An annotation summarizes the important points of a message and can serve as a reference the next time the same message is received. Message annotations generally contain the following information:

- Action performed to resolve the problem.

- Starting and finishing time of the action.

- Any pre- and post-action values.

Annotations also can be used to record any difficulties encountered along the way toward resolving the problem, verbal or written instructions received by the operator in handling the problem, and communications sent to users or groups affected by the problem. The Annotations window contains all annotations related to a single message.

Acknowledging Messages: After completing work on a message, the operator can move it from the Message Browser (or View Browser) window and store it in a history database for future reference. This is done by acknowledging a message.

Typically, the operator acknowledges a message because:

- Work on the message is finished and any related problems are resolved.

- Another message is in the Browser that describes the same event.

- The message is no longer needed because it has low severity and requires no action.

When the message is acknowledged, the status of the corresponding message group and node changes. Acknowledged messages can be moved back to the active Message Browser by unacknowledging them. After unacknowledging a message, the operator can continue to work with it.

Automatic Acknowledgment: The OperationsCenter administrator can configure an automatic acknowledgement for messages with either automatic or operator initiated actions. When the action is completed for a message with an automatic action and an automatic acknowledgement, the message is sent directly to the history database. The message disappears from the Message Browser window, without operator intervention, as soon as the action finishes successfully. The operator can review automatically acknowledged messages using the History Message Browser and return them to the Message Browser window by unacknowledging them.

The operator can generate different types of reports on the status of the environment, including a report about all OperationsCenter severe error messages. The operator can select a short or detailed form and send the output to a printer, a file or display terminal. The short form report contains report date, time and type; all message attributes, including message text; and the original message text.

In addition to this information, the detailed report contains all operator instructions and message annotations.

The following report types are available:

Active Messages: One or more active messages selected from either the Message Browser or View Browser windows.

History Messages: One or more history messages selected from the History Message Browser window.

All Active Messages — Short Report: Contains information on all active messages.

All Active Messages — Detailed Report: Contains information on all active messages, including all operator instructions and message annotations.

All History Messages — Short Report: Contains information on all history messages.

OperationsCenter Error Report: Contains OperationsCenter server error messages.

OPERATIONSCENTER CONSOLIDATES AT A CENTRAL POINT A LARGE NUMBER of management activities for systems distributed across the organization. The customization and configuration capabilities of HP OpenView OperationsCenter enable the application to be adapted to meet the specific requirements of virtually any organization.

OperationsCenter is designed to provide a secure operating environment. Each operator has a password to ensure that only authorized persons have access. Operator profiles control the activities of each operator on the management system and managed nodes. Only the information needed by a particular operator is collected and displayed on that operator's console.

Because OperationsCenter runs on top of the HP OpenView SNMP platform, other HP OpenView applications can be added to address other management tasks.

For example, HP offers Hierarchical Storage Management (HSM) through its OmniStorage software, which allows users to manage online storage of files between magnetic and optical disk drives. OmniStorage is tightly integrated with OperationsCenter. Problem and error notifications from OmniStorage can be reported automatically through a color change on the map of a remote OperationsCenter console. This improves an administrator's productivity through central management and monitoring.

Another HP OpenView application, OmniBack, allows users to manage multiple backup domains from a single OpenView management station. The integration of OmniBack with OperationsCenter extends enterprise-wide problem management to include the handling of backup-related events. This solution improves the productivity of system administrators through single-point exception handling and sitewide access to applications on the network.

The management tasks performed from within the OperationsCenter environment also can be extended through the integration of third-party management applications or custom programs developed in-house.

CHAPTER

5

Remote Monitoring and Data Collection

AS NETWORKS EXPAND, THE ABILITY TO PERFORM REMOTE MONITORING becomes more important. Problems can be identified and resolved from a management console, rather than by sending a technician to remote locations, which is expensive and time-consuming. The ability to monitor the performance of remote local area network (LAN) segments has been made easier with SNMP's Remote Monitoring Management Information Base (RMON MIB) standard.

RMON provides a common platform from which to monitor multivendor networks. Hardware- and software-based RMON-compliant devices placed on each network segment monitor all data packets sent and received. Although a variety of SNMP MIBs collect performance statistics to provide a snapshot of events through the use of agents, RMON enhances this monitoring capability by keeping a past record of events that can be used for fault diagnosis, performance tuning and network planning.

REMOTE MONITORING

The RMON MIB is a set of object definitions that extend the capabilities of Simple Network Management Protocol (SNMP). RMON is not used to manage the devices on the network directly; instead, probes equipped with RMON agents passively monitor data transmitted over LAN segments. The accumulated information is retrieved from the HP 4995A LanProbe II/Ethernet monitor or HP 4985A LanProbe II/Token Ring, or another SNMP agent that reports to another central network management system such as OpenView, using SNMP commands.

RMON enhances the management and control capabilities of SNMP-compliant network management systems and LAN analyzers. The probes view every packet and produce summary information on various types of packets, such as undersized packets, and events, such as packet collisions. The probes also can store information for further analysis by capturing packets according to predefined criteria set by the network manager or test technician.

For instance, there might only be interest in examining NetWare packets running over Ethernet to track down the source of an intermittent problem with opening files at a remote server. According to an established threshold, an alarm can be generated if there is more than one file-open error per 100 file opens. Packets that match the filter criteria are stored in the probe's memory, while those that do not match are discarded. At any time, the RMON probe can be queried for this information by HP NetMetrix applications or the SNMP-based management console so that detailed analysis can be performed in an effort to pinpoint where and why an error occurred.

RMON OBJECT GROUPS

The RMON MIB is organized into object groups with associated variables (Figure 5-1):

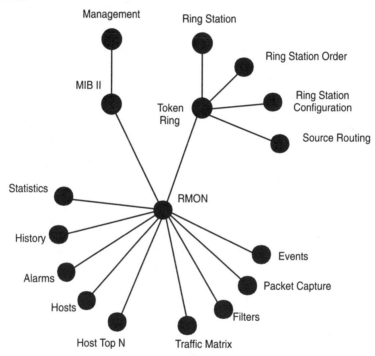

Figure 5-1: RMON Object Group

Statistics Group: Maintains low-level usage and error statistics such as number of packets sent, broadcasts and collisions.

History Group: Provides user-defined trend analysis based on information in the statistics group.

Host Table Group: For each host, contains counters for broadcasts, multicasts, errored packets, bytes sent and received, and packets sent and received.

Host Top N Group: Contains sorted host statistics, such as a complete table of activity for the top broadcasters or error generators. N indicates the number of nodes specified by the network manager.

Alarms Group: Allows a sampling interval and alarm threshold to be set for any counter or integer recorded by the RMON agent.

Filters Group: Provides a buffer for incoming packets and user-defined filters.

Packet Capture Group: Allows buffers to be specified for packet capture, buffer sizing, and the conditions for starting and stopping packet capture.

Event Group: Logs events such as packet matches or values that rise or fall to user-defined thresholds.

Traffic Matrix Group: Arranges usage and error information in matrix form to permit the retrieval and comparison of information for any pair of network addresses.

Full compliance with the Ethernet RMON MIB specification (RFC 1271)[1] requires that the vendor provide support for every object within a selected group. Because each group is optional, when selecting RMON MIB agents, users should determine the features they require and verify that those features are included in actual products.

Statistics Group: The Statistics Group provides segment-level statistics. For an Ethernet segment, for example, these statistics show packets, octets (or bytes), broadcasts, multicasts and collisions on the local segment, as well as the number of occurrences of dropped packets by the agent. Each statistic is maintained in its own 32-bit cumulative counter. Real-time packet size distribution is also provided.

The RMON MIB includes error counters for five different types of packets. With regard to Ethernet, for example, the following type of errors are counted:

- **Undersizes (runts):** Ethernet packets of less than 64 bytes, which are usually caused by a collision on the network. A normal Ethernet packet is 1518 bytes. Excessive runt packets may indicate that the transmitting station is not configured properly.

---

[1]All RFCs are available and downloadable from the Internet.

- **Fragments:** A packet whose total length is less than 64 bytes (excluding framing bits) and is not an integral number of octets in length or which has a bad frame check sequence.

- **CRC/Alignment Errors:** Cyclic Redundancy Check (CRC) is the last 32 bits of information contained in a packet/frame and is used for detecting transmission errors. When the CRC value of an incoming frame is not identical to the CRC value of an outgoing frame, a bit flop is said to occur, which generates a CRC error. This is usually caused by faulty cable, as when an impedance mismatch occurs, causing a reflection on the cable, which in turn causes the bit flop. An alignment error is a packet that is not an integral number of bytes in length and is between 64 and 1518 bytes in length (including the frame check sequence but excluding the framing bits) or which has a bad frame check sequence. An alignment error is most often caused by a frame collision on the network, although loose or noisy cable also can be the cause.

- **Collisions:** Refers to data sent by a device on the network without regard for any other devices that also may be trying to transmit. When two or more devices try to transmit at the same time, a collision occurs, a situation that causes the signals to collide and the data to become garbled.

- **Oversizes (giants):** A packet that exceeds the maximum 1518 bytes (excluding framing bits but including the frame check sequence) and which has a good frame check sequence. This type of packet can be caused by a node that is not configured properly.

These error counters provide useful network management information beyond that provided by typical network interface cards, for example. Because runt and giant packets are counted by the RMON MIB agent, they usually are reliable indicators of configuration problems in the transmitting station.

History Group: With the exception of packet size distribution, which is provided only on a real-time basis, the History Group provides historical views of the statistics provided in the Statistics Group. The History Group can respond to user-defined sampling intervals and bucket counters, allowing for some customization in trend analysis.

The RMON MIB comes with two defaults for trend analysis. The first provides for 50 buckets (or samples) of 30-second sampling intervals over a period of two minutes. The second provides for 50 buckets of 30-minute sampling intervals over a period of 25 hours. Users can modify either of these or add additional intervals to meet specific requirements for historic analysis. The sampling interval can range from one second to one hour.

Host Table Group: A host table is a standard feature of most current monitoring devices. The RMON MIB specifies a host table that includes node traffic statistics: packets sent and received, octets sent and received, as well as broadcasts, multicasts, and errored packets sent. In the host table, the classification *errors sent* is the combination of undersizes, fragments, CRC/Alignment errors, collisions and oversizes sent by each node.

The RMON MIB also includes a host time table that shows the relative order in which each host was discovered by the agent. This feature is not only useful for network management purposes, but also assists in uploading those nodes to the management station of which it is not yet aware. This reduces unnecessary SNMP traffic on the network.

Host Top N Group: The Host Top N Group extends the host table by providing sorted host statistics, such as the top 10 nodes sending packets or an ordered list of all nodes according to the errors sent during the last 24 hours. Both the data selected and the duration of the study is defined by the user at the network management station, and the number of studies is limited only by the resources of the monitoring device.

When a set of statistics is selected for study, only the selected statistics are maintained in the Host Top N counters; other statistics over the same time intervals are not available for later study. This processing — performed remotely in the RMON MIB agent — reduces SNMP traffic on the network and the processing load on the management station, which would otherwise need to use SNMP to retrieve the entire host table for local processing.

Alarms Group: The Alarms Group provides a general mechanism for setting thresholds and sampling intervals to generate events on any counter or integer maintained by the agent, such as segment statistics, node traffic statistics defined in the host table, or a user-defined packet match counter defined in the Filters Group. Both rising and falling thresholds can be set, each of which can indicate network faults. Thresholds can be established on both the absolute value of a statistic or its delta value, so the manager is notified of rapid spikes or drops in a monitored value.

Filters Group: The Filters Group provides a generic filtering engine that implements all packet capture functions and events. The packet capture buffer is filled with only those packets that match the user-specified filtering criteria. Filtering conditions can be combined using the boolean parameters **and** or **not**. Multiple filters are combined with the boolean **or** parameter.

Users can capture packets that are valid or invalid or that are one of the five error packet types. With the proper protocol decoding capability at the management station, this filtering essentially provides distributed protocol analysis to supplement the use of dispatched technicians with portable protocol analyzers.

The monitor also maintains counters of each packet match for statistical analysis. Either an individual packet match, or a multiple number of packet matches through Alarms, can trigger an event to the log or the network management system using an SNMP trap. Although these counters are not available to the History Group for trend analysis, a management station may request these counters through regular polling of the monitor so that trend analysis can be performed.

Packet Capture Group: The type of packets collected depends on the Filter Group. The Packet Capture Group allows the user to create multiple capture buffers and to control whether the trace buffers will wrap (over-write) when full or stop capturing. The user may expand or contract the size of the buffer to fit immediate needs for packet capturing, rather than permanently commit memory that will not always be needed.

The network manager can specify a packet match as a start trigger for a trace and depend on the monitor to collect the results without further user involvement. The RMON MIB includes configurable capture slice sizes to store either the first few bytes of a packet (where the protocol header is located) or to store the entire packet (which may reveal application errors). The default slice setting specified by the RMON MIB is the first 100 bytes.

Notifications (Events) Group: In a distributed management environment, traps can be delivered by the RMON MIB agent to multiple management stations that share a single community name destination specified for the trap. There are seven traps specified for SNMP (RFC 1157): link up, link down, warm start, cold start, authentication failure, EGP neighbor loss and Enterprise-specific. Three additional traps are specified in the RMON MIB: rising threshold, falling threshold and packet match.

The Notifications (Events) Group allow users to specify the number of events that can be sent to the monitor log. From the log, any specified event can be sent to the management station. Events can originate from a crossed threshold on any integer or counter or from any packet match count.

The log includes the time of day for each event and a description of the event written by the vendor of the monitor. The log overwrites when full, so events may be lost if they are not uploaded to the management station periodically. The rate that the log fills depends on the resources the monitor dedicates to the log and the number of notifications the user sends to the log.

Traffic Matrix Group: The RMON MIB includes a traffic matrix at the media access control (MAC) layer. A traffic matrix shows the amount of traffic and number of errors between pairs of nodes — one source and one destination address per pair. For each pair, the RMON MIB maintains counters for the number of packets, number of octets, and error packets between the nodes. Users can sort this information source or destination address.

TOKEN RING SUPPORT

Initially, RMON defined media-specific objects for Ethernet only. Media-specific objects for token ring are now available and those for the Fiber Distributed Data Interface (FDDI) are anticipated in the near future.

The token ring RMON specification (RFC 1513) adds four extensions to the original RMON specification (refer to Figure 5-1): source routing statistics, station configuration control, station configuration and station order.

Source Routing Statistics: The extension for source routing statistics is used for monitoring the efficiency of source-routing processes by keeping track of the number of data packets routed into, out of and through each ring segment. Traffic distribution by hop count, provides an indication of how much bandwidth being consumed by traffic-routing functions.

Station Configuration Control: The extension for station configuration control provides a description of the network's physical configuration. A media fault is reported as a fault domain, an area that isolates the problem to two adjacent nodes and the wiring between them. The network administrator can discover the exact location of the problem — the fault domain — by referring to the network map. Faults that result from changes to the physical ring, including each time a station inserts or removes itself from the network, are discovered by comparing the start of symptoms with the timing of physical changes.

The RMON MIB not only keeps track of the status of each station, it also reports the condition of each ring being monitored by a RMON agent. On large token ring networks with several rings, the health of each ring segment and the number of active and inactive stations on each ring can be monitored simultaneously. Network administrators can be alerted to the location of the fault domain should any ring go into a beaconing (fault) condition.

Network managers also can be alerted to any changes in backbone ring

Network managers also can be alerted to any changes in backbone ring configuration, which could indicate loss of connectivity to an interconnect device such as a bridge or to a shared resource such as a server.

Station Configuration: The ring station group collects token ring specific errors. Statistics are kept on all significant MAC-level events to assist in fault isolation, including ring purges, beacons, claim tokens, and error conditions such as burst errors, lost frames, congestion errors, frame copied errors and soft errors.

Station Order: Each station can be placed on the network map in a specified order relative to the other stations on the ring.

BENEFITS OF RMON

The RMON MIB facilitates the gathering of information from network devices, which can be used for fault diagnosis, performance tuning and network planning.

Although the standard MIB is designed to provide real-time protocol management for devices that use the External Gateway Protocol (EGP), Internet Protocol (IP), Internet Control Message Protocol (ICMP), Transmission Control Protocol (TCP) and Simple Network Management Protocol (SNMP), the accumulation of historical performance data requires that the network management station or LAN analyzer constantly poll every network device and store the accumulated data. In many cases, however, historical data is more appropriately gathered at the network device itself, and only retrieved occasionally by the network management station or LAN analyzer. This is exactly what the RMON MIB is designed to do. It reduces the processing overhead inherent in SNMP polling which, in turn, reduces network overhead traffic.

Despite the apparent simplicity of SNMP, the RMON MIB demonstrates that SNMP agents can be quite complex and offer a rich feature set. This complexity is necessary to allow the agents to monitor the network in a beneficial manner. Because RMON agents are programmable, a single management station can observe and manage a large network with many segments.

By expanding the reach of the RMON MIB beyond Ethernet to also include token ring, the Internet standards community has enabled a wider audience to benefit from this potentially powerful network-monitoring standard.

DATA COLLECTION

HP offers several RMON-compliant tools that monitor and collect data: LanProbe II hardware, Power Agent programs, and a suite of applications called NetMetrix. These tools can be used separately or in combination.

They also can be integrated into the SNMP-compliant OpenView network management platform.

LANPROBE II

Hewlett-Packard was the first vendor to fully support RMON through its hardware-based HP 4995A LanProbe II, an Ethernet monitor that supervises various network segments to which it is attached, allowing network managers to supervise large networks. With the development of the draft standard for RMON MIB extensions for token ring (RFC 1513), Hewlett-Packard introduced the hardware-based HP 4985A Token Ring LanProbe II monitor. The HP 4995A Ethernet LanProbe II supports all nine feature groups of the RMON MIB, while the HP 4985A Token Ring LanProbe II supports the nine RMON groups, plus the four token ring RMON MIB extensions.[2]

The LanProbe II's packet capture buffer size can be specified, according to need. Buffer use can be optimized by saving on a portion of the frames captured (packet slicing). When the capture buffer is full, packet capture can stop, or continue with wrap around. Multiple studies can be performed simultaneously.

Protocol decodes for the most common LAN protocols are provided and are useful for diagnosing problems such as client-server connectivity, protocol mismatches and excessive broadcasts. They can help pinpoint problems directly related to the performance of a node — problems that might otherwise go undetected or unreported.

Read and write access to and from the HP LanProbe is controlled through four levels of passwords (community names) and by a list of valid client IP addresses. The security feature:

- Restricts access to network performance data and/or captured data files.

- Controls access to measurement setup, including historical studies, alarms, and SNMP trap destinations.

- Restricts access to remote probe setup, including IP address, community names, and downloading of firmware updates to the probe. With built-in security, the network is less likely to be compromised by unauthorized access.

---

[2]Both LanProbe II monitors use the Intel 386 processor and come with 4 MB of memory. Memory configurations of up to 8 MB are available to accommodate larger networks and allow more packet-filters to be run simultaneously. LanProbe III and LanProbe III Plus are lower-cost probes for collecting RMON data on Ethernet segments. They come with 1 MB and 4 MB of memory, respectively.

Out-of-band access to the LanProbe II is available through direct RS-232 or modem connection. This is a critical alternative for troubleshooting if in-band network access is unavailable, or if troubleshooting must be done from a remote location.

HP Probe Manager, which is a fully integrated OpenView-based management application, manages the SNMP RMON and extentions in both types of LanProbe II monitors. Probe Manager enhances other OpenView applications by providing troubleshooting, operational, and planning features that focus on the node, segment or network level.

Probe Manager allows multiple managers to collect data from a single probe or a single manager to control multiple probes. This allows flexibility to manage from a central point or from numerous locations.

The following features of Probe Manager are fully integrated into the OpenView menu bar and map:

- Automatic historical data collection and reporting.

- Baselining.

- Alarm on all RMON MIB variables (with the ability to set traps on multiple destinations).

- Rich set of protocol filters and split-screen protocol decoding.

- Multiple probe output for consolidation on a single graph.

- Out-of-band access to LanProbe II.

- Remote, simultaneous firmware download to LanProbe II.

- Multiple security levels.

Probe Manager includes decodes for such popular network protocols as TCP/IP (and associated protocols), Novell NetWare, Banyan Vines, DECnet, AppleTalk, OSI, 3Com and XNS. Another management application, ProbeView/SNMP, runs under Microsoft Windows and provides similar functionality to Probe Manager.

PROBEVIEW

An enhanced version of ProbeView is available from HP. In addition to providing centralized analysis of network traffic statistics collected by LanProbes, ProbeView/SNMP 2.0 supports all nine RMON groups for standard collection of Ethernet traffic statistics. It maps all IP-addressable nodes, including servers, bridges, hubs and routers. It also can depict upper-layer traffic over time on a LAN segment. Note, that it can support RMON-equipped traffic monitoring devices from other vendors such as

Cabletron, Chipcom, Hughes LAN Systems and SynOptics. Ostensibly, there are two advantages with embedded RMON over conventional probes: lower costs, because equipment is consolidated; and custom control of devices through integration.

POWER AGENTS

Power Agents are software-based, RMON-compliant data collectors that run on UNIX-based workstations. They are available for Ethernet, token ring and FDDI.

Power Agent software plays a role similar to the one LanProbe II plays in hardware, collecting the same information as the LanProbe II. However, Power Agents go a step further than the LanProbe II: they not only collect data, they process the packets to provide detailed and high-level information regarding network traffic.

Power Agents also incorporate a rich set of private MIB extensions, which are available through the NetMetrix applications. These extensions include:

- Information from all 7 layers of the network protocol stack.

- Protocol distribution.

- Correlation between time, protocol, source and destination.

- Network trending.

- Out-of-band access to and from a remote station running the Power Agent.

HP LanProbe II segment monitors and Power Agents can be used together distributed throughout a LAN as well as a geographically dispersed through the WAN. Their packet capture with filtering and decoding capabilities allows early detection of suspect traffic patterns and identification of faulty network devices. Because HP LanProbe II segment monitors and Power Agents use the network only when information is requested, they do not burden the network with unnecessary overhead.

LanProbe II monitors and Power Agents can be managed by the HP NetMetrix suite of distributed monitoring and analysis applications for UNIX- or DOS-based systems, which run under HP OpenView. Figure 5-2 depicts the relationship of LanProbe II, Probe Manager, Power Agent, NetMetrix and ProbeView.

HP NETMETRIX

Control, visibility and easy-to-read information are essential characteristics of tools for internetwork monitoring and analysis. These characteristics are inherent in the suite of HP NetMetrix applications. Through LanProbe

II segment monitors and/or Power Agents, the RMON-compliant NetMetrix applications monitor and collect data at remote segments, refine the data into useful information, and present the information in visually useful formats. The tools permit proactive management and, in reactive situations, permit rapid inference so the operator can take corrective action promptly.

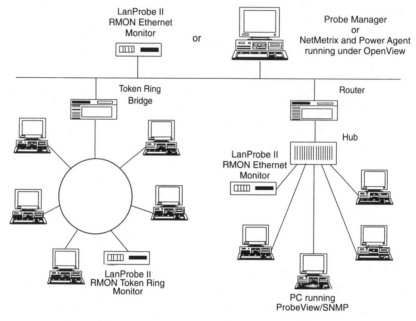

Figure 5-2: *Remote Monitoring Configuration*

HP NetMetrix complements SNMP management functions for Ethernet and token ring networks. RMON-compliant LanProbe II/SNMP segment monitors, Power Agent, and NetMetrix provide vendor-independent monitoring of the network.

NetMetrix applications run on workstations under UNIX to provide a range of capabilities for tracking and correlating status and performance statistics from multiple remote LANs. With support for Ethernet, token ring and FDDI, HP NetMetrix applications provide end-to-end visibility of large internetworks, as well as small workgroups.

NetMetrix applications integrate with each other to provide a comprehensive, cohesive toolset. There are six applications, which are available separately: Internetwork Monitor, Load Monitor, Network File System (NFS) Monitor, Protocol Analyzer, Traffic Generator and Enterprise Utilities.

Internetwork Monitor: The Internetwork Monitor gathers data from RMON agents running on each segment in the network. The data is integrated and correlated to provide various internetwork views that provide end-to-end visibility of network traffic, both LAN and WAN. The operator can switch between many different views.

For example, the operator can switch between a media access control (MAC) view (which shows traffic going through routers and gateways), a network view (which shows end-to-end traffic), or apply filters to see only traffic of a given protocol or suite of protocols. These traffic matrices provide the information necessary to configure or partition the internetwork to optimize LAN and WAN use.

The Internetwork Monitor provides the following views:

Segment View: provides a picture of all segment-to-segment traffic. A simple, flat map is constructed with each segment on the network represented as a dot. Lines connecting the dots depict the intersegment traffic, varying in color and thickness to indicate load. Statistics can be displayed for any line (Figure 5-3).

MAC Level View: expands the depiction of segments, showing each node of each segment separately and indicating node-to-node intrasegment data traffic. It also shows total intersegment data traffic from routers and gateways. This combination allows the operator to see consolidated internetwork traffic and how each end-node contributes to it (Figure 5-4).

Network Level View: shows end-to-end data traffic between nodes, across segments. By connecting source and ultimate destination, without clouding the view with routers and gateways, the operator can identify immediately specific areas contributing to an unbalanced traffic load (Figure 5-5).

Because the Internetwork Monitor gets its data from remote monitors, it does not produce the same level of detail as the Protocol Analyzer and the Load Monitor. But it does provide the big picture — showing traffic between each node and each segment. The Internetwork Monitor is most appropriate for very large networks with monitoring stations on each segment.

Load Monitor: The Load Monitor examines and categorizes network traffic. Monitoring traffic patterns can help the operator recognize potential problem areas or identify the cause of elusive performance bottlenecks. Load Monitor lets the operator see network load by time interval, source node, destination node, between pairs of nodes, by protocol type, or by packet size (Figure 5-6).

When data has been saved for a day, for example, using the Protocol Analyzer, the Load Monitor can be used to analyze the data file. Through a display window, the collected data load is analyzed and displayed in a strip chart showing the peaks and valleys of network usage.

Then, with the Load Monitor's zoom feature, another window is opened showing the different protocols in use. The operator can point to any time of day in the first graph and see, in the second window, the protocols, nodes and programs in use at that time.

Measurements are displayed in a variety of graphs and tables. A zoom feature allows correlational analysis of the statistics, which lets the operator pinpoint traffic patterns. By arranging any combination of Load Monitor measurements in a desired sequence, the operator can drill down four layers deep.

As the operator drills down from the top level to increasingly more detailed, microscopic views of suspect data, an investigation can be narrowed to the data needed for decision making.

For example, the operator can see which node is generating most of the load on the network at the time interval at which it is most heavily loaded

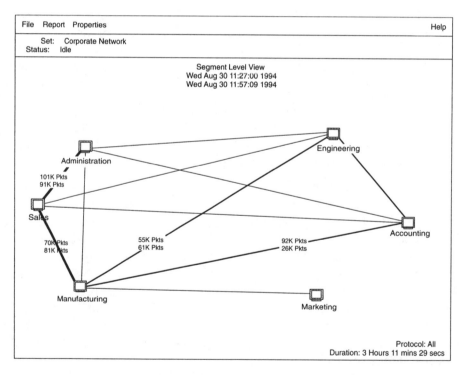

Source: Hewlett-Packard Co.

Figure 5-3: Internetwork Monitor: Segment View

and what applications comprise that load. This information can be used to determine the optimal location for a bridge or router to ease real or potential bottlenecks on the network.

Network File System (NFS) Monitor: The NFS Monitor is a necessity for any network experiencing NFS-related problems. It is essentially a smart protocol analyzer specializing in NFS. It lets the operator explore client-server relationships as well as evaluate NFS performance improvement strategies so that servers can be distributed across the network effectively.

It measures and graphs NFS load; NFS response time for client and server retransmits, rejects and errors by client and server; NFS procedure; and time interval. The results are presented in line graphs, bar and pie charts, for easy interpretation and comparison.

A zoom feature allows the operator to explore and correlate any combination of these measurements in relation to client, server and procedure over time or at a specific time. For example, the operator can explore cli-

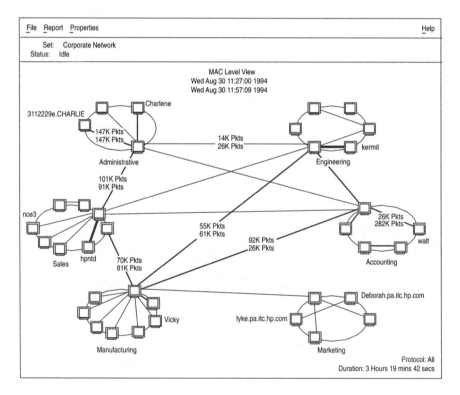

Source: Hewlett-Packard Co.

Figure 5-4: Internetwork Monitor: MAC Level View

cnt-server load distribution, compare server performance, and evaluate NFS enhancement techniques.

Protocol Analyzer: Protocol Analyzer captures, decodes and displays all protocol layers of all packets in real time. It provides the operator with an array of capabilities to keep the network up and running.

Protocol Analyzer contains seven-layer decode suites for more than 100 protocols; including: TCP/IP, NFS/SunRPC, DECnet, DEC LAT, IPX, SNMP, SNA, Novell NetWare, XNS, Banyan Vines, AppleTalk and OSI. It also decodes token ring management and FDDI Station Management (SMT) frames.

Extensive menu-based filtering lets the operator sift through packets before or after trace capture at any layer of the protocol stack. Triggering, pretriggering, flexible capture buffer controls and dump-to-disk functions assure that the operator gets the required trace. Packets can be displayed in summary, detail or hexidecimal format.

Side-by-side views of traces in both detail and summary formats speed problem identification and resolution. Multiple views let the operator see

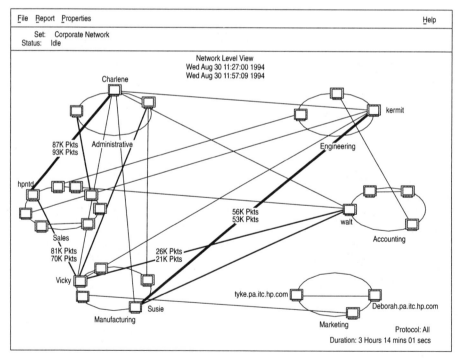

Source: Hewlett-Packard Co.

Figure 5-5: Internetwork Monitor: Network Level View

packet dialogues side by side. A developers' kit is available for custom decodes.

Traffic Generator: Traffic Generator lets the operator generate a precise traffic profile to simulate load on the network (Figure 5-7). This provides the operator with the opportunity to test and validate system configurations and management station alarms from such devices as routers, bridges and hubs before money is spent on them, or observe the effect of added nodes before they create problems. Traffic Generator works simultaneously with all other NetMetrix applications, allowing the results of tests to be viewed in real time.

The operator has complete control of transmission through a program editor and a packet editor. Through the programming interface, the operator can set such variables as bandwidth, packet composition, packet

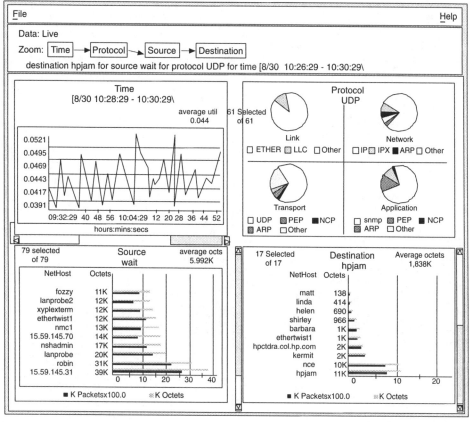

Source: Hewlett-Packard Co.

Figure 5-6: Load Monitor

sequence, filtering and conditional responses. Captured packets even can be modified and retransmitted.

With the ability to customize and replay network data, the operator has virtually unlimited possibilities for network capacity planning.

Enterprise Utilities: Enterprise Utilities allow the user to consolidate and present multiple segment information, configure RMON alarms, provide complete token ring RMON information, as well as perform baseline measurement and long-term reporting.

Alarms can be set on any RMON variable (Figure 5-8). Notification through traps can be sent to multiple management stations. Baseline statistics allow long-term trend analysis of network traffic patterns that can be used to plan for network growth.

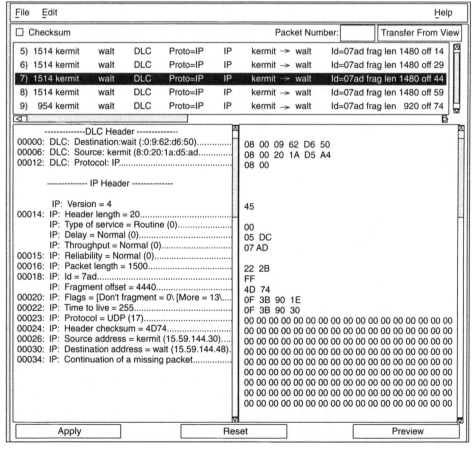

Source: Hewlett-Packard Co.

Figure 5-7: *Traffic Generator*

The application's token ring utilities display status and error table information as well as nodes in order of Nearest Active Upstream Neighbor (NAUN), allowing the operator to understand the fault domain. Ring status provides indications of normal operation and beaconing. The token ring remove capability provides the operator with additional troubleshooting and control over the token ring network. The application's automatic report generation facility sends easy-to-read reports to the management console screen to a printer.

NetMetrix Monitoring/Analysis System

The combination of LanProbe II, Probe Manager, Power Agents and NetMetrix constitutes the HP NetMetrix Monitoring/Analysis System. This integrated approach provides the network manager with several benefits:

- A comprehensive and independent view of network performance that significantly enhances the management information typically available from bridges, routers and hubs.

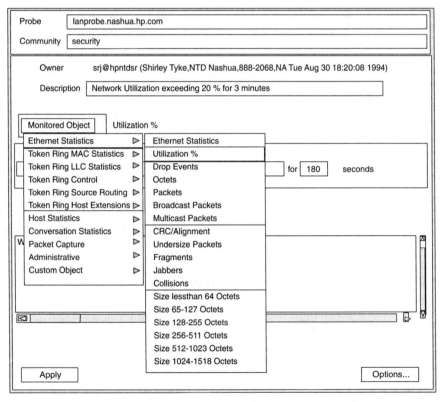

Source: Hewlett-Packard Co.

Figure 5-8: Enterprise Utilities: Alarm Settings on RMON Variables

- Visibility of non-IP and non-SNMP devices and protocols.

- Reduced bandwidth consumption by network management activities, because the probe is remote at the monitored network and its statistics can substitute for echo packets and SNMP requests sent periodically and repeated across the network.

- Monitoring hardware and software are remotely controllable either over the LAN, or through a out-of-band connection to allow troubleshooting to continue during network outages.

More than 150 predefined high-level packet-type filters are provided with HP NetMetrix. They can be combined in various ways for highly selective data capture. Filters can be downloaded simultaneously to multiple probes.

Together, LanProbe II and NetMetrix can perform such tasks as tracking all IP addresses and detecting duplication automatically, generate alarms based on user-definable thresholds for critical network parameters, and alert network administrators to anomaly occurrences.

Any remote HP LanProbe II or Power Agent can be managed from a centrally located Probe Manager console. Configuration management includes:

- Changes to IP address tables, subnet masks, and default gateways.

- Warm and cold starts.

- Out-of-band configuration.

- Downloadbable firmware updates, alarms and filters.

The convenience of performing all these operations remotely, from a single menu on the NetMetrix console to multiple collectors, allows the network management environment to be easily updated.

Like Probe Manager, HP NetMetrix allows multiple managers to collect data from a single probe or a single manager to control multiple probes. This allows flexibility to manage from a central point or from numerous locations. NetMetrix also can be configured to manage the RMON-based probes of other vendors.

RMON VS. X WINDOWS

The HP NetMetrix applications use both the SNMP-based RMON MIB and the X Windows protocol for building a distributed network monitoring and analysis system. Although each has its advantages and disadvantages, the NetMetrix applications combine them to provide the best of both worlds.

The obvious advantage of RMON is its interoperability: any RMON-compliant management station can access any RMON monitoring agent. And, a management station can collect data from multiple RMON agents and correlate the accumulated information to provide an enterprise-wide view. However, there are at least four disadvantages of RMON:

- It consumes significant bandwidth, especially as the frequency of polling increases.

- Its MIB is limited to providing MAC layer statistics; it does not provide network layer statistics.

- The limitation of the MIB and SNMP structure makes extensive retroactive analysis of the data impossible — test and packet capture must be predefined and are limited.

- Performance is slow, because the data must be polled and is retrieved relatively slowly across the network.

The primary advantage of the X Windows protocol is that it allows processing power to be distributed out onto the remote segments. Not only is this approach more efficient, saving network bandwidth, it enables more powerful monitoring and analysis applications to operate over the network. The disadvantage of X Windows is that, because it is a standalone process, it does not interoperate with any other applications. This makes X Windows impractical for providing an enterprise-wide view, and it only interoperates with management stations by being started from their topology views.

In supporting RMON and X Windows, NetMetrix applications provide the optimal solution for network monitoring and analysis: RMON can be used for statistical data collection and correlation into an enterprise-wide view, while X Windows can be used for running more powerful analysis applications that are distributed to remote segments. The user can switch seamlessly between the two modes.

Hewlett-Packard is developing tools for intelligent network analysis. These tools examine all packets and automatically identify the problems. Such tools will require intelligence at the local site because all packets cannot be sent to the management console for analysis without creating network bottlenecks. Having a powerful processing engine at the remote site will facilitate the advanced analysis applications of the future.

WITH CONSTANT MONITORING OF EACH AND EVERY PACKET ON THE network, HP NetMetrix applications, in conjunction with LanProbe II (and newer LanProbe III) monitors and Power Agents, can provide the data necessary to monitor performance, plan for growth, and detect and resolve faults. Support for both Ethernet and token ring RMON MIB groups extends the LanProbe's value in monitoring heterogeneous network environments. Power agents are available for Ethernet, token ring and FDDI.

The RMON MIB offers a standardized, flexible and economical solution to monitoring network performance. Because many network equipment vendors support RMON, products already purchased may only have to be upgraded through agent software instead of being replaced entirely. This means that SNMP-supported network management systems, including Hewlett-Packard's OpenView will be able to monitor an ever-expanding base of network devices from multiple vendors.

According to HP sources, the company eventually will migrate the best functions of ProbeView to NetMetrix. Right now no further development work is planned for ProbeView. When the applications are fully melded, HP will issue a new release, probably under a new product name.

CHAPTER

6

Problem Management

WITH NETWORKS CONTINUOUSLY EXPANDING TO KEEP PACE WITH ORGANI-
zational demands, the chance for performance problems increases expo-
nentially. Ordinarily, alarm conditions are passed on immediately to the
network operator for action. However, many of these alarms are not usually serious enough to warrant operator intervention. Often, the sheer
number of alarms that the network operator must contend with hinders
problem resolution and prolongs network downtime. Problem management
can be greatly enhanced with an alarm service that correlates, filters and
upgrades alerts automatically. To present only intelligently preprocessed
information to network operators — capabilities not available with Simple
Network Management Protocol (SNMP).

SNMP is based on the client-server model: servers own specific resources
and clients request services or information from these resources. In this
model, servers are called agents, and clients are called managers or management stations. The agent interfaces directly to the operating system
and/or the networking layers to obtain and manipulate the network management information for the resource being managed. The agent reveals
management information by communicating with managers through
SNMP.

Typically, SNMP-based agents run on gateways and routers, as well as
important servers or mail gateways, to allow monitoring of overall network
connectivity. Dedicated agents also may monitor specific hardware or applications. The manager or management station is application software
that runs at a central location; typically, the organization's Network Operations Center.

SNMP uses a request/reply protocol, implementing simple fetch/store
operations. Fields are provided in SNMP to permit elementary authentication and the correlation of replies with corresponding requests. When an
agent receives an SNMP message, it uses the supplied community string[1]

---

[1]This is a simple password used by the agent running on the node. The password is required
from the management system (i.e., the manager) before the agent can provide information
about the node.

to determine if the requested operation is allowed. In general, SNMP Get, GetNext and Set messages are generated by a manager and Get_Response and Trap messages are generated by agents. Figure 6-1 illustrates these roles.

An agent can send a trap to the manager if something important, such as a link failure, occurs; however, this is the exception rather than the rule for many management devices. More often, the manager sends an SNMP request to the agent to obtain information (Get, GetNext) and/or change the value of some variable (Set). To each of these requests, the agent responds with a Get_Response packet. Normally, an SNMP-based manager polls agents for information, relegating agents to a passive role. Only in a few cases will an agent take the initiative and send a trap to the manager to report state changes. If the manager receives the trap, it can take appropriate action to obtain more information. Although the SNMP standard discourages use of additional traps, it does not place restrictions on their use.

Many management environments rely on polling to monitor important devices continuously. In fact, polling is fundamental to the operation of SNMP. However, this can be a burden on the network because large quantities of available bandwidth can be consumed with management-specific traffic. The challenge in using SNMP is to minimize the frequency and scope of polling operations and still obtain all of the information necessary to identify and resolve problems.

This is the role of NetLabs' NerveCenter, an advanced rules-based alarm service that enables the operator to monitor the network for events, errors and traffic conditions. NerveCenter goes beyond SNMP in that it deter-

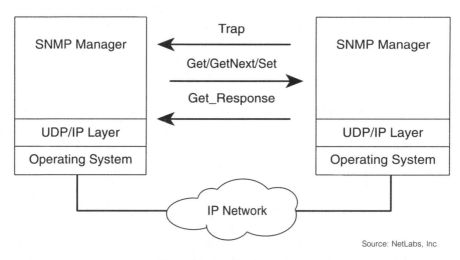

Source: NetLabs, Inc.

Figure 6-1: **SNMP Operation**

mines whether the condition is serious enough to require operator intervention. For example, in the case of a temporary workstation malfunction that merely necessitates a system reboot, NerveCenter withholds the alarm, saving valuable operator time and network resources.

LEVEL OF INTEGRATION

NetLabs' SNMP-based NerveCenter is available as part of the company's DiMONS management platform. It is also interoperable with HP's Network Node Manager as an add-on module. In the near future, NerveCenter will be integrated more fully into Network Node Manager and behave as a third-party application, taking advantage of the underlying platform services of OpenView using application programming interfaces (APIs) for tasks such as mapping and discovery.

Even as an add-on module, NerveCenter greatly enhances the capabilities of Network Node Manager. Currently, OpenView managers are flooded with alarms when a crisis occurs and do not have an effective way of dealing with them. Just one failed router, for example, could generate hundreds of alarms down the line. NerveCenter's ability to correlate event information enables it to see the relationship between those events and point network operators in the right direction for quick problem resolution at the source.

When NerveCenter is fully integrated into the OpenView platform, other third-party applications also will be able to take advantage of it. For example, as NerveCenter isolates problems, information about those problems could be passed to various trouble-ticketing applications.

NERVECENTER

NerveCenter offers two methods of detecting events, errors and traffic conditions: trap messages from SNMP agents and polling based on user-defined conditions.

The operator can configure alarms to filter traps or the results of polls, and then implement corrective action automatically when predefined conditions occur. The operator defines these conditions through a graphical user interface (GUI). Simple conditions can be described, such as thresholds, as well as more complex conditions, such as values that increase over a specified time interval. By using Boolean parameters, conditions can be defined that are actually a combination of several conditions.

The network operator can set up automatic actions based on alarms. These include logging data, sending e-mail, beeping a pager, starting corrective actions and launching other applications. After set up, NerveCenter automatically handles all the monitoring and response details. The network operator can even devise instructions to guide other operators in the handling of specific situations. These instructions will be displayed whenever the situation occurs.

NerveCenter can be adapted to monitor and take automatic actions in a way that is consistent with how the networked environment already is managed. Keeping this in mind, NerveCenter includes these features:

Multiple severity levels: Colors can be defined for each level of alarm severity.

Dynamic selection of monitored and polled elements: The operator determines which devices and connections are monitored and polled. New elements can be configured into NerveCenter without affecting those already being monitored and polled.

Classes of devices and connections: NerveCenter uses the concept of Property Groups to allow the creation of different classes, such as Key Router, T1 lines or All Workstations in Accounting Department. These classes can be used to define the scope of polls and alarms.

Predefined alarms: NerveCenter comes with predefined alarms to get operators started immediately. New alarms can be added, while predefined alarms can be modified as changing needs require.

CONNECTION MONITOR

The Connection Monitor feature in NerveCenter alerts the operator of network connection interface problems. Often, the problem can be corrected before network users are even aware of it. Connection Monitor does this by providing several levels of network connection information. Physical interface parameters can be monitored, such as those for traffic and performance. In addition, logical connections can be monitored.

For example, an alarm can be set to signal the operator when a particular network service is disrupted, such as a Telnet connection. In this case, the physical network may be operating correctly, but a network configuration problem could exist. Going beyond simple alerts, Connection Monitor can be instructed automatically to take action if such a problem occurs.

ACTION ROUTER

When network problems occur, service requests must be forwarded to the appropriate person for corrective action. The Action Router feature in NerveCenter automatically routes service requests generated by the active alarms. In addition to routing, the operator can configure the service request through the GUI to include the time of day, the problem location, problem characteristics and problem severity.

When routing is established, operator intervention is not needed to correctly route requests. Action Router can notify the appropriate person by sending e-mail messages or by paging them. Paging even can be set up on a case-by-case basis. For example, Action Router can be configured to notify one person during the day and someone else if the problem occurs during the evening.

THE NERVECENTER MODEL

The basic NerveCenter concepts use the SNMP management model of traps and polling. This model is illustrated in Figure 6-2.

TRAP MASKS

The network administrator responsible for configuring the SNMP management platform defines masks to filter the SNMP traps received by the system to isolate items of interest. One of the challenges of managing with SNMP is that there can be many traps that are of interest under special conditions, but not of general interest all the time. NerveCenter masks allow the operator to define what to look for in their unique environment, given the network operator's specific management responsibilities. A single NerveCenter mask can filter for traps of a specific category, or for a vendor-specific trap within a category.

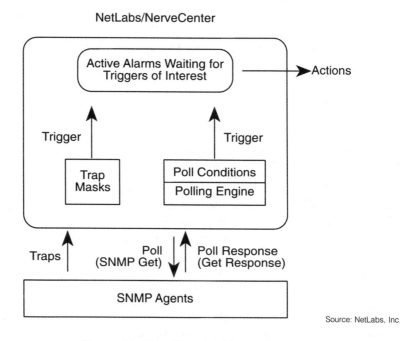

Source: NetLabs, Inc.

Figure 6-2: NerveCenter Model

There are seven types of SNMP traps, numbered 0 through 6[2]. These traps include notification of:

Cold start: indicates that the node is initializing and that the node's agent configuration or protocol may be altered.

Warm start: indicates that the node is initializing and that neither the node's agent configuration or protocol will be altered.

Link down: indicates a failure in one node of the communications links in the agent's configuration.

Link up: indicates that one of the communications links in the agent's configuration has come up.

Authentication failure: indicates that the node received a protocol message that is not authenticated. (SNMP implementations must be able to both recognize and suppress this type of trap.)

EGP[3] neighbor loss: indicates that an EGP peer of the node sending the trap is down and that the peer relationship no longer exists.

Enterprise-specific: indicates the occurrence of an event defined by the node vendor. These traps include a secondary trap field that identifies which vendor-defined trap occurred.

There is also an All Traps trap that filters all SNMP-defined and vendor-defined traps.

Each vendor using SNMP has the option of defining traps for their specific needs. These enterprise-specific traps send information about a particular device or type of device from that vendor. To understand the trap, the network operator must know the enterprise-specific numbers being used by the vendor and be able to capture all the trap information for analysis. Often, operators do not have the time or the necessary tools to decode these traps. NerveCenter masks can be set up to perform this decoding automatically each time a trap is received.

To configure a mask, the operator fills in the fields of a graphical form provided by NerveCenter. While most of the form involves naming and documenting the condition for which a given mask is filtering, the key entry in the form is the mask string. The mask string has the following format:

---

[2]The SNMP standard (RFC 1157) defines seven categories of traps, numbered 0 through 6. These are called the major trap numbers.

[3]The External Gateway Protocol (EGP) is an inter-domain routing protocol used by IP routers to connect multiple IP subnetworks over point-to-point serial links and X.25 data networks. EGP neighbor loss indicates a router problem.

SNMP <major_trap_no> <FROM <enterprise><minor_trap_no>>

Minor_trap_no is one of the seven SNMP trap categories. ALL or -1 can be entered to indicate that this mask applies to all SNMP-defined and vendor-defined traps. The enterprise variable specifies which vendor device sent this trap. This variable consists of the object identifier for the vendor device (for example, 1.3.6.1.4.1.9) or the MIB name for the object identifier (for example, cisco).

A mask will set a flag (called a trigger) when receiving a trap, if the enterprise in the trap is the same as or is the child of the enterprise variable specified in the mask string. For example, 1.3.6.4.1.9.1.3 is the child of 1.3.6.4.1.9 and would raise a trigger if 1.3.6.4.1.9 is specified in the enterprise field. The minor_trap_no is a vendor-defined positive integer that identifies the trap. A minor_trap_no of -1 specifies all traps the vendor defines for a device. This is particularly useful for monitoring critical network devices.

TRIGGERS

When an interesting trap has been detected by an active mask, NerveCenter will raise a trigger, which is a flag that the alarm system will use to identify what trap has been received, so that specific actions can be taken in response to the trap. A single mask can raise a trigger for all traps of a particular category, or just for a specific vendor's traps within a category.

There are many predefined masks that come with NerveCenter. One of these predefined masks raises a trigger for every trap that arrives, regardless of the category of the trap or vendor (i.e., specifies ALL in the major_trap_no portion of the mask string). This is a useful mask for those environments where it is desirable to log every trap received from the network.

POLLING AND POLL CONDITIONS

Network operators define what management information base (MIB) information should be collected through polling and under what conditions the response to the poll should raise a trigger. All triggers are processed the same by NerveCenter, whether they are the result of having received a trap or whether a poll response causes a condition to evaluate to *true*, thus raising the trigger.

Polls can collect information about any SNMP base object[4] and the operator can create as many polls as required. Any single poll collects

---

[4]A base object consists of a set of attributes, which are children of the base object. The base object can be managed and the values of its attributes (for each base-object instance) can be polled.

information about only one base object. When a poll is set up, the operator specifies its polling rate, trigger names, and trigger definitions or poll conditions. When the values returned in a polling operation are evaluated and found to match the specified conditions in the poll conditions field for the poll, the poll sends a true trigger to NerveCenter for use by the active alarms. The operator also can configure the poll so that when the values returned in the poll do not fulfill the conditions specified, the poll issues a false trigger.

When setting up poll conditions, the operator selects the base object and attributes whose values are to be retrieved. The operator then specifies the instance values and their relationships to each other which will cause a trigger to be raised. Poll conditions consist of one or more relational expressions. To create a relational expression, an attribute is selected from the Attributes list presented by the NerveCenter GUI. Next, a relational operator is selected, and then, if appropriate, a value or threshold is specified for the object instance of the attribute.

The relational operators provided include:

== The condition is true when the value of the object instance equals the value specified by the network operator.

!= The condition is true when the value of the object instance does not equal the value specified by the network operator.

<= The condition is true when the value of the object instance is less than or equal to the value specified by the network operator.

>= The condition is true when the value of the object instance is greater than or equal to the value specified by the network operator.

present The condition is true when the object instance is present. The value for this condition is not specified by the network operator.

not present The condition is true when the object instance is not present. The value for this condition is not specified by the network operator.

increased<= The condition is true when the increase in the value of the object instance since the last poll is less than or equal to the value specified by the network operator.

increased>= The condition is true when the increase in the value of the object instance since the last poll is greater than or equal to the value specified by the network operator.

decreased<= The condition is true when the decrease in the value of the object instance since the last poll is less than or equal to the value specified by the network operator.

decreased>= The condition is true when the decrease in the value of the object instance since the last poll is greater than or equal to the value specified by the network operator.

NerveCenter also allows the addition of multiple expressions to a single poll condition through the use of Boolean parameters. In this way, poll conditions can be created that automatically can evaluate the MIB data in virtually any combination. The Boolean parameters include: **AND, OR, AND- NOT** and **OR- NOT**

A poll can monitor all the nodes and lines in the network that have the base object specified by the network operator in the poll. It is also possible to restrict a poll to a smaller group of nodes or lines by using Property Groups.

PROPERTY GROUPS

NerveCenter uses property groups for two purposes:

- To learn what base objects a node's agent knows about and can be polled for. (The base objects are listed in the property group.)

- To limit the scope of individual alarms and polls.

A property group is a list of text strings. These text strings include the names of base objects and user-defined properties. NerveCenter requires that each node that is to be monitored must be assigned a valid property group. A selection of basic property groups is provided with NerveCenter. The network operator can use these groups or create unique property groups.

When the operator defines a poll or alarm, a property to be associated with it also can be defined. This can be the base object to be polled or monitored, some other base object, or a text string that has been added to a property group. The poll or alarm will apply only to those nodes and lines that contain in their property group the specified property.

For example, if the network operator wants to monitor as a group all nodes that support the RMON MIB, NerveCenter can recognize automatically most of these nodes from looking at the map database. The operator can configure additional nodes to have the RMON property group assigned to them. Later, when the operator defines polls and alarms to monitor the nodes, a property can be specified for each poll and alarm. If a property is specified that already is included in the RMON property group, all nodes assigned to that property group will be monitored.

In addition, the network operator arbitrarily can assign a text string to any MIB-based property group, creating a new group. For example, if the operator only wants to monitor certain key nodes which support RMON, the RMON property group can be copied and a string added, such as key_rmon_nodes, as a property to this second group. Polls and alarms then can be restricted to monitoring only nodes with this new property.

THE STATE DIAGRAM

With NerveCenter, the network operator has the ability to combine the evaluation of traps and poll conditions in a way that models the behavior of the environment and determines at each step in the model the appropriate action for the alarm system to take. This is accomplished by using a state diagram. State diagrams and their components are created using the GUI. Figure 6-3 shows a sample alarm state diagram.

Some thought must be put into building NerveCenter alarms.[5] NerveCenter will be able to automate most of the analysis of MIB data performed manually today, but careful design will allow much more to be accomplished than has been possible.

STATES

Each state diagram manages a MIB base object. There will exist for each active alarm, one instance of the state diagram for every instance of the base object that is being monitored. Every state within an alarm is assigned a severity and an associated color.

NerveCenter contains six states named to reflect problem conditions: Critical, Major, Minor, Warning, Inform and Special.

NerveCenter also contains six states named to reflect traffic conditions: Saturated, VeryHigh, High, Medium, Low and VeryLow.

When creating multiple-state alarms, the likely behavior of the network and the optimal actions the network operator would like to take should be considered.

Suppose, for example, that an alarm is designed that checks devices on the network to see if they are operating. When a device does not respond to a poll, NerveCenter generates a no-response trigger. The trigger causes the alarm to transition to a first warning state for that device. A second trigger causes the alarm to transition to a second warning state for that device.

If the device responds to a third poll after missing the first two, the question arises: Should the alarm be designed so that it returns to the ground state when the third poll is answered, or so that it transitions down to the next lower warning state, or so that it remains at the current warning state pending the next poll?

The answers depend on the organization's performance requirements and conditions in the network, such as the quality of the links. If this alarm is simply used to confirm that the node is alive, a return to ground state can be specified as soon as the device answers, regardless of previous failures to respond. If a warning that the device missed two polls is required, the

---

[5]In this context, *alarm* is used to denote a single state diagram defined within NerveCenter.

alarm can be held at the highest severity state for the device until the network operator resets it. If the alarm is required to maintain a state that reflects the recent history of successful and unsuccessful responses to polling, it can be made to transition to next-higher and next-lower states as polls are answered or missed. The results then are logged.

TRIGGERS AND TRANSITIONS

Whenever an active alarm detects a trigger that will move it from the current state to the next state, the transition is made automatically. There may be multiple triggers that can cause a transition; in this case, the first trigger raised will do so.

If an alarm receives a trigger from a poll or mask monitoring a particular base object and transitions to a new state for that instance, and then receives a trigger from a poll or mask monitoring a different base object, the alarm will ignore the second trigger for that alarm instance even if the alarm definition specifies a transition. This focuses the behavior of any given alarm on evaluating conditions specific to a base object.

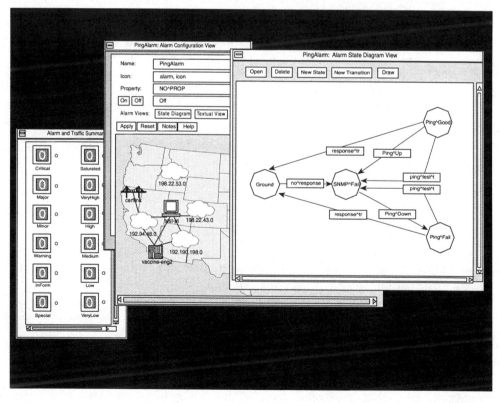

Source: NetLabs, Inc.

Figure 6-3: Alarm State Diagram

ACTIONS

When a transition occurs in an alarm (i.e., the current state changes to one of the next available states as defined by the diagram and triggers), any one or all of the following actions can be taken automatically by NerveCenter:

- Generate an audible beep.

- Display the alarm information so network operators can stay informed of status.

- Log the information to a file.

- Invoke an operator-defined application.

- Invoke a UNIX script.

- Send mail messages that contain the protocol data associated with the alarm transition to a list of specified recipients.

- Dial a pager and relay a numeric code that corresponds to the alarm that has triggered the action.

- Issue a trap or trigger, causing additional evaluation within NerveCenter or on a remote platform and notifying the operator of what to do next.

- Open the detailed notes associated with an alarm for more information, which might include explicit instructions to the operator of what to do next.

- Turn a poll on or off, giving operators the ability to automatically do follow-up checks.

- Issue an SNMP set.

INTEGRATED CAPABILITIES

The basic components of NerveCenter give it flexibility for monitoring SNMP-managed networks. By integrating the capabilities of trap monitoring, intelligent polling and automatic actions, the network can be monitored more completely with the result that problems will be diagnosed and resolved more quickly. The basic features of NerveCenter can be used to build more complex features.

MONITORING CONNECTIONS

NerveCenter includes several predefined alarms for monitoring the performance and status of physical and logical connections. Because of the way NerveCenter processes SNMP instance data, it can distinguish between multiple interfaces or ports in a single node and identify connections specific to an interface or port. These individual connections then can be monitored for status and performance.

Performance alarms shipped with NerveCenter use traffic severity levels. Traffic alarms use polls that issue triggers if traffic is at a specified level. The traffic classifier alarm can even differentiate between lines of different speeds in performing its analysis. This alarm uses relative polling, because it measures the increase in the number of octets (8-bit bytes) since the last poll. This alarm can be customized to represent the line speeds and traffic within the network.

ISOLATING SPECIAL INTEREST TRAPS

When handling SNMP traps, NerveCenter masks not only define the trap number that specifies the category of trap, but the minor_ trap_no within a category. This allows NerveCenter to evaluate automatically the information within a trap to see if a trigger should be raised. This is particularly useful when processing a vendor's enterprise-specific traps. In many cases, vendors use the minor number to represent a specific trap for a particular device, or — when proxy agents are in use — a particular device represented by the proxy.

The ability to evaluate this information automatically and take appropriate action gives network operators a significant head start in detecting and diagnosing error conditions. Of course, because NerveCenter only takes action when explicitly told to do so, informational traps can be handled in a totally different manner than traps that are more indicative of error conditions.

INTELLIGENT NOTIFICATION

The Action Router feature of NerveCenter allows the operator to specify how actions should be handled based on such criteria as time of day, severity of alarm, and the node from which the alarm originated. There are two components to the Action Router: rules with the associated actions to take, and an engine that evaluates the status of specific alarms to see if the rules apply.

To compose a rule, a conditional statement is specified by the network operator along with an associated action statement. A conditional statement can be a compound statement that evaluates any of the following condition types individually, or as joined by the logical operators **AND** and **OR**:

- Alarm.

- Severity.

- Node.

- Property Group.

- Trigger.

- Time.

- Day.

Within a condition, relational operators are used to determine how Action Router evaluates the data it receives relative to the value the network operator has set. For Alarm, Severity, Node, Property Group and Trigger, the following relational operators are used:

=	equal
<>	not equal

For Time or Day, the network operator can use the following relational operators:

=	equal
<>	not equal
<	less than
>	greater than
<=	less than or equal
>=	greater than or equal

To configure NerveCenter alarms to use Action Router, the network operator can modify them to specify Action Routing as the desired alarm action for a specific transition. The Action Router will then apply the additional rules specified before invoking the desired action.

REDUCING MANAGEMENT BANDWIDTH

Polls defined within NerveCenter do not automatically monitor all the nodes within their scope if the result of the poll will have no effect. They monitor only those object instances that are currently in an alarm state and that can be affected by the poll trigger.

This rule exists so that polls do not needlessly monitor nodes that are currently in a state that is not of interest to the specific analysis at hand. For example, suppose that an alarm can transition from Ground to State A to State B to Ground. The poll that generates the trigger that returns the alarm to Ground from State B will not be issued if the node is currently in State A.

In this way, NerveCenter uses the information accumulated about a node to optimize the amount of polling performed at any given time. By keeping a record of the node's history as represented by transitions through a state diagram, it is possible to avoid retrieving information that the operator of the management system should and probably will ignore. NerveCenter takes efficient, intelligent notification one step further and continually avoids generating network traffic to capture useless information.

USING NERVECENTER WITH OPENVIEW

From the perspective of an HP OpenView administrator, configuring HP OpenView Network Node Management to interoperate with NerveCenter is very straightforward. Because NerveCenter generates traps to notify management platforms and other applications of specific conditions, Network Node Manager need only be configured to understand the NetLabs-specific traps.

As part of the standard Event Configuration within Network Node Manager, the operator would load the NetLabs MIB and then add NetLabs enterprise events and associate the proper actions. To support adding NetLabs specific traps, NetLabs provides a MIB. The operator can then specify any actions that are deemed appropriate upon receiving a NerveCenter event.

Another configuration modification that network administrators may want to make is to suspend polling for thresholds within HP's Network Node Manager, because NerveCenter provides more power and flexibility through its finite state mechanisms. NerveCenter ships with sample alarm definitions to enable network operators to put NerveCenter to work handling the basic thresholds provided with Network Node Manager. These sample alarms then can be modified to take over operator-defined threshold polling as well.

The collection of MIB data should be evaluated to determine what can be handled more efficiently by NerveCenter. NerveCenter provides guidelines to assist network operators in this analysis. In addition to these guidelines, NetLabs provides facilities to keep the internal data store of NerveCenter automatically synchronized with Network Node Manager's data to minimize any NerveCenter-specific administration and to automatically derive the proper property groups needed by NerveCenter from the OpenView topology information.

NETLABS HAD PREVIOUSLY OFFERED ITS DIMONS PLATFORM TO COMPETE with Hewlett-Packard and other platform providers. Now the company has abandoned its efforts to compete as a platform provider in favor of providing management applications that can run on multiple platforms, including HP OpenView. NetLabs will integrate NerveCenter with the OpenView platform in stages. Full integration with OpenView is expected in mid-1995.

Network managers need not wait for full incorporation of NerveCenter capabilities into OpenView to reap its benefits. Using NerveCenter as a third-party application now with HP Network Node Manager extends problem management capabilities beyond those available with NNM alone, providing the benefits of automated data evaluation. Bandwidth required for network management is minimized because NerveCenter correlates, filters and upgrades alerts automatically to provide only intelligently preprocessed information to network operators. This significantly enhances the value of the information presented, since it allows network operators to more readily determine if the condition is serious enough to warrant intervention. HP also intends to add NerveCenter capabilities to its OperationsCenter systems management application and OpenView/DM platform for the management of the telecommunications environment.

NetLabs has released Version 2.0 of NerveCenter, which includes the ability to manage 80,000 nodes, up from 5,000 nodes supported by the previous version. This scalability will allow users of OpenView Network Node Manager to be much more productive. An administrator can distribute network-management tasks across multiple domains to detect local events and forward them to a central network-management station for cross-domain coordination.

CHAPTER 7

Managing the
Physical Network

COMPANIES OF ALL TYPES AND SIZES HAVE COME TO RELY ON THEIR NETWORKS to support mission-critical applications. As LANs, voice and enterprise networks experience dynamic growth and change, the ability to effectively monitor and control them becomes increasingly important. To cope with this situation, network management activities must be proactive, efficient and support the daily needs of all network users.

To meet these needs, ISICAD Inc. offers a single-workstation solution, combining the following applications:

- COMMAND for management of the network's physical components and connectivity.

- COMMAND HelpDesk for implementing and tracking service requests.

- Integration with a standard network management system (NMS) or element management system (EMS), such as HP's Network Node Manager or Cisco's CiscoWorks, for monitoring the logical aspects of the network.

Working together, these applications share and update data, offering an automated process to increase the productivity and effectiveness of available network management staff.

Specifically, COMMAND is a physical network management tool that collects detailed information from the network's many components and makes it available to network managers and system operators through a relational database management system (RDBMS). It includes automated design tools that allow planners to lay out entire networks using standard and operator-definable equipment and cable/cableway symbols. It also issues trouble tickets, work orders, service schedules, status/tracking reports, transaction logs for change management, and inventory and asset valuation information.

LEVEL OF INTEGRATION

COMMAND can be integrated with HP OpenView to provide information concerning the physical connectivity for every device on the network. COMMAND provides menu bar integration with HP OpenView Network Node Manager, general interoperability with the OpenView platform, and data sharing with other OpenView applications. With this level of integration, COMMAND complements HP OpenView's ability to monitor network performance and traffic, and identify problems by providing information about both the active devices monitored by the HP OpenView system, and passive devices that are invisible to the logical management system (Table 7-1).

A COMMAND-OpenView link provides real-time, dynamic correlation between physical and logical components of the network. Over this link,

Network Node Manager (logical)	COMMAND (physical)
Real-time, transient asset and connectivity data	Same, plus permanent, "as defined" asset and connectivity data, plus operator-defined data
Network performance monitoring	N/A
MIB equipment only	MIB, plus non-intelligent equipment, plus new technology equipment before standards are defined
Logical map	Physical trace, including connectivity and cabling, with logical comparison
N/A	Physical location (i.e., floor, closet, rack)
N/A	Work orders
Integrated EMS links only	Additional EMS links through APIs
Bitmap display	CAD drawing display
IP addresses as discovered	IP addresses as assigned by network manager
Proprietary database	Standard relational databases
Single data storage point	Access to multiple databases and drawing servers

Table 7-1: Logical vs. Physical Network Management

COMMAND information can be retrieved while Network Node Manager is in operation. When Network Node Manager alerts the operator to a node failure, for example, COMMAND provides drawings of the node's physical location, as well as other helpful information such as the circuit listing and a complete connectivity matrix for all of the node's used and available ports.

Through the COMMAND-HP OpenView link, companies can solve network problems more quickly, minimize downtime, and improve network management, diagnostics and repair activities. The link between COMMAND and OpenView is augmented by helpdesk capabilities that provide a comprehensive network management solution.

THE NETWORK ENVIRONMENT

COMMAND addresses the following five areas:

Premises and Backbone Infrastructure: Fundamental to effective network management is the management system's ability to document and manage all of the equipment, interfaces, and connections in the enterprise network. COMMAND documents and provides detailed information about the entire networking infrastructure, including the actual location of network devices, their technical characteristics, and their physical connectivity. All of this information is kept up-to-date and is accessible through an on-line RDBMS, saving operators, technicians and network managers time performing daily tasks.

Integration with Network Management Systems: COMMAND is the physical network management core that can be optionally integrated with a variety of applications to provide a comprehensive network management solution. This allows network problems to be solved quickly, minimizing downtime and improving network management, diagnostic and troubleshooting activities. The result is the ability to document and manage the physical relationship of all network devices, both intelligent and non-intelligent, including those that cannot be actively managed by Network Node Manager.

Integrated HelpDesk and Troubleshooting: Optional COMMAND HelpDesk software may be fully integrated with COMMAND. In addition to providing a workflow process that guides end users through the problem reporting process, COMMAND HelpDesk assigns the problem to support staff, tracks its resolution, builds a database for ongoing helpdesk management, and notifies the end user when the service request is complete. A technician can view the current status of any service request or open new trouble tickets.

Network Design and Management: COMMAND allows the network manager to place and connect devices graphically for an accurate picture of the network's design. Rule-based auto-configuration capabilities allow the most appropriate end-to-end circuit to be established. COMMAND automatically traces the patches and cross-connections necessary to complete the circuit, easing design and change management. Complete documentation about the location and connectivity of every physical component is also provided to facilitate effective troubleshooting.

Bandwidth and Virtual Circuit Management: An optional WAN management module for COMMAND provides the ability to create and trace circuits/links between customer premises equipment (CPE) and telco central office components. Channel availability and bandwidth allocation also can be monitored. This includes the ability to capture the relationship of one circuit riding on another circuit, both virtual and physical.

COMMAND OPERATION

In daily operation, the Network Management System (NMS) collects device and alert data from simple network management protocol (SNMP) agents residing on network devices such as routers, wiring hubs and adapter cards. Abnormal conditions trigger alarms, which tell COMMAND HelpDesk to open a trouble ticket and display the physical location of the alarmed device(s). The NMS inserts logical data about the device into the trouble ticket, and COMMAND inserts the physical location and connectivity data (Figure 7-1).

The following scenario illustrates this automated process:

1. Based on continuous real-time monitoring of the intelligent devices on the network, the network management system — in this case, HP's Network Node Manager — triggers an alarm when a device goes down.

2. The NMS furnishes specific logical data about the device — such as IP address and equipment name — to the trouble ticket. COMMAND inserts physical data, such as:

   • Device location, such as building, floor or workgroup.

   • Connectivity.

   • Asset information.

   • End-to-end circuit trace for all components — both active and passive — connected to the device.

3. COMMAND also can print out a detailed circuit trace showing the location of the device for use by repair technicians.

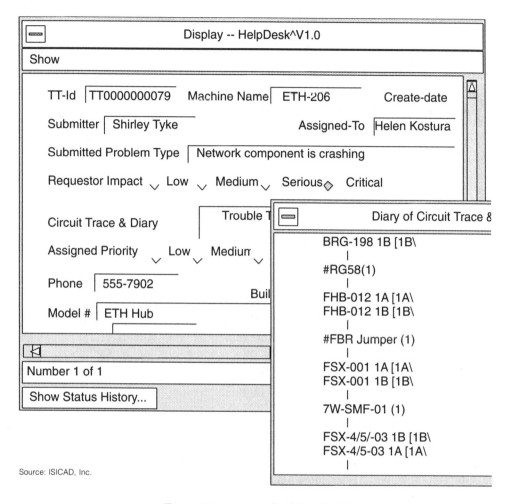

Figure 7-1: *Auto-populated Trouble Ticket*

4. Technicians can query COMMAND's database at any time for historic information, such as a log of previous work orders against the device.

5. COMMAND HelpDesk automatically routes the trouble ticket to a central station or to the appropriate technician, based on a predefined workflow.

6. All trouble-ticket information, including the resolution, is logged automatically into a knowledge database to aid in ongoing helpdesk management.

7. Using COMMAND's HelpDesk standard forms or operator-definable forms, network end users can enter service requests and report problems.

8. The trouble ticket automatically polls COMMAND for connectivity and asset information, then routes the data appropriately via e-mail. An on-screen notifier enables the administrator or end user to check the status of the request.

INTEGRATED GRAPHICAL ENVIRONMENT

COMMAND incorporates an integrated graphical environment for the management and presentation of network management information, built on an interface of pulldown menus, dialog boxes and other productivity tools. COMMAND combines this graphical representation of the network infrastructure with dynamic links to standard relational databases for management of network and telecommunications assets — both intelligent and non-intelligent — and connectivity.

USER INTERFACE
COMMAND operates from a graphical user interface (GUI) built on industry-standard OSF/Motif and X11. Pull-down menus and dialog boxes aid navigation, while less often used functions can be accessed from hot-keys or from groups of menu commands.

All pull-down menus are operator-definable, allowing the addition and modification of options to run macros, launch other applications, or generate SQL queries. In addition, graphical navigation, such as zooming into a close-up view of a network segment, is done by pressing on-screen buttons or clicking with the mouse.

NETWORK REPRESENTATION
The key interface into COMMAND data is the graphical representation of the network, which can map the network infrastructure to an operator-defined level of detail. Graphical views and intelligent operator-defined symbols are the major components of this interface. Operators can use them to visually navigate the infrastructure, quickly adding or locating equipment and connections. This reduces troubleshooting time and allows network monitoring to be delegated to less skilled staff.

Graphical Views: Up to eight graphical views or drawings of the network may be open at a time, such as multiple floors or buildings. The operator can activate any one of the views selectively, using the others in the background as a reference. Each drawing can contain up to 256 layers that can be displayed individually. This allows the operator to display only the voice circuits, for example, or only the workstations. Drawings can reside anywhere on the network, including multiple hosts.

A comprehensive set of drawing tools is included with COMMAND, allowing the operator to create symbols and graphical models of any desired complexity. Among these are:

- Create lines, polylines, arcs, circles, points, symbols and text.

- Rotate, scale, align and mirror graphics objects.

- Move, edit, copy, search for and delete graphics objects.

- Assign colors to objects (up to 256 colors).

- Move objects among 256 layers, which can be selectively displayed.

- Edit text within symbols.

- Store, retrieve, copy, edit and manage drawing files.

- Plot or print drawings at operator-definable real-world scale and standard drawing sizes. Output can be to a pen plotter, electrostatic plotter or printers.

In addition, drawings may be imported from CAD systems using industry-standard DXF or IGES formats. With the optional CADSCAN module, COMMAND also can display and edit RLC raster images, such as scanned blueprints, and use them as backgrounds.

Navigation Aids: To organize a project, the COMMAND operator can create a hierarchy of drawings, beginning with an enterprise or topological map. This could represent a campus, a city or an entire hemisphere. From this top level, the operator can move down to other maps or network representations with increasing levels of detail, such as a floor plan or wiring closet. Navigation among these drawings can be done quickly by drilling down to the next-lower level, entering the drawing name, or selecting it from a list. In addition, operator-defined views of drawings can be saved and recalled by name to display only the desired portion of the drawing.

Operator-Defined Symbols: A symbol is a graphical representation of an element in the COMMAND database, such as a router or a hub. It is composed of vector-based graphics and associated database information that relates to the symbol. The symbol could represent a type of workstation, a lower-level drawing, or a macro program. When adding an instance to the graphical representation of the network, all operator-defined symbols are available from on-screen catalogs, which can be grouped by type (such as all fiber-optic multiplexers) or by make and model of equipment (such as all AGS+ components for a Cisco router).

COMMAND offers the following types of symbols:

Equipment: Equipment symbols can be created in both plan (horizontal) and elevation (vertical) views. For example, the same piece of equipment can be modeled on a floor plan and in a rack. Symbols can be updated automatically to change all instances to a new graphic while preserving existing attribute information. They can be also placed automatically when using the auto-discover capability of Network Node Manager. In addition, equipment symbols display whether ports are assigned or free (for example, red for assigned and green for free). When COMMAND is linked to Network Node Manager, symbols also can change color to indicate alarm status, based on an operator-definable color table.

Drill Up/Drill Down: A specialized symbol or defined boundary area can be used in any COMMAND drawing to drill down to one or more subdrawings, which may display more detailed configuration information, or drill up back to the parent drawing. For example, a campus drawing might be used as the top level, with drill down capability in each building, going into progressively more detail through floor plan, department, wiring closet and equipment rack. Multiple instances of the same piece of equipment on different drawings are referenced to a single database entry for proper asset management.

Executable: A specialized symbol can be designated that launches a particular operator-defined macro. Macros are scripts that are used to automate fairly routine tasks. Rather than manually going through repetitive steps, these steps can be scripted and carried out automatically by a macro.

MODELING

COMMAND provides a modeling capability that allows the network infrastructure — equipment, circuits and connectivity — to be graphically represented.

COMMAND models a variety of networks equipment and services, including:

- Voice (PBX, telephone, patch panels).

- Data (servers, bridges, routers, PCs).

- Video (full-motion, broadcast).

- Fire (sprinkler controllers).

- Security (alarms).

- Various topologies (star, ring, bus).

EQUIPMENT MODELING

To enforce its rule-based circuit model, COMMAND includes a variety of predefined equipment categories to be used when adding network or telecommunications equipment. Each type defines a relative number of connectors/ports to maintain logical integrity in the COMMAND model.

These predefined equipment categories are:

- **End Item:** station equipment such as a workstation, server or telephone.

- **Connector:** passive equipment such as a floor box or wall outlet.

- **Node:** equipment with no physical ports, providing a pointer to a location from which a list of equipment can be generated.

- **Patch:** cross-connect equipment with internal mapping, such as a patch panel.

- **MUX:** equipment that creates a composite circuit and must be used in pairs, such as multiplexers.

- **Black Box:** operator-defined equipment that concentrates or distributes connections, such as a fan-out box.

- **Multiplexer/Bus:** an end piece of equipment with a bus into which other equipment is directly attached, such as a hub or PC with add-in cards.

CIRCUIT MODELING

When a network infrastructure has been documented with COMMAND, useful analysis and troubleshooting information is readily available. This can take the form of a circuit trace, traces of associated equipment or software, and a complete routing of cabling and cableway information.

Circuit Traces: When a particular item of equipment has been identified by selecting it on a graphical representation of the network, as the result of an SQL query, or from an alarm generated by HP's Network Node Manager, the operator quickly can display a complete circuit trace, either in graphic or text form (Figure 7-2). When COMMAND is linked to Network Node Manager, these same capabilities can be launched from that platform as well.

Options for a circuit trace include:

- **Graphics Trace:** displays a new window with a graphical circuit schematic.

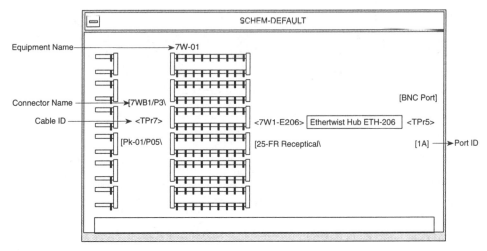

Source: ISICAD, Inc.

Figure 7-2: *Circuit Trace*

- **Textual Trace:** displays the circuit trace in text format.

- **Trace with Equipment Locate:** activates the graphical representation of the network on which the equipment is located, zooms in and flashes the equipment, then generates a separate graphic or text window with the circuit trace.

- **Client to Server Trace:** after the operator specifies the source and destination connectors, COMMAND presents the circuit that links them.

- **Filtered Trace:** the operator specifies which type(s) of equipment should be displayed in the circuit trace, filtering out all others.

- **Logical Trace:** a circuit trace based on equipment association rather than port connectivity. This is useful if the infrastructure has not been detailed to the connector level. Optionally, the logical circuit may be highlighted/flashed on the base drawing for quick identification.

Graphic circuit traces are intelligent drawings, just like the primary COMMAND drawings, from which SQL queries and other information can be extracted. They also can be plotted or printed and used to fill out a trouble ticket with COMMAND HelpDesk. The same methodology as circuit traces can be used for process traces as well. For example, the client portion of a database software package can be traced back to its associated server in order to pinpoint a problem.

PHYSICAL CONNECTIVITY MODELING

Modeling COMMAND provides sophisticated cable management that can be used alone or as part of a comprehensive network management strategy. It allows the operator to design cable layouts faster and more accurately.

Groups of cables can be routed through cableways, which consist of several connected straight segments that record directional and compartment/level changes. Their lengths are calculated automatically as the cableway is defined. Cableways may represent a physical object, such as a conduit or cable tray, or merely a defined route, such as a microwave link. They can contain such intelligence as total capacity and maximum cable weight.

Equipment can be connected with cables, either individually or in bulk operations, and the cables can be routed manually or automatically through cableways. Information such as cable type, identifier and number of lines in the cable is stored in the system and selected by the operator from an on-screen list. Connectivity even can be documented down to the pin level. There is no limit on the number of connections that may be documented in a COMMAND project.

The operator can select connected equipment in a number of ways, including single and multiple picks off the screen drawing, by a rectangular window drawn around the equipment, or by all the equipment in an operator-defined region. Cable routing may be determined manually or automatically, using either the shortest route through defined cableways or a predefined route, such as a backbone. Patching is also supported, both through internal equipment mapping and external patch cabling.

ASSET MANAGEMENT

An often overlooked benefit of the documentation provided by a physical NMS is its value as an asset management tool. Increasing amounts of money are tied up in network equipment, which continues to be added at an accelerating pace to keep up with organizational needs. Network documentation gives companies the ability to know the exact location of their equipment — whether it is on the floor or in inventory — what it is worth, and how much capacity is available. Along with better inventory management and control, the asset management database can help companies control operating costs by permitting more efficient use of resources. Accountability is enhanced by the ability to generate depreciation schedules, track departmental chargebacks and project growth.

COMMAND provides the means to manage network telecommunications and other assets of a project. By providing each piece of equipment with a unique identifier, such as network name, the network administrator is able to track inventory with such information as equipment owner, serial number, cost center, date installed and configuration. Because these identifiers are operator-definable, they can be linked to a specific corporate process for asset management. Reports can be generated with stock counts, based on given criteria, such as *all PCs in accounting*. SQL queries related to asset information also can be launched.

At this writing, ISICAD and NetLabs are planning to integrate their network management software products to facilitate asset management across the enterprise network. This integration allows operators to run NetLabs' AssetManager application on the COMMAND physical network management system, allowing them to compile asset information on logical and physical network elements. Although COMMAND operators can take advantage of the auto-discovery capabilities of OpenView to load management information base (MIB) data about Simple Network Management Protocol (SNMP) devices, that data is limited to management attribute information on Internet Protocol (IP) nodes. With AssetManager, operators can load much more information about IP and non-IP devices into the COMMAND database.

ZONES

Asset management can be enhanced by the definition of optional zones, or positional properties, in a COMMAND graphical representation of the network. They can be defined either by dragging a rectangle to indicate a zone region or by picking the boundary of an existing region, such as an office. Zone IDs are assigned by the operator, and all assets within that zone inherit the ID. Equipment can be selected by zone ID, and when assets are moved to another zone, the ID is updated to keep the inventory current.

LOCATE EQUIPMENT

Based on the equipment identifier or the results of a database query, COMMAND can automatically load the drawing on which a particular piece of equipment is located, zoom in on the equipment and highlight/flash it, as well as display attribute information. When COMMAND is linked to HP's Network Node Manager, these same capabilities can be launched from that platform as well. In addition, a reverse locate enables COMMAND to identify located equipment on the OpenView map.

MAC MANAGER

COMMAND's Media Access Control (MAC) Manager function allows an administrator to move and connect equipment through simple processes that do not require detailed knowledge of the network infrastructure or database (Figure 7-3).

ISICAD achieves this by providing an open architecture environment in which the network manager can define a rule-based set of instructions for COMMAND to follow whenever the operator performs the defined operation, such as moving a workstation.

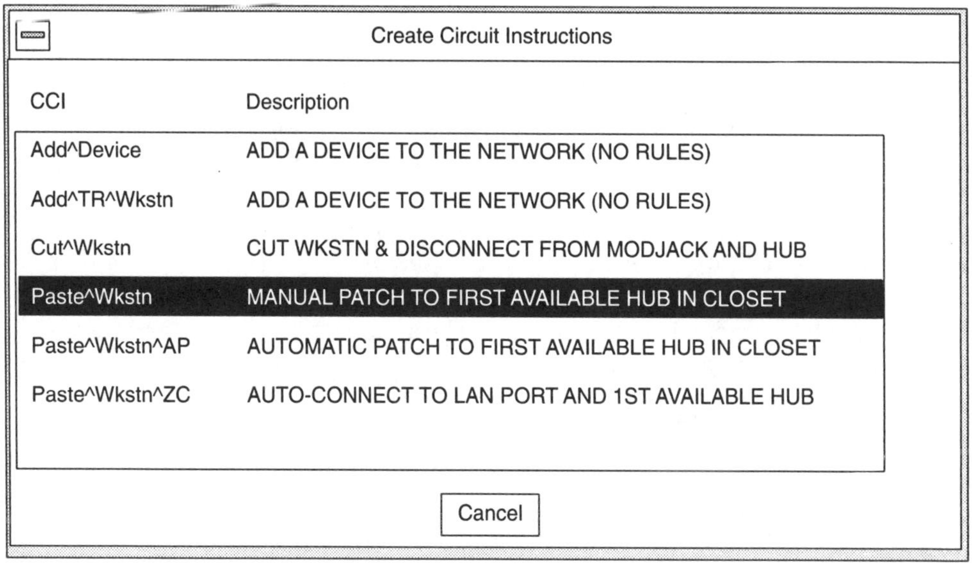

▭	Create Circuit Instructions
CCI	Description
Add^Device	ADD A DEVICE TO THE NETWORK (NO RULES)
Add^TR^Wkstn	ADD A DEVICE TO THE NETWORK (NO RULES)
Cut^Wkstn	CUT WKSTN & DISCONNECT FROM MODJACK AND HUB
Paste^Wkstn	MANUAL PATCH TO FIRST AVAILABLE HUB IN CLOSET
Paste^Wkstn^AP	AUTOMATIC PATCH TO FIRST AVAILABLE HUB IN CLOSET
Paste^Wkstn^ZC	AUTO-CONNECT TO LAN PORT AND 1ST AVAILABLE HUB

Cancel

Source: ISICAD, Inc.

Figure 7-3: MAC Manager

Rules can be based on industry standards, or company or vendor requirements. They also can include error-checking, such as preventing:

• A data line from being connected to a telephone jack.

• An Ethernet port from being connected to a token ring network.

• A workstation from being added to a Novell network.

When these processes are created they can be listed on a pull-down menu. That way, the operator merely can select an appropriate item and follow the prompts to complete the move or connection. If an error occurs during execution, COMMAND will roll back the process to its beginning to preserve data integrity.

MAC Manager provides the system administrator with a scripting language, which includes system variables such as drawing name and current connector number, along with up to 50 operator-defined variables. The results of SQL queries also can be passed to a variable and used as part of the script. Execution of the script can be controlled with instructions such as *If...Else, GoTo*, and requests for operator input. COMMAND macros also can be run from within a MAC Manager script.

Using MAC Manager, the system administrator can automate processes such as connecting and disconnecting equipment completely, creating new graphic instances in a drawing, changing object color, and invoking an action based on the result of a database query. When equipment is moved, its attributes move with it, automatically keeping the database up-to-date.

In a typical implementation, the system administrator first defines a set of instructions as ASCII text files, based on industry standards or the particular organization's or vendor's rules for moving and connecting equipment. Corresponding function names are then added to the COMMAND pull-down menus for simplicity of operation.

When these are in place, the system operator then selects the appropriate function as needed from the menu, such as Move Workstation or Move Phone. Depending on the instruction set, the operator may answer prompts, such as Select Workstation, as the process proceeds step by step. Depending on the choices made, the function can perform different operations, based on an *If...Then* structure.

COMMAND CUSTOMIZATION

COMMAND provides a customizable environment through the use of scripts, macros and other operator-definable processes. Any of these can be added to the menu.

The Script function provides an interactive interface to UNIX shell scripts, complete with operator-defined variables and screen prompts, to accomplish tasks such as:

- Initiate a trouble ticket inquiry.

- Locate and display a network component "Device View" in HP's Network Node Manager.

- Locate the source of a network alarm.

- Invoke SQL queries and Xterm sessions.

Macros also may be created and stored, then invoked by selecting the macro file name or selecting a drawing symbol that has a predefined hot link to the macro file.

The operator also can manipulate a database from within COMMAND, including loading or removing records from a table, querying the database, and getting information about a database table.

Other items that can be customized include:

- Input/output screens.

- Forms, reports and work orders.

- Rule sets.

- Directories.

- Site-specific symbols.

- Database applications.

- SQL scripts.

WAN MANAGEMENT

The optional WAN Management Module provides the ability to model and manage wide-area circuits or links and to track bandwidth allocation. The add-on module offers tools for troubleshooting and fault isolation to reduce the costs associated with supporting enterprise networks. It also provides capabilities for documenting WAN equipment and topology.

PHYSICAL MODEL

Customer premises equipment (CPE) and wide-area nodes can be modeled, along with physical connectivity attributes such as cable type. In addition, other asset information can be incorporated in the database, including maintenance contract telephone numbers and configurations. The level of detail is operator-definable; COMMAND merely requires that CPE or WAN nodes be attached at each end of a circuit.

Premises and wide-area assets can be incorporated into a single project. Typically, the router is used as the dividing line between LAN and WAN. One piece of equipment can be displayed on multiple drawings, such as a premises floor plan and a wide-area closet on two different drawings, with a single entry in the relational database.

LOGICAL MODEL

Between the end pieces of equipment, one or more virtual circuits can be laid out, with or without the use of drawings. Sublevels of detail also can be modeled, with one circuit riding over another facility, such as a 64K service that is part of a 256K circuit, which in turn consists of a series of T1 or T3 segments. Additional information can be tracked on the logical circuit, such as circuit identification, carrier and contact name.

CIRCUIT ROUTING

When the physical, logical and virtual circuits have been laid out, the relationship between them can be established by COMMAND's routing system. This is a semiautomatic process in which COMMAND graphically builds a circuit schematic based on connectivity information it has been given, then queries the operator at each decision point by presenting a list of possible paths before continuing to the next hop. The schematic is updated dynamically as each segment is being routed, and a change log also may be activated to record the routing at the same time. Using this system, a typical WAN circuit may require only three or four decision points before it is completely routed.

COMMAND also checks the available bandwidth for each circuit segment — both channelized and unchannelized — and either allocates the bandwidth required or informs the operator that the necessary bandwidth is unavailable. At a later time, additional submaps or facilities may be built if more detail is desired. Intermediate equipment also can be added to an existing circuit as required.

WAN CIRCUIT TRACE

When the WAN model is in place, a graphical or textual circuit trace can be generated automatically at any time, bringing in components from one or more drawings. A circuit trace includes equipment, physical and virtual circuits, and port connectivity. On the circuit trace are text labels that identify the segment and equipment that completes the circuit. As with all COMMAND circuit traces, these objects have intelligence and can be queried further for detail from the database, or the whole trace can be printed as part of a work order.

BANDWIDTH ALLOCATION TRACKING

With COMMAND's WAN module, the bandwidth allocation for circuits can be modeled. Bandwidth is tracked by channels using the formula: *channel bandwidth x the number of channels = the total capacity of the circuit.* Circuits can be modeled using channelized or unchannelized bandwidth.[1]

The channels of a circuit are categorized as available, *reserved* or *used.* Available channels are marked as *used* as the circuit is routed over them, or set to *reserved* using the channel allocation tool. Channels are made available again by unrouting the circuit from the facility.

Accessing the channel allocation tool displays the list of channels for the selected circuit, along with their status. *Used* channels show the circuit that is routed on them. Any available channels can be set to *reserved* to mark them for future use. For a used or reserved channel, an owner (such as a department, group, cost center, project or software application) can be assigned and optionally associated with a flat-rate cost for chargebacks.

---

[1] Channelized bandwidth refers to the partitioning of the available bandwidth into separate channels. In the case of a T1 line, there can be 24 channels of 56/64 Kbps each. The total bandwidth of a T1 line is 1.544 Mbps. Taking out 8 bps for inband management, the unchannelized bandwidth of a T1 line is 1.536 Mbps.

USER INTERFACE

The WAN module can be accessed from COMMAND's standard pull-down menus by detaching a floating menu of WAN tools. Included are circuit definition and routing functions, along with a variety of predefined standard SQL queries.

RELATIONAL DATABASE MANAGEMENT

COMMAND provides links to industry-standard relational databases. Using IP socket technology, COMMAND allows databases to be distributed across the network. Asset and connectivity information are stored in multiple database tables that can be accessed from COMMAND through SQL queries. The results of these queries are used in many ways, including displaying graphical information such as a circuit trace, maintaining a transaction log, and generating work orders and reports. In addition, operator-defined information that is stored in other databases, such as equipment costs and maintenance schedules, can be quickly accessed from the COMMAND menu and maintained as part of a particular project.

DATABASE STRUCTURE

The COMMAND database is organized as a collection of tables:

Equipment: defines equipment types, default connectors, equipment instances in the project, and operator-defined "info tables" that can be used for maintenance and inventory information.

Media: includes media types (such as cables, optical fiber, and microwave) and line information within the various media.

Media paths: includes cableways, media segments, nodes, and routing information.

Change logs: used to define work orders and track tasks associated with changes to equipment, ports, cables and locations.

Data/drawing integrity: handles communication between the database and drawings, tracking drawing locations, and maintaining system integrity.

Quick Start: temporarily stores data that is used to auto-populate drawings based on equipment and connectivity information that has been supplied by an outside source.

DATABASE QUERIES

COMMAND provides an interactive interface to SQL that enables the system operator to generate sophisticated database queries and display the results in different ways. A set of predefined queries are provided with the system, and the operator may create an unlimited number of additional queries, using a combination of standard SQL functions and specialized COMMAND functions, such as changing object colors or performing a circuit trace, on the results of the query. As part of the query execution, COMMAND can display operator prompts for input to be passed as a parameter to the query, thus extending the power of the query function. SQL queries can be saved to a file by name and then displayed on COMMAND pull-down menus.

Predefined queries are provided with COMMAND that can retrieve information in the following categories:

- **Equipment:** such as flashing all PCs on the drawing.

- **Cable:** such as listing all unused cables of a specific type.

- **Cableway:** such as reporting available cable tray capacity based on cross-section or weight.

- **Connector:** such as highlighting all the components connected to a selected component.

- **Zone:** such as highlighting the free outlets within a specified zone.

- **Change log**.

CHANGES, WORK ORDERS AND REPORTS

At the operator's option, changes to the COMMAND database can be tracked in a change log. This information, along with complete database information, can be output in the form of work orders and reports. Several of these are predefined, including:

- Cable, cableway, equipment or connection schedules, which generate a detailed listing of all cables, cableways, equipment or connections, or a subset specified by the operator.

- Network value reports, which detail bills of quantities and associated costs for a project, or a subset specified by the operator.

- Bill of quantities, which lists components that appear in project drawings, with total cost for each drawing and a grand total for the project.

- Textual circuit trace.

Using standard database tools, the operator can create additional reports from the COMMAND database.

QUICK START

Integrated into COMMAND is a suite of tools and utilities called Quick Start. With these tools and utilities, the operator can implement a new project more efficiently by incorporating existing data. Any combination of the tools may be selected, depending on the specific situation.

CONNECTOR NAMING

After an equipment type has been defined for the COMMAND database, system operators typically provide names for the connectors, as well as mapping information. If an equipment type has many connectors, such as patch panel, creating names can be a long task. The COMMAND system has a default connector naming convention (e.g., 1A, 2A, 3A, 1B), but most operators have more descriptive names they may wish to use (e.g., Port-1, IN, OUT, BUS). This utility provides the ability to specify a pattern and increment for naming the connectors, similar to the equipment naming capability. Operators have the ability to specify starting and ending connectors as well.

On several categories of equipment it is beneficial for system operators to pre-map the connectors so that the mapping does not have to be recreated each time they place the equipment. This tool allows the operator to map the connectors more easily.

DATA LOADING UTILITIES

Much of the information about the network may reside in different formats. These formats include paper documentation, other database systems, bar code systems and NMS information. The purpose of the data loading utilities is to provide a mechanism to capture that data and load it into the COMMAND system. When this data is captured, it can be used to generate graphical representations of the networks with equipment, connectivity, location and asset information. The more information that is available from these other sources, the more the utility will be able to perform automatically.

When this data has been collected in a COMMAND-compatible flat file format, it can then be loaded into the database and processed by the utility.

FLAT FILE GENERATORS

To assist in creating the flat files needed for the data loading utilities, ISICAD provides a variety of programs and procedures to create these files. Quick Start contains the following flat file generators:

- **Discovered Devices — HP OpenView:** Using the APIs provided by HP for the OpenView platform, it is possible to select information about objects that have been discovered by OpenView. The Quick Start program takes the output from this mechanism and formats it properly for data loading. This information may be used to generate the physical network diagram in COMMAND, with automatic placement of discovered equipment by one of the following methods:

- Place into designated named zone or region location.

- Replace specified text with a given piece of equipment.

- Place equipment at a designated text marker location.

- Place upon an existing piece of equipment, such as a floor box.

- Place by pick and drag into position.

- **Converting Paper Documentation to Electronic Formats:** Because a lot of network documentation may be in paper form, Quick Start provides a suggested methodology for inputting that data in the format needed for the data loading utilities. This methodology describes data input forms that can be set up in a PC spreadsheet package or a database environment and used to input the data. This data then can be extracted in the correct format and used to generate the COMMAND drawings.

System operators may provide their own programs and procedures to create the flat files needed for the data loading utilities. The format of the file is documented and available for their use.

INTEGRATED NETWORK MANAGEMENT

As noted, COMMAND can be linked to HP's Network Node Manager, providing a two-way connection that allows integrated network management from a single console. Generally, the link is used for automatic discovery of network equipment, monitoring and responding to alarms, determining the physical location of equipment, and generating a circuit trace. All of these options can be installed directly in the OpenView menu system for access.

AUTO-DISCOVERY

As part of setting up a COMMAND project or updating an existing network configuration, the auto-discovery process in COMMAND reads the database generated by Network Node Manager and assigns information such as graphic symbol, zone and physical location to each discovered component. Through the Quick Start tools, the components then are placed in proper position on the COMMAND drawing.

ALARMS

When linked to Network Node Manager, COMMAND can display alarms and equipment status on a physical drawing, such as a floor plan, to graphically indicate where the fault is located. Alarms may be exported directly to COMMAND, or COMMAND may read OpenView's event log directly, depending on the particular implementation.

The operator may choose to cycle through the alarm process manually or set up continuous monitoring with a specified polling rate, such as every 30 seconds. A color table can be set up to indicate device status in a range of colors determined by the operator.

PHYSICAL LOCATION

When a component has been selected in Network Node Manager, either manually or by an alarm, the operator can choose a physical locate command from the menu. This will launch COMMAND if necessary, load the correct drawing, and zoom in on the identified piece of equipment, which is highlighted on the screen. From this point, any COMMAND function can be run against that component, including auto-population of a trouble ticket with information from the COMMAND database.

CIRCUIT TRACE

When a component has been selected in Network Node Manager, either manually or by an alarm, the operator can choose a circuit trace command from the menu. This will launch COMMAND, if necessary, and generate a circuit trace in the form selected from the following options:

- Graphic trace.

- Graphic trace and physical equipment locate.

- Textual trace.

- Textual trace and physical equipment locate.

- Client to server trace.

- Filtered trace.

- Logical trace.

- WAN circuit trace, if the optional WAN module is installed.

In all cases except the textual trace alone, an intelligent graphic window is displayed and a schematic is wrapped within the new window.

COMMAND HELPDESK

COMMAND HelpDesk is an optional software package for automating network helpdesk and troubleshooting operations, based on Remedy Corp.'s Action Request System (ARS). It is designed to integrate with COMMAND and other network management systems, such as HP's Network Node Manager, providing a specific workflow that will assist network operators and technicians in reporting and resolving network problems.

In addition, it assigns the problem to support staff, tracks its resolution, builds an experience database for ongoing helpdesk management, and notifies the requester when the problem is resolved or the service request is completed. It also can activate a pager when certain types of problems are reported. COMMAND HelpDesk runs on UNIX servers and allows trouble ticket submittals from X-workstations and PCs running Microsoft Windows.

WORKFLOW

When Network Node Manager detects a network device failure, a trouble ticket for that device can be created automatically. The trouble ticket is populated automatically with asset and connectivity information from COMMAND's database, including an end-to-end circuit trace of all the physical components connected to the specified device. Auto-routing sends the ticket to the appropriate technician, while the requester can query the status of the trouble ticket at any time.

COMMAND HelpDesk features pull-down menus and a standard Motif interface that enables end users throughout the network to enter network service requests and trouble tickets using a standard or operator-definable set of forms. The trouble ticket includes end user information, a problem description, and detailed information showing the device's actual physical location. The form then is routed automatically to a central support person or directly to a technician, depending on the nature of the problem and how the workflow has been designed.

Customizing tools allow helpdesk administrators to set up COMMAND HelpDesk to meet corporate or specific site standards, such as setting operator access rights, customizing windows, and specifying which type of requests are sent to individual support personnel.

The administrator or a technician can access COMMAND's physical infrastructure database to get a historical record about network equipment and its connectivity. COMMAND also provides an actual drawing or floor plan of the device's location so it can be easily located by the technician performing the work.

OPERATOR PRIVILEGES

The COMMAND HelpDesk includes two groups of operators: Write License and Submitters.

Under the Write License group, operators can be subgrouped into administrators and support staff. Administrators can perform tasks such as design schemas and forms, define filters, set user permissions, and control trouble ticket process flow. Support staff personnel can read and write all tickets in the database, per the permissions defined by the administrators. These two types of users are configured into the HelpDesk system through the use of operator and group IDs with associated assigned privileges.

The Submitters have the ability to submit tickets into the HelpDesk. They also can view and modify the tickets they have submitted, but do not have the ability to view or edit any other ticket in the system.

COMMAND API LINKS

One major benefit of COMMAND is its ability to seamlessly link with other software, such as HP OpenView and Remedy Action Request System. Together, these products provide the network administrator with an integrated environment on a single platform.

Links between COMMAND and other software are accomplished through a series of Application Program Interfaces (APIs). These consist of an API Gateway, which is the core, and one or more other API interfaces linked to specific third-party products. Only one API Gateway is required for each server, regardless of how many other APIs are running on that server.

The API Gateway is a set of operator-customizable scripts and programs that allow third-party applications to physically locate equipment inside COMMAND and generate a connectivity trace, including managed and unmanaged devices. The API Gateway also enables the graphic display of network alarm status in the COMMAND drawing.

The individual, application-specific API links (such as OpenView or HelpDesk) work with the API Gateway to provide the operator with access to COMMAND from the application's own menu or to integrate other third parties into a comprehensive network management system.

For example, within OpenView the operator can select COMMAND from a pull-down menu. ISICAD's OpenView API then passes OpenView information to the COMMAND API Gateway, which will:

1. Check the database type, such as Oracle or Unify.

2. Use OpenView's data to see if the equipment ID exists in the COMMAND database.

3. If the equipment is found, the corresponding drawing and graphic symbol will be identified.

4. COMMAND will be launched, if not already running.

5. The API Gateway will then do one of the following:

- Locate and flash the requested equipment on the screen.

- Generate a graphical circuit trace, with or without a locate.

- Generate a textual circuit trace, with or without a locate.

Similarly, the API link can be used to display the alarm status from Network Node Manager in the COMMAND drawing. The objects can be mapped to operator-definable colors to indicate the alarm condition. Operators can scan through an entire drawing or portions of a drawing, using continuous or single-pass monitoring without leaving COMMAND.

The API system also can be used to launch HelpDesk from COMMAND. Operators can submit and review trouble tickets and network service requests without leaving COMMAND. Any ticket submitted to the HelpDesk is supplemented with the manufacturer and model from the COMMAND database, as well as a textual circuit trace showing the physically connectivity. This enables the technicians and support staff handling trouble calls to have complete information as soon as they view the ticket. The HelpDesk environment can be extended to supplement the trouble ticket with any additional information from the COMMAND database.

With the integration with OpenView, ISICAD has provided menu bar access to the HelpDesk using the same tools that are used in COMMAND. This gives the OpenView operators the ability to submit and review tickets in the HelpDesk database.

WORKING COOPERATIVELY, OPENVIEW, ARS AND COMMAND PROVIDE managers with a comprehensive view of a network, including hardware, software, connectors, data and other important management details, such as when warranties on a particular item expire or whether software on a computer has been registered. The amount and type of information stored in COMMAND's database is at the discretion of the network manager.

The level of integration between the three products makes them easy to use as a system. If OpenView detects a problem, for example, it automatically can launch parts of the ISICAD package to track down the culprit. When the loose connector, software conflict, or other offender has been located, ARS comes into play, pulling information from both COMMAND and OpenView and then using e-mail or its own built-in notification system to send a trouble ticket or warning notice to the network manager.

From a single workstation, the manager continuously can monitor the status and performance of network devices, document and track the physical location of components, and submit and manage trouble tickets and network service requests.

Each function can be accomplished from any of the applications, providing automated coordination of key tasks. The result is faster resolution of network problems, reduced network downtime, and more efficient diagnostic and troubleshooting activities. The resultant savings in time and money can be substantial.

In addition to working under OpenView and other management platforms, COMMAND can be integrated with other third-party applications, such as NetLabs' AssetManager. This integration allows users to run NetLabs' AssetManager application from within COMMAND, allowing them to compile asset information on the logical and physical elements of their networks — COMMAND monitoring the physical cabling infrastructure and AssetManager compiling data on logical local-area network connectivity, desktop computers and software. The combined system enables COMMAND users to input more data about IP and non-IP devices into the COMMAND database and eventually load more data about third-party network nodes in the database as NetLabs adds support for those nodes. The integrated products offer network managers up-to-date information for reporting, accounting, inventory control and asset management from a single point of control.

At this writing, ISICAD plans to release a revised version of COMMAND. It will consist of a modular suite of six scalable software products that offers connectivity and asset management from the wiring closet to the WAN and out to remote offices. This is in contrast to the present version of COMMAND, which is a single-workstation software product for mapping on-premises physical network connectivity.

The six modules of COMMAND and their functions are:

- **Equipment Manager:** allows users to document their networks and track the physical relationships between network devices spread across the enterprise. This is the core module on which the others depend and runs on a UNIX workstation.

- **Connectivity Manager:** allows users to detail physical connectivity down to the port and patch level.

- **WAN Manager:** allows users to document virtual connectivity across the enterprise so they can track bandwidth allocation and utilization, service levels from different carriers, and the services and applications that use particular circuits.

- **Desktop Access:** provides a native Windows front-end for managing remote office environments, allowing users to access remote, UNIX-based COMMAND servers without requiring X Window System terminal emulation. Administrators can use this tool to manage remote-office network changes and keep track of network assets as well as perform chargebacks for asset management.

- **Info Manager:** an object-oriented database front-end that allows users to build screens, forms and reports with data from Oracle and Sybase databases without having to write fourth-generation language (4GL) code.

- **Report Works:** works with Info Manager to provide ad hoc report generation on specific network devices or events.

Among other things, the revised COMMAND will allow users to keep track of more network assets. It also will facilitate the reporting of moves, adds and changes. More importantly, it makes COMMAND applicable to the enterprise, not just specific management domains.

Noticeably absent from all of these products is the capability to track PC assets, both their hardware and software components. There are several reasons for this, primarily that PCs were conceived and designed as standalone machines. There was no need to treat the installed base in the aggregate and the means to track assets was not built into the system components. As the need developed to share data with or accept instructions from other machines, an overlay of an entirely new software and hardware system was required — a network. With PCs interconnected over the network, asset management became a neccessity.

Hardware inventory starts with identification of the major kinds of systems that used in the distributed computing environment — from the servers all the way down to the desktop computers as well as their various components, including the CPU, memory, boards and disk drives. The utilities that come with servers generally provide this kind of information, along with various performance metrics.

Hewlett-Packard launched its suite of Asset Management Services in September 1994. Under the service, companies can contract with HP to gather information about hardware, software and other resources in a customer-specific relational database that resides at HP. The service not only helps track systems, software and personnel resources, it includes consulting and management services as well. The HP service modules include inventory (using bar-code techniques), software license management, hardware asset management (down to the board level for most PCs), utilization management for hardware and software, obligation management for lease and maintenance contracts, and financial management for depreciation and chargeback. Customers can obtain reports categorized by user and/or location that graphically illustrate asset information. This information is used to help customers make decisions on such issues as hardware and software standardization, technology upgrades and migration, maintenance and budgeting.

After the initial inventory, HP will update the asset information to include ongoing changes. To maintain database accuracy, HP uses a mixture of internally developed and third-party tools that reside on network servers and automate reporting of configuration changes. These changes can be loaded into the customer's asset database over public and private networks, the Internet, or dialup serial connections. HP also offers an 800 number, online forms, customized fax service, and e-mail services to facilitate customer reporting of moves, adds and changes. The company also will do periodic physical inventories to ensure that all changes have been properly recognized and that the database is current and accurate.

HP plans to make information from its Asset Management Services available to users of its OpenView management platform. OpenView users will be able to read information from the service's database when and if that information is pertinent to systems management routines. At the same time, the Asset Management Services database will be able to retrieve data from an OpenView database to provide more complete asset reporting. In addition, the service database will be able to share asset information with ISICAD's COMMAND, which is used to create a model of a network's physical infrastructure.

CHAPTER
8

Systems Management

HEWLETT-PACKARD OFFERS A PORTFOLIO OF UNIX-BASED OPENVIEW SOLUTIONS for the management of host and distributed computer systems. These solutions provide system management control for organizations that are moving away from mainframe architectures or implementing multivendor client-server environments. This chapter discusses other complementary systems management tools including: PerfView, PerfRX, GlancePlus, OmniStorage, OmniBack, OpenSpool and Software Distributor.

These applications run on the OpenView Simple Network Management Protocol (SNMP) platform, which includes the main OpenView graphical user interface (GUI). Not only can these applications be integrated into OperationsCenter, an integrated structured query language (SQL) database allows these applications to share important network data with Network Node Manager.

PERFVIEW

In the past, managing the performance of large, distributed, multivendor environments was inefficient because the operator had to monitor every node actively or react to user complaints of erratic service. PerfView facilitates performance management through the use of management-by-exception techniques, implemented through alarming, which allows the operator to concentrate only on the areas that require the most attention.

Initially, PerfView was designed only for monitoring the performance of UNIX systems and ran as an application on the HP OpenView management platform. Here, PerfView provides a framework from which information systems managers can gain control over the performance of diverse, geographically dispersed systems, while minimizing the amount of human and system overhead required for effective performance management.

Starting with version 3.0, PerfView also can run as a standalone performance management system for UNIX-based networks, databases and applications, as well as systems. This is accomplished with the addition of HP's Data Source Integration (DSI) technology, which allows operators to monitor the performance of any resource in the distributed computing environment through a proxy agent. Even MVS mainframes can be monitored.

APPLICATION COMPONENTS

The HP PerfView distributed performance management solution consists of two components:

- Motif-based HP PerfView performance analysis software, which runs on HP 9000 computer systems and provides alarm monitoring, filtering and analysis.

- HP PerfView intelligent agent software, which collects and monitors performance metrics on HP, Sun or IBM nodes.

AUTO-DISCOVERY

PerfView's auto-discovery feature automatically identifies systems and network devices in the TCP/IP environment and builds a map. The software tracks ongoing changes and dynamically updates the map to reflect those changes. The hierarchical user interface enables the operator to assess the entire environment's status, characterize existing and potential performance problems and resolve problems.

MANAGEMENT BY EXCEPTION

Using management-by-exception techniques, PerfView automatically identifies and helps resolve existing and potential performance problems in real time, before they affect system and network users. Alarms notify a central station of conditions that require operator attention.

Intelligent agents on each monitored system capture and log performance metrics and determine if exception conditions exist. Special algorithms compare current service levels, such as response times and transaction rates, resource utilizations, and bottleneck indicators, against predefined alarm thresholds. When an exception condition occurs, the agent notifies the central analysis workstation by sending an alarm.

A unique set of global or application-level alarms can be defined by the operator for each monitored node. Only when a predefined condition occurs does the agent send an alarm and supporting data to the PerfView analysis software. This minimizes system and network overhead.

Not only can the operator choose the metrics that are appropriate for each node, but the graphs can be customized to highlight the most interesting metrics for one or more nodes (Figure 8-1). This is accomplished by choosing from a list of available metrics and altering the color and line styles of the graphs to emphasize the appropriate information.

Real-time and recent historical performance data from one or more monitored nodes also can be compared graphically (Figure 8-2). Pan and zoom features allow the operator to isolate important information and determine the source of bottlenecks.

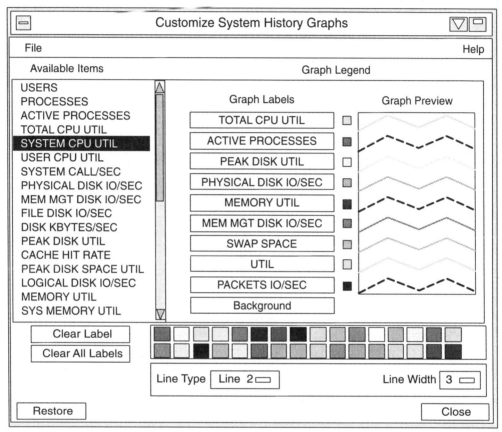

Source: Hewlett-Packard Co.

Figure 8-1: Customizable Graphs

PerfView also can automatically initiate local actions such as paging or electronic mail messaging when an alarm condition occurs. All of these capabilities give operators the ability to handle larger environments by letting them focus on specific nodes only when problems exist.

PROBLEM IDENTIFICATION

PerfView's alarm filtering capability allows the operator to identify potential performance problems before they affect service levels, such as response time, transaction rates and job turnaround. The operator receives notification of a problem through the graphical map, where alarms are displayed.

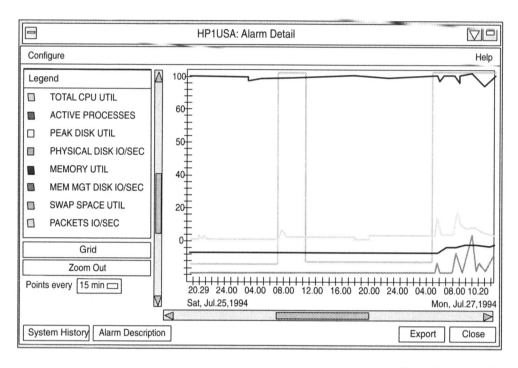

Source: Hewlett-Packard Co.

Figure 8-2: PerfView Alarm Detail

The software also allows the operator to monitor, examine and compare the performance of selected nodes within the environment to isolate a problem to one or more nodes. The operator can then use node-specific performance monitors, such as HP GlancePlus to determine the cause and resolve the problem, often before users notice any deterioration in service.

For example, a central helpdesk performs first-level environment management and documents more complex performance problems. A specialist receives these problems for further analysis and resolution. In addition to the detailed information that PerfView provides, the specialist can then use the same interface to access the integrated GlancePlus performance monitor.

DSI AGENTS

To manage the performance of various resources, DSI agent software is used. When operator-defined performance thresholds are exceeded, the DSI agent running on that resource sends an alarm to the PerfView management console. Through a remote procedure call (RPC), the console instructs the DSI agent to send raw performance data to it from the resource as well as from other network resources that might have been affected. PerfView then filters out the irrelevant performance data and summarizes only the relevant data, then time-stamps it and logs it into system memory.

With this information, PerfView operators can correlate graphically performance data across the network and gauge the interaction of other resources and the impact they have on one another. The operator can use this information to balance loads among diverse computing resources, which should result in optimized service to end users.

For example, PerfView might be used to monitor the interaction between MVS mainframes and UNIX servers during the migration to a distributed client-server environment. Bringing all the performance data together into the same analysis environment facilitates correlation, which would be difficult or impossible to do with separate monitoring tools for each type of system.

Interfaces provide for the integration of third-party performance monitors, user-defined information, and application information to enable the management of other systems in the environment. This integrated approach results in a consistent way of monitoring and acting on network, system and performance information, which increases efficiency and reduces training requirements.

HP PerfView software is available alone or bundled with HP OpenView Network Node Manager. It also integrates with HP OpenView OperationsCenter and other network and system management products.

The DSI agents complement the functionality of existing systems management platforms such as OperationsCenter. The agents allow users to integrate their legacy application data sources into the PerfView environment. This provides the advantage of using the same interface for monitoring the performance of legacy applications, newly developed in-house applications, or HP-provided applications.

PerfView's DSI capability can be used to automate the transaction monitoring function of an order entry production system, for example. Although a transaction monitor may be able to time itself when it runs transactions, it still might require that a systems administrator watch the response time and track the results. With DSI, this application can be incorporated into PerfView, providing the systems administrator with the ability to simultaneously monitor the performance and tracking of dozens of such systems.

Although there are several standalone tools that monitor applications, databases and other resources, the advantage of PerfView with DSI is that it consolidates these capabilities into a single product. It works with UNIX-based computers, including Sun SPARCstations, the HP 9000, and IBM's AIX-based RS/6000. There also is support for IBM MVS and compatible mainframes.

PERFRX

A continuing challenge for information systems managers is to achieve optimum use of computing resources while maintaining service levels for their system users. The solution must allow systems managers to examine performance and utilization data and turn this data into useful information.

HP offers PerfRX Analysis Software as the solution. It helps operators better understand the computing environment by providing a hierarchical approach to guide operators from the system level perspective down to the application and process level for more detailed analysis. It offers an interface to an extensive set of performance metrics collected from managed nodes by HP Performance Collection Software.

RESOURCE USAGE

PerfRX allows systems managers to graphically view, analyze and document comprehensive, long-term historical system resource utilization data as well as in-depth data on CPU, disk, memory, transaction rates and response time.

PerfRX's point-and-click capability is used to identify the actual applications or processes using system resources. With this information, systems managers can take appropriate action, such as balance system workloads, support system purchase decisions, and improve and maintain service levels.

DATA MANIPULATION

Collected data can be displayed in graphs to view specific information in daily, weekly or monthly time periods using line, pie or stack charts. A zoom capability lets the operator focus on a specific time period to identify and isolate the processes or applications that were using system resources. Metrics such as CPU, memory and disk use are available in tabular as well as graphical format. Metrics data can be exported to spreadsheet or ASCII file formats. From there, the data can be imported into spreadsheet, database, statistical analysis or reporting applications.

GRAPHING OPTIONS

The cause of system bottlenecks can be identified using the graphing options to represent historical system resource utilization data. The operator can turn on or off the lines that represent the various metrics, adjust the granularity of the graph to view any trends or anomalies in system activity, and adjust the Y-axis of the graph to take a closer look at lower-level activity details.

The operator can create custom graphs to examine trends and compare workloads. The operator does this by choosing the graph type, metrics, and data for display and analysis. Line, pie and stack charts (Figure 8-3) can be output to black-and-white or color printers and incorporated into management reports. These graphs can even be saved as templates for future use.

PerfRX operates as a standalone application or integrates with PerfView.

GLANCEPLUS

Performance monitoring and tuning are becoming increasingly important in all types of UNIX installations. Several HP-UX commands provide the means to quickly ascertain what is taking place on the computer system, including:

iostat provides I/O statistics on devices such as disks and terminals, as well as CPU use.

netstat provides network statistics.

ps provides a list of processes and information about each process.

vmstat provides virtual memory statistics and CPU utilization.

However, these commands only produce snapshot results; they do not provide very much information, and are not intended for obtaining information gathered over an extended period of time. If the operator wants to obtain more information about the computer system over a period of a day, week or month, HP-UX accounting can be enabled. At the end of a defined period, an accounting report is produced which provides the amount of system resources consumed by a user or application during that period.

To take the analysis beyond that which is available through HP-UX commands and accounting, an add-on product must be used, such as HP PerfView (previously discussed) or HP GlancePlus.[1]

GlancePlus is a real-time performance monitoring and diagnostic tool. It offers far greater functionality than HP-UX commands and accounting. For instance, with GlancePlus the operator can graphically display the amount of CPU, memory, disk and network being consumed on the system and obtain information on specific processes. In addition to providing the operator with the means for viewing online system activity, GlancePlus can be used to identify and resolve performance bottlenecks when they occur, and resolve other problems expeditiously.

---

[1]PerfView centrally manages system performance in the distributed computing environment and would be used on a large network of systems. GlancePlus is used to manage and tune the performance of host systems, from workstation clusters to high-end multiuser systems.

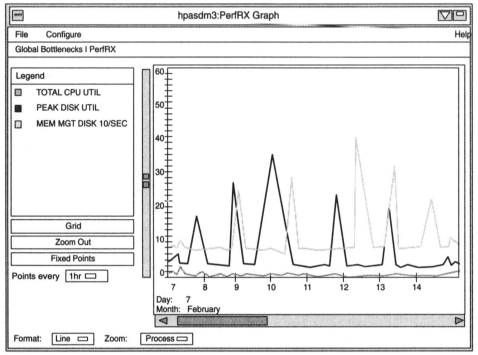

Figure 8-3: PerfRX Graphs

INFORMATION GATHERING

Bar graph summaries of system activity appear at the top of each screen. The bar graphs show usage levels of important system resources, including CPU, memory, disk, and swap space, so the operator quickly can assess how the system is performing.

The CPU, disk and memory detail screens provide a detailed view of system activity. The software highlights top users of CPU and disk to help the operator resolve potential resource bottlenecks. Disk I/O rates and queue lengths by disk device can be viewed to determine whether disks are in balance. The operator also can see how much disk activity is due to virtual memory I/O and swapping.

If a performance problem is suspected, the operator can further examine how the mix of applications is using system resources. The operator also can view detailed information on individual processes, including CPU and memory usage and time spent waiting for different system resources. With this tool, a picture is provided of how major resources are being used and who is using them. This information enables the operator to choose alternative system and kernel configurations or processing priorities and schedules, so problems can be resolved quickly. With the online help facility, performance data can be interpreted readily.

The GlancePlus application can be run whenever a performance problem is suspected; or, the tool can run continuously to evaluate how the system behaves over time, using running counts and averages.

The operator-defined filtering capability permits information gathering to be tailored to meet specific needs. For example, filtering can be implemented by program and user name to see how current users matching the criteria are using system resources. Because the thresholds can be turned on or off during filtering, only the most interesting processes of that filter can be shown. This information helps the operator determine how specific user and program workloads are affecting the system.

HP has integrated its Process Resource Manager (PRM) into GlancePlus. This application lets network administrators define workload groups and allocate minimium CPU resources to them over the HP-UX operating system. While GlancePlus lets the network administrator define performance thresholds that trigger alarms — when CPU usage reaches a certain level, for example — PRM is used to make changes in the allocation quickly. PRM works with other HP network and systems applications as well, including HP PerfView and HP PerfRX.

EXPERT FACILITY

The expert facility in HP GlancePlus software (for MPE/iX systems only) informs the operator when the software detects a problem, explains how it arrived at this conclusion, and suggests possible solutions. Upon request, the software provides the operator with a process-level breakdown of those using or needing scarce resources. The expert facility also provides a way for novice operators to learn about performance issues and for advanced operators to verify their conclusions.

In networked environments, HP GlancePlus software enables the operator to monitor NFS and HP-UX diskless activity to determine which client nodes are loading the servers. The operator also can examine how LAN activity is affecting system performance.

GLANCEPLUS PAK

If historical data collection is required, HP GlancePlus Pak software is used. It offers the online diagnostic capabilities of GlancePlus and adds HP Performance Collection software to provide the historical data collection capability.

HP Performance Collection software gathers and classifies data on the host system. It runs as a process and gathers more than 100 performance metrics. The metrics can be accessed directly on the host system and exported into three formats: the ASCII file format for reporting on the host systems; the data file format for import into third-party database, spreadsheet and graphics packages; and the binary format for programmatic processing.

The collection software offers archiving and logfile management facilities to help the operator manage the data. Its summarizing capabilities allow the operator to keep, on average, a year's worth of global and application data in 7 MB to 10 MB of disk storage space.

By importing the data into a graphics package and plotting it, the operator can see the trends in system usage and plan for future growth. The operator can see which applications are using resources and how each one is performing. The software provides the flexibility to choose the data and format needed for analysis. In addition, the operator can define the data sampling intervals and durations for the graphs.

OMNISTORAGE

The data storage requirements of many organizations is increasing, not only in terms of the amount of data to be stored, but in terms of the need for fast and convenient access. Typical applications that need access to large amounts of online data include CAD/CAM and document management. Also, organizations planning to re-engineer the IT infrastructure expect a Hierarchical Storage Management (HSM) solution that can support the client-server environment.

Huge amounts of data — hundreds of gigabytes or even terabytes — cannot be managed efficiently without the help of intelligent software solutions. HP OpenView OmniStorage is a hierarchical storage management solution that provides all applications on networked systems with unlimited online storage through the migration of files between magnetic disks and optical disk libraries, according to predefined rules. In addition, it provides unattended and automated operations.

HIERARCHICAL STORAGE MANAGEMENT

OmniStorage provides the required online storage capacity by integrating and combining the advantages of magnetic hard disks and optical disk libraries. This balances the cost, capacity and efficiency of the different storage media according to its usage.

OmniStorage ensures that expensive magnetic hard disks only contain the most frequently used data. Infrequently used data is migrated automatically to optical disk libraries. When accessed, data migrated to optical library systems is transparently and automatically migrated back to magnetic disk. In addition to automatic file migration, multiple files and whole directories can be migrated manually through commands.

DISASTER RECOVERY

Information is stored on optical disks in a self-contained, standard HP file system format. Optical disks can be removed from a library, put into another one, and read and processed by another system.

OmniStorage contains backup and restore capabilities to efficiently save the data managed by it. In case of magnetic disk crash, only the magnetic portion of the data has to be restored from backup media. The links to the data migrated to optical storage can be rebuilt directly from optical storage, greatly reducing recovery time.

CUSTOMIZATION

OmniStorage operation can be customized to the individual needs of users and applications. For example, migration can be controlled through file size and access time; individual files or complete directories can be excluded from migration. The whole system can be dynamically reconfigured.

SERVER PLATFORM

HP OpenView OmniStorage is supported on an HP 9000 as the server platform. Client systems in a networked environment are supported in two ways:

- **Native network migration:** Data migration is provided directly between client disks and optical disk libraries managed by the storage server. Native network migration is available for HP 9000 (Series 700 and 800) clients.

- **Migration via NFS:** File systems on any system with OmniStorage installed can be exported to other systems in the network. This function is available for HP and non-HP systems capable of NFS.

SYSTEM COMPONENTS

HP OpenView OmniStorage contains several components (Figure 8-4).

Library Manager: The Library Manager manages the optical storage (libraries and disks). It controls the mounting and unmounting of platters, and it maintains a database that keeps track of the managed jukeboxes and the optical disks.

Very Big File System: OmniStorage uses a file system type called Very Big File System (VBFS), which is an extension of the standard HP-UX file system. It provides a transparent view to all managed data, independent of its physical location (i.e., magnetic and/or optical storage). Embedded in the file system is information that tracks such attributes as migration priorities, read-ahead strategies, and segmentation of very large files. System administrators can specify this information on a per file, directory, or file system basis.

Ager: The Ager controls the transparent outward migration of files based on criteria established by the system administrator. System-level default configuration values can be inherited and customized.

In addition to determining the migration priority of files, these configuration values establish the threshold levels, called water marks, which are expressed as a percentage of used magnetic disk storage space. The Ager migrates files from magnetic disk to optical storage when reaching the water marks.

To do this, the Ager is triggered in either of two modes: Active Mode or Bulk Mode. By default, the Ager runs in Active Mode. When magnetic disk storage reaches an established limit, called the High Water Mark (e.g., 80), the Ager migrates files to optical storage, freeing up magnetic storage until it reaches another limit, called Active Low Water Mark (e.g., 60).

The Ager runs in Bulk Mode during off-peak periods, at which time the Ager migrates files to optical storage until the Inactive Low Water Mark is reached (e.g., 50). At that time, the Ager continues to copy files until the Bulk Water Mark is reached (e.g., 40). These copies allow the Ager to simply delete the file copies on magnetic disk when the disk fills again.

Queuer: The primary responsibility of the Queuer is to satisfy requests from the VBFS file system, the Ager and OmniStorage utilities in migrating data between the optical storage and magnetic disk storage. The Queuer determines the priority of migration requests (i.e., migrate in versus migrate out).

OPERATIONSCENTER INTEGRATION

The integration of the OmniStorage application with OperationsCenter provides the benefit of using the management capabilities of OperationsCenter to set up and monitor OmniStorage from a central point. Problem and error notifications from OmniStorage can be reported automatically through a color change on the map of a remote OperationsCenter console, improving an administrator's productivity.

OmniStorage complements HP OmniBack and HP OmniBack Turbo, which are the HP OpenView backup and recovery solutions.

OMNIBACK

The rapid growth in computer networks has caused the virtual disappearance of homogeneous environments. At the same time, the growing number of distributed, networked computing environments has awakened systems administrators to the importance of central backup and recovery. As increasing amounts of data are spread across heterogeneous networks, the availability and protection of data becomes critical. Not only are operating costs in this type of environment on the rise, but data can become lost easily, causing disruption to normal business operations. Therefore, a software solution that supports multiple platforms is a necessity.

HP's OmniBack product family offers backup and recovery options that protect data against hardware and software failures, disasters and human errors, while reducing operating costs. These products are OmniBack, OmniBack/Turbo and OmniBack/Link.

BACKUP MANAGEMENT

Both HP OmniBack and HP OmniBack/Turbo provide network backup management in mixed environments of HP-UX, Apollo Domain and SunOS (backup clients only). In addition, they can backup and recover files from or to disks that are mounted on supported platforms such as NFS file systems. MS-DOS PC integration into the OmniBack environment is achieved through interoperation of OmniBack with Plan-B/UX from Quest. PC data stored on the HP-UX server via LAN Manager/X also can be backed up and recovered.

OmniBack provides a common OSF/Motif-based graphical user interface for both backup and restore. In the networked environment, OmniBack can backup multiple systems simultaneously. Centralized control of

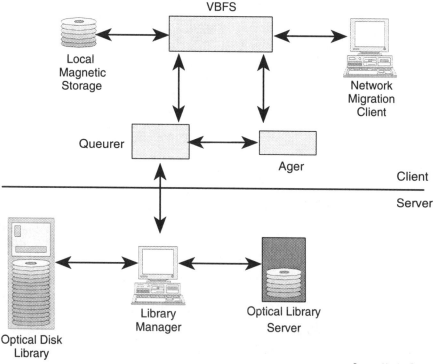

Source: Hewlett-Packard Co.

Figure 8-4: OmniStorage Components

175

networkwide backup for mixed-vendor environments lowers operating and resource costs by reducing time spent on backup and recovery.

Through its support of DAT/DDS devices and HP's Rewritable Optical Disk Library Systems, OmniBack provides the means to implement unattended network backup, eliminating operator intervention and further reducing costs.

OmniBack enhances media management by providing overwrite protection, log file analysis, media labeling, and the ability to recycle backup media. The journaling and scheduling capabilities OmniBack and OmniBack/Turbo relieve the operator of the time-consuming tasks of tracking, logging, and rescheduling network and system backups.

OmniBack's data compression facility reduces media costs by increasing media capacity. This feature also increases backup performance while reducing network traffic.

Offline database backup of file-system based databases is performed by both OmniBack and OmniBack/Turbo. In addition, OmniBack/Turbo allows backup of databases based on raw disk. Online database backup can be handled by OmniBack/Turbo when certain database products are used, such as Oracle.

HIGH-SPEED OPTION

High speed backup is a major requirement for systems with large amounts of online data. High speed backup also increases system availability. OmniBack/Turbo offers all the functionality of OmniBack with the addition of a high-speed component for local data backups (Figure 8-5). OmniBack/Turbo's high-speed component offers up to 20 GB/hour raw disk backup performance on local data, depending on the backup device configuration.

INTEGRATION COMPONENT

OmniBack/Link, the OpenView integration component, allows OmniBack to send problem or error notifications directly to the HP OpenView management station. This permits central management of multiple OmniBack servers by Network Node Manager or OperationsCenter. Central backup and recovery is provided for both systems and workstations on a LAN, through OmniBack and OmniBack/Turbo.

When problems or errors are reported to the OpenView management station, the operator or administrator is notified by a color change of the respective OmniBack symbol on the OpenView map. Direct access to the OmniBack application is provided through graphical application symbols and menu bar tasks on the OpenView map.

OPENSPOOL

The administration of the UNIX print service is complicated and time-consuming, especially in networked, heterogeneous environments. Not only does access to various printers and plotters require detailed knowledge of routing procedures, but the print facility is inflexible. For example, the HP-UX print facility does not permit specific pages of a document to be printed. The printing of a text file cannot be restarted at a specific page number. There also is not a way to establish print priorities or to change print requests already in queue.

The HP OpenView OpenSpool family — consisting of OpenSpool, OpenSpool/SharedPrint and OpenSpool/Link — provides the functionality lacking in traditional UNIX print services. OpenSpool provides an integrated print management system for mixed environments. It supports HP-UX, Sun Solaris and IBM AIX platforms, and integrates PCs via LAN

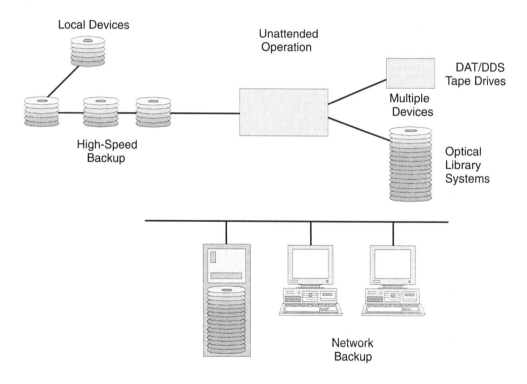

Source: Hewlett-Packard Co.

Figure 8-5: HP OmniBack/Turbo

Manager/X. OpenSpool provides the same end user and operator functionality across all of the supported platforms.

Queue and device servers can be located anywhere in the network, making use of distributed CPU power. Single point administration (Figure 8-6) simplifies previously complicated tasks and provides capabilities that enable any print or plot device anywhere in the network to be shared, thereby maximizing all available output devices.

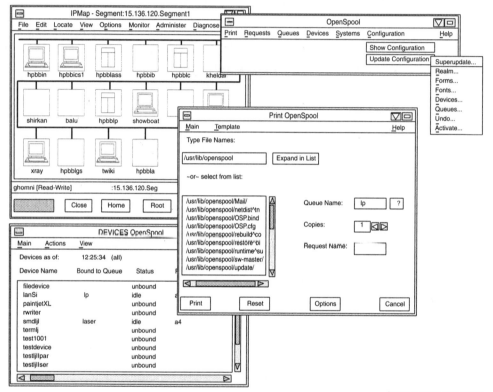

Source: Hewlett-Packard Co.

Figure 8-6: HP OpenSpool Interface

FUNCTIONALITY

End users can handle their print or plot requests using familiar commands. All HP-UX applications calling **lp/lpr** can be used without changes; because OpenSpool emulates the **lp/lpr** commands, it can be used without having to modify existing applications. The OpenSpool administrator can delegate queue or device management tasks to the end users. Security is addressed by restricting end-user access to print queues and print requests. This protects certain forms, such as checks.

OpenSpool allows print priorities to be established. It displays the status of print jobs and permits the changing of print requests until the request is finally printed. It can restart the printing of text files at a specific page number and offers advanced print options like *keep after print*, as well as font and electronic form handling. It offers templates for repetitive tasks, and accepts and manages various paper types and sizes. It integrates user-defined filters, models, and fonts to serve special printing needs.

OpenSpool can log account information as well as events. An administrator can determine the resource consumption of a particular department or workgroup, then apply charges accordingly.

CONVERSION FILTERS

HP OpenSpool/SharedPrint provides the integration of special document and bitmap conversion filters into the OpenSpool facility. Among other things, this allows the printing of:

- PostScript files on PCL devices.

- ASCII text on both PCL and PostScript devices.

- PCL files on PostScript devices.

- CGM files on HP-GL/2 devices.

These bitmap formats can be printed on PCL, PostScript, and RTL devices: Starbase, TIFF (including Group 3/4 JPEG, LZW, Packbits), GIF, JFIF, XWD and XBM.

OPENVIEW INTEGRATION

HP OpenView integration is performed through OpenSpool/Link, allowing central monitoring of the print management system from Network Node Manager or OperationsCenter.

OpenSpool print management stations are displayed on the OpenView map. Direct access to the OpenSpool application is provided through graphical symbols and menu bar tasks on the OpenView map. Problems and errors from OpenSpool are reported automatically to the OpenView management station. The operator or administrator is notified by a color change of the respective OpenSpool symbol on the OpenView map.

SOFTWARE DISTRIBUTOR

Productivity is hampered when everyone is working with different software versions and data sets. Yet keeping distributed systems updated with the latest software can be a costly and painstaking chore; more so in the client-server environment, where it is essential that application revision changes at both ends be synchronized. With vendors upgrading software more frequently, administrators seem to be making a full-time job of installation and maintainance. In fact, software distribution currently costs companies millions of dollars every year in media, travel costs and time spent by skilled personnel.

HP OpenView Software Distributor focuses on improving the productivity of administrators by eliminating or automating time-consuming software installation and update activities. Software Distributor assists administrators in managing every aspect of software configuration, verification, and removal, significantly reducing costs in media duplication, travel and time.

DISTRIBUTION OVERVIEW

Packaged software is placed in a depot for distribution over a network, or it can be placed on CD-ROM or tape media for distribution to non-networked systems. One or more distribution depots contain software that is available for installation to other systems, called target systems, in the network. The controller system manages the software distribution process (Figure 8-7).

Software Distributor supports products that are organized into products, subproducts and filesets (collections of files). This hierarchical organization allows the administrator to specify installation of a product without inspecting the individual files within the product. When disk space is limited, it allows the administrator to specify partial product installation through the selection of subproducts or filesets.

Distribution Depots: Distribution depots are repositories of software available for installation, and often are used as the source of an installation task. The depots can be configured to support the policies of the organization as follows: from a centrally located software warehouse, to multiple depots arranged hierarchically, to a fully distributed solution on servers throughout the environment.

Software Distributor allows depots to distribute software packages to multiple target systems simultaneously and allows depots to be distributed on various servers. It also allows administrators to manage (create, populate, list, verify and remove) distribution depots. System administrators can control the access to individual software products on the depot.

Software Distributor helps the administrator locate available depots and retrieve detailed information on software products in the depot catalog. This information consists of product name, revision, descriptions, hardware and software dependencies.

Target System: The system on which the software is installed is called the target system. Typically, the target system is the users' desktop computer. Software Distributor will, by default, only install compatible software on a target system. It checks the target operating system types, revisions and machine attributes to determine if the product can be installed.

Software Distributor automates the task of analyzing each target machine by performing a series of checks between the target machine and the software that is to be installed. The target system can be checked to ensure all file systems used during the installation are mounted and available.

A detailed disk space analysis evaluates the disk space on the target machine against the amount necessary for the software to be installed. By default, software will not be installed on a target unless there is enough disk space. Additional checks also can be performed.

Software Distributor checks the request to ensure the target system has the authorization to install the selected software. Requests from unauthorized target systems are denied.

If the link is broken between the source and target during a software download, the administrator is notified. The administrator is able to recover from the error and resume the software installation.

Software Distributor supports the unique configuration of each target system. The administrator can perform this configuration as part of the installation task or can defer the actual configuration to another time. Multiple software versions can be supported on a single target system through this configuration process.

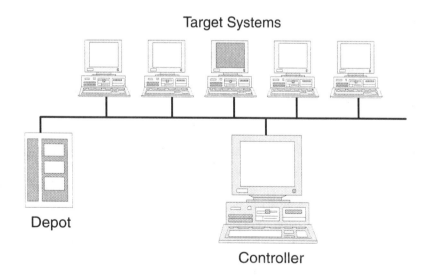

Target Systems

Depot

Controller

Source: Hewlett-Packard Co.

Figure 8-7: *Software Distribution Environment*

Controller System: The controller system is any system using Software Distributor to manage the software distribution process. When the administrator chooses a Software Distributor command to perform a distribution task, the controller initiates the task, providing the necessary information to one or more target systems. The administrator has the option to compress software files that are transferred during installation from a depot, which reduces network load.

The administrator can save policy definitions, software selections, and target selections to named files. Previous sessions can be retrieved from the files to enhance productivity and streamline redundant tasks.

A Software Distributor task operating on multiple targets displays progress information for each target. The interactive interface provides detailed information about each target's status.

Software Distributor provides comprehensive verifications of installed software on each depot or target system. From their central locations, administrators can build processes that monitor the integrity of the software within their networks.

SOFTWARE MANAGEMENT

Part of managing software is knowing what applications are installed throughout the distributed environment, which allows for better planning of software purchases and license conformance.

From a central location, administrators can generate reports on the installed software within their network. Software Distributor stores the installed software information for each system in the Installed Products Database (IPD).

Each depot also has a catalog of software available for installation, and it contains all the information provided in the product packaging. Software Distributor can list the available products, along with their attributes, in various formats.

From a central location, the administrator can remove obsolete or unnecessary software products within the network. Software Distributor provides removal of software, target-specific configurations created by the product, and product files on depots or target systems. It understands software dependencies, and will not cause side effects on other products unless forced to by the administrator.

INDUSTRY STANDARD

Software Distributor is the basis for the electronic Software Distribution Services (SDS) for OSF's Distributed Management Environment (DME). It is also the basis for the IEEE's Posix 1003.7.2 Software Administration Standard. Software Distributor follows these common interface and data format standards, providing common software packaging and management processes between different vendor platforms.

ADMINCENTER

To ease the task of administrating distributed systems and applications, HP offers AdminCenter, a centralized configuration- and change-management software product for the OpenView framework. AdminCenter automates system-administration tasks such as configuring new systems, servers, users and software. By providing a single view for an administrator's entire management domain, AdminCenter significantly reduces the time and cost needed to perform these activities.

AdminCenter complements HP's OperationsCenter. Whereas OperationsCenter addresses problem management and operations in a management-by-exception fashion, AdminCenter addresses proactive configuration and change in a management-by-objective fashion. AdminCenter uses a process-oriented approach to perform several dissimilar tasks with each change. For example, an administrator can set the computing environment for a new employee by initiating a series of linked actions that load application software onto the employee's desktop system and issue a login ID and network password.

With its initial release in early 1995, AdminCenter offers complete inventory functionality and manages the following system objects: software, file systems, peripheral devices, users and groups, passwords, systems (including operating-system kernals), and print spoolers. AdminCenter also maintains inventory information for these objects. HP-UX, IBM AIX and Sun Solaris systems and PCs can be managed by AdminCenter.

POLICY SETTING

AdminCenter is highly scalable, serving the system management needs at the workgroup, site, region and enterprise levels. With "administrator-privilege policy setting," companies can allocate varying degrees of responsibility to administrators in different management domains. For example, a local administrator might be allowed to add and configure a new printer, but not be allowed to do operating-system configuration and performance tuning, which require greater technical expertise. Policy setting allows AdminCenter to adapt to a company's existing management policies and organization, permitting a faster rollout of the solution companywide.

The software also features configuration policy setting to verify that any configuration change complies with predefined guidelines and policies. This gives both the Information Technology (IT) organization and local administrators consistent control over system and network resources. For example, a policy that restricts classes of users to specific login ID ranges and passwords can be applied and enforced, ensuring consistent network access based on organization structure. Additionally, administrator errors are minimized.

Synchronization

AdminCenter ensures that administrators have an accurate and current understanding of the status of all system and software objects and are informed of any changes. AdminCenter's synchronization feature takes a snapshot of the status of the managed environment to determine what may have changed recently, such as an unauthorized addition to a password file that would grant access to confidential information. The administrator is notified of any changes to the managed environment and can either acknowledge and approve the changes or reset the configuration to reflect pre-change conditions.

Change Orchestration

AdminCenter offers inventory information at a glance, including past, present and planned changes. It offers a log of historical activity for audit purposes and can access the current state of the environment with a query capability. For advanced planning of the changes, AdminCenter features a simulation mode that shows an administrator how a planned change will impact the managed environment before the change is initiated. The ability to see the effects of a change before making it could increase network performance and availability by decreasing the outages experienced during changes. In addition, a virtual change feature recognizes complex dependencies by allowing administrators to plan and prepare changes to occur in a specific sequence.

For example, an administrator who plans to install a new order-entry application in a week may not want to wait until then for other operators to start setting it up, preparing the system resources and issuing end-user assignments. The administrator could prepare AdminCenter for application installation at a future date and then set up (and simulate, if needed) user logins and passwords for application access to occur after step one had been completed. The administrator would continue the process with other dependent resource assignments and complete them all before the application was ever installed.

AdminCenter is a critical pillar in the HP OpenView strategy to provide end users and application developers with an Integrated Network and System Management (INSM) framework based on universal management processes. A future release of AdminCenter will offer complete integration points so that other HP and third-party OpenView applications can take advantage of its unified process for configuration and change. AdminCenter's model-based reasoning technology offers a relatively easy way to integrate other applications. An application integrator need only define the objects to be used, their attributes, their relationships to other objects, and the actions to be taken. AdminCenter automatically handles database schema definitions, user interface creation and presentation, logfile creations, checks against predetermined policies and synchronization.

THESE SOLUTIONS, WHICH MAY BE INTEGRATED INTO NETWORK NODE MANAGER and/ or OperationsCenter, provide centralized system management control for organizations that are moving away from mainframe architectures to distributed computing or multivendor client-server environments.

Some of these solutions provide the necessary tools for viewing and monitoring system and network performance, and implementing long-term performance trend analysis. Others provide the means to manage storage, backup, print and software distribution processes. All run on the OpenView platform and may be augmented by third-party solutions, which also may be integrated with Network Node Manager and/or OperationsCenter.

Managing the Distributed UNIX Environment

MOST POWER USERS KNOW THE ADVANTAGES OF THE 32-BIT MULTITASKING UNIX operating system in academic and engineering environments. However, because networked UNIX systems lack comprehensive management tools, users often must struggle with problems of limited productivity, throughput and resources. In fact, this lack of manageability has stalled mainstream acceptance of UNIX systems in the business environment. After all, a global systems management solution is a prerequisite for handling the mission-critical applications entrusted to legacy mainframes.

THE PROBLEM WITH UNIX

Traditional UNIX users were skilled programmers who did not think the absence of an integrated suite of management utilities was a serious liability. Although UNIX offered rudimentary utilities that could be implemented with the operating system's arcane command-line syntax, there were no verification or cross-checking techniques that business people require to safeguard important data. For example, native UNIX would write over data backed up on a tape drive without realizing that critical data was being overwritten. With UNIX's **cron** utility, jobs can be scheduled based on date and time of day, but there is no provision for checking whether they have completed successfully. And because native UNIX does not automate the handling of operating system messages, they must be handled by an operator or not at all. Reports have to be printed in their entirety because native UNIX makes no provision for selecting only portions of reports to be printed. And in UNIX, there is no concept of a common database for system management policies and statistics.

Of course, management tools for UNIX are available from many vendors. There are tools for managing printing. There are tools for managing disk space and for performing backups to tape. There are tools for monitoring and fine-tuning system performance. There are tools for managing the distribution of software and for automating hardware and software inventory. There are tools for software license monitoring and metering.

There are even tools for file transfers between UNIX and DOS and machines using other operating systems. However, these and other solutions are aimed at specific UNIX tasks, lack a consistent user interface, and usually must be purchased separately. Until recently, UNIX users had to make do with gluing together separate tools from several vendors, and usually were not able to solve the entire problem.

Not only did these tools have to be purchased from different vendors, they had to be matched with a specific version of UNIX. Currently, there are dozens of variations of UNIX. To complicate matters, many enterprises have non-UNIX systems as part of their environment. Systems such as IBM's MVS and OS/400 and Tandem's Guardian also have to be managed uniformly.

What is urgently needed in this era of distributed computing is an integrated system-management solution for the entire UNIX corporate environment — one that leverages the power of UNIX and other systems, making the operating system more attractive for downsizing important mainframe applications and creating new applications. An integrated, feature-rich solution would encourage companies to implement UNIX systems and, in some cases, help them prolong their investments in perfectly useable legacy systems by providing linkages to the open environment.

A SOLUTION FOR UNIX

Recognizing this need, Computer Associates International, Inc. (CA), an HP Premier Partner, has created an integrated solution for the UNIX environment. Its CA-Unicenter is a system-management solution[1], that is integrated with HP OpenView. Unicenter leverages the power of UNIX, making the operating system more attractive for downsizing important applications from mainframes, creating new applications, and enabling the enterprise to maximize the return on investments made in UNIX systems.

Together, the HP OpenView applications portfolio and CA-Unicenter provide a comprehensive collection of management functions for HP-UX systems. This integration extends the automation capabilities of each product and expands the scope of management across the enterprise. A few examples demonstrate how integration adds value to both products:

---

[1]CA-Unicenter is comparable in many ways to HP's OperationsCenter. CA-Unicenter is designed to manage more than just UNIX platforms. OperationsCenter, by comparison, focuses on UNIX platforms only. Also, the functional areas covered by CA-Unicenter are broader than OperationsCenter. This makes CA-Unicenter complementary to OperationsCenter.

- **Security Administration:** A security administrator can monitor security exceptions throughout a distributed environment from a central point. Using color or blinking alerts, security violations tracked by CA-Unicenter can be represented on the graphical network map of HP's Network Node Manager.

- **System Administration:** A system administrator can be notified of performance problems before users are affected. A CA-Unicenter helpdesk problem entry can be generated automatically based on I/O bottlenecks, severe memory constraints, and other performance thresholds detected by the HP PerfView application throughout the network.

- **Application Errors:** Manual intervention is eliminated when application errors are detected and resolved programmatically. HP OperationsCenter can monitor an application's log files, triggering recovery job streams from CA-Unicenter to restore data and rerun errant processes.

The integration of the HP and CA management applications comes just in time: The prevalence of low-cost reduced instruction set computing (RISC) workstations and more than 20,000 DOS and Windows applications adapted to UNIX makes the operating system appealing for mission-critical business applications. Specifically, in addition to handling a broad range of information processing needs, UNIX systems make it easier to perform distributed processing, operate client-server networks, and implement distributed databases. With the corporate network rapidly evolving into the system that runs the applications, integrated management systems are assuming a vitally important role. And, with integrated management, the case for UNIX is now too compelling to ignore.

APPLICATIONS INTEGRATION

The OpenView and CA-Unicenter applications are integrated in several ways. To communicate, both product sets monitor and generate **syslog** messages. Events that are tracked by CA-Unicenter, such as failed jobs, are forwarded to HP OpenView. Conversely, HP Network Node Manager informs CA-Unicenter of SNMP events, which Unicenter also can monitor.

The command line interface is another point of integration. The functions of both Unicenter and OpenView are invoked through line commands and shell scripts. Each product executes these commands or scripts automatically through triggers and automated message/action routines.

OpenView and Unicenter also are integrated through log files. HP OperationCenter polls flat files to search for certain events. Unicenter database information, such as the number of scratch tapes available, is extracted into a flat file and detected by HP OperationsCenter for further analysis.

Finally, integration is achieved through the graphical user interface (GUI). Through the use of Motif standards, the Unicenter GUI and HP OpenView desktops are modified to include icons for each other's programs. For example, the Unicenter security icons can be launched from the HP OpenView Windows Manager, or the HP Glance performance monitor can be launched from the Unicenter performance icon.

CA-UNICENTER CAPABILITIES

Like OpenView, Unicenter uses a Motif-based GUI (Figure 9-1). Unicenter comes with integrated functions for security management, storage management, production control, performance management and accounting, data center administration and helpdesk. Together, these functions establish a structured environment for networked UNIX systems that is required to support business-critical processing.

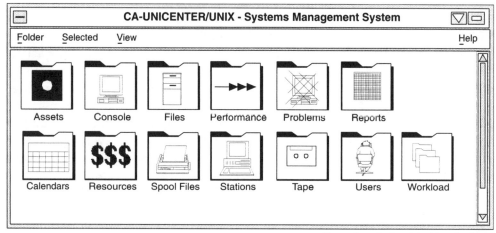

Source: Computer Associates International, Inc.

Figure 9-1: Motif-based GUI of CA-Unicenter

SECURITY MANAGEMENT

Security always has been a concern in the UNIX environment. Until now, there was virtually no way to tell when an unauthorized access attempt occurred. Password protection and permission schemes were vulnerable. There were no controls on file use by time-of-day or day-of-week. Any security features that were implemented at great effort and expense still could be bypassed by a super user, who could then access any resource and change any management controls.

CA-Unicenter offers a level of security that meets the needs of business processing. Under CA's policy-based approach to security, files are protected not by the physical attributes of the file as in HP-UX, but by their description in a common, fully encrypted relational database that is not visible from the UNIX directory. This means that newly created files are protected automatically, not at the discretion of each creator, but consistent with the defined security needs of the organization.

For example, CA-Unicenter provides global enforcement of both user access and asset access controls. Through a graphical calendar, various assets can be made available to select users only during specific hours of specific days. Whereas HP-UX has only three access modes for each asset — Read, Write and Execute — CA-Unicenter provides more precise control of each asset or group of assets, providing Delete, in addition to Read, Write and Execute (Figure 9-2).

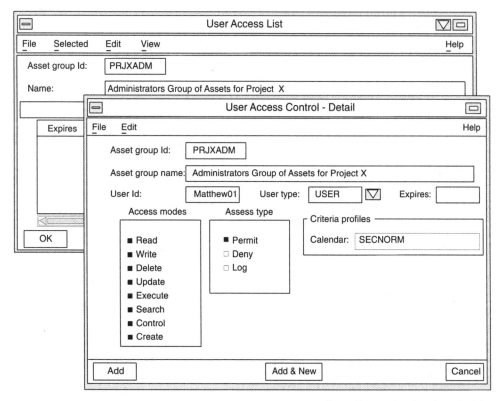

Source: Computer Associates International, Inc.

Figure 9-2: Setting File Access

For each asset or group of assets a different permission type may be applied: Permit, Deny and Log. Permit allows a user or user group to have access to a specified asset. Deny allows an exception to be made to a Permit, not allowing writes to certain files, for example. Log allows an asset to be accessed, but stipulates that such access will be logged. Default permissions (Permit and Deny) allow security to be phased in. The security administrator can protect only a subset of the assets on the system and leave HP-UX security in control of the rest, or enforce a policy of protection by default, whereby no asset may be accessed unless it is defined to the security function and access is specifically given to authorized users.

The Security function supports many additional password controls not provided on the base UNIX system. These password controls are included in CA-Unicenter:

- User-controlled password change.

- Effective date and time restrictions.

- Must change password interval.

- Minimum number of days between password changes.

- Effective date for new login IDs.

- Absolute login ID expiration date.

- Criteria profiles for customized system entry determination.

CA-Unicenter provides enhanced password controls that include these options and enforcement policies:

- Provision of an exclude list for obvious passwords.

- Password masking ability to encourage unusual character combinations.

- Random, machine-generated passwords.

Aside from a full suite of password controls and tracking features, CA-Unicenter provides the ability to determine whether a single login ID can have multiple terminal sessions on the same system. It also allows the security administrator to specify appropriate enforcement actions to be taken when a user's login ID exceeds the system limit for violations, including:

- **Cancel:** The access attempt is denied and the process that attempted the unauthorized access is cancelled.

- **Logout:** The access attempt is denied and the process group and all child processes associated with it are cancelled. If a logged-in user is associated with the attempt, he will be logged out.

- **Suspend:** The access attempt is denied and the process group and all associated child processes are cancelled. In addition, the login ID is suspended and the user is locked out of the system until suspension is lifted by the security administrator.

Through the Console Management function, CA-Unicenter provides the means to review real-time and historical violation activity online, along with other system activity.

Because all security authorization decisions are based on user access to different assets — including files, commands, and special UNIX utility functions — the super user attribute is not used by Security Management to determine access. Therefore, the special capabilities of a super user can be controlled by CA-Unicenter, and can be delegated to work against a specific set of secured files or users.

STORAGE MANAGEMENT

The native UNIX environment is not very friendly when it comes to managing data on disks and tapes. When disk space is exhausted or a job needs an archived file, work stops. Local backups are often so time-consuming that operators often do not bother to do it. Remote backups tend to clog the network unless carried out after normal business hours, in which case all of the systems must be left running. Tapes are not protected against overwrites, which can result in the loss of important data.

CA-Unicenter brings robust storage management tools to the UNIX environment, ensuring that files are backed up at the right time and that tapes are labelled properly and write-protected to prevent data loss. An integrated file manager system tracks the online, backup and archive versions of every HP-UX file, regardless of the medium on which the file resides.

By tracking file residency, CA-Unicenter's automated storage management (ASM) provides for the seamless movement of files from backup to archive and back to the system when needed. Through the common file catalog of ASM, the archive facility can locate and initiate the restoration of an archived file without user intervention. Any user request, process or program attempting to access an archived file is suspended until the file is restored and then allowed to continue without failure.

ASM also ensures that users have enough disk space to accommodate new files. When a file system reaches a predefined threshold of X percent full, ASM is initiated, using the common file catalog to determine which files eligible for archive currently are backed up.

CA-Unicenter then simply updates the catalog to indicate that the files have been archived and deletes them from the disk file system, freeing needed disk space. The automatic restoration feature stands ready to replace any files that are needed later.

Files backed up or archived to tape can be assigned an expiration date. Each tape has an internal label that is validated each time it is mounted. File location information, stored in the ASM common file catalog, is compared with the tape label to determine whether the tape can be overwritten. If so, it is considered expired and may be removed from the tape backup or archive pool for reuse. Tapes removed in error cannot be overwritten and new retention criteria are established for expired tapes when they are reused.

In the movement of files for backup and archival storage, CA-Unicenter overcomes many of the limitations of the UNIX **tar** program. It offers file compression of up to 70 percent and an encryption scheme to prevent loss of data resulting from tampering. And whereas **tar** is limited to writing data in 5KB blocks, CA-Unicenter's ASM function uses dynamic block adjustment to optimize performance based on media type and available memory.

The CA-Unicenter backup program also is much faster than other options, with an average transfer rate of approximately 2 GB per hour.

PRODUCTION CONTROL

CA-Unicenter provides automated production control of ongoing and scheduled processes within the UNIX system. This frees the system administrator from continuously setting up and executing background process groups, collating and distributing reports, and monitoring console messages to detect errors and take action on unusual conditions.

Workload Management: The UNIX scheduler (**cron**) is based on date and time-of-day, and does not recognize predecessor/successor relationships. Furthermore, submitted work is not tracked, so it is hard to know what is happening at any given time. CA-Unicenter overcomes these limitations, offering tools for workload planning, workload processing, and calendar- and event-based scheduling.

The workload planning component of CA-Unicenter provides a central location for the information needed to manage and process production work. It contains the job and jobset profiles, workload sequencing information, job dependencies, processing requirements and priorities for jobs. This component also provides the ability to monitor and balance the load on a given node, and route units of work to the least busy eligible node on the network.

The workload processing component provides automatic submission of recovery jobs or jobsets should a scheduled job fail. Integration with console management provides facilities that enable administrators to define specific actions that should be performed in the event of an interruption, which also can speed job recovery and restart.

With calendar-based scheduling, jobsets are identified and dates selected for when they will run. For example, the system administrator may want to schedule the weekly archiving of all files not accessed in the past 60 days with the objective of freeing at least 100 MB of disk space. This jobset would consist of the following discrete jobs:

1. The first job triggers the manual process of gathering scratch tapes for the archive.

2. The second job archives all files not accessed in 60 days.

3. The final job triggers a manual task to review the results to make sure the archive satisfied the objective of freeing at least 100 MB of storage.

Event-based scheduling runs predefined workloads when dynamic events occur in the system, such as the close of a specific file or the start or termination of a job. Events can be customized to trigger predefined actions. For example, all files in a directory can be archived automatically after the last print job or a database update performed after closing a particular spreadsheet.

Console Management: CA-Unicenter provides a graphical interface through which the system administrator can view all system console traffic. Depending on the size and complexity of the UNIX system, the console may process hundreds or even thousands of messages per minute. Through the console management facility, policies can be defined that highlight important messages, automatically respond to messages, and identify unusual conditions requiring additional information.

The console management facility includes **syslog** messages for all running programs or user processes, as well as CA-Unicenter status information. Each message entry includes the login ID or program name of the message originator, the date and time the message was issued, and the host name where the message was issued (Figure 9-3). This facility enables a single person to administer an entire network of UNIX computers.

There are several actions supported by CA-Unicenter, any combination of which can be used to document the automated processing of an input or output console message. Among these message actions are:

AUTORPLY: automatically answers a query that has been directed to the system console with a predefined response.

DELAY: causes message action processing to wait a specific amount of time before proceeding to the next action.

DISCARD: prevents an unwanted message from being displayed on the operator console, and does not record the message in the console log.

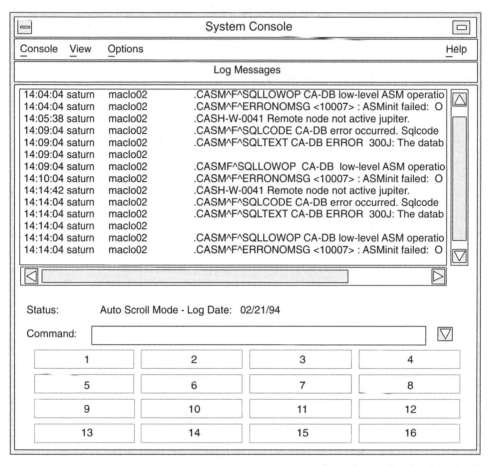

Source: Computer Associates International, Inc.

Figure 9-3: View of Messages at the Console

EVALUATE: performs message selection based on the text value. If a match is found, a new task is built to perform the actions associated with the match. If no match is found, a SENDOPER action is performed.

GOTO: enables non-consecutive actions to be chained together, optionally based on the success of a prior message action.

SENDOPER: sends a message to the operator console, without waiting for a reply.

Spool Management: The UNIX spooler (**lp**) is cryptic with hard-to-remember commands for manipulating the spool. CA-Unicenter eliminates the need to remember several commands and command keywords, substituting a single English-like command and graphical interface for manipulating and viewing all spooled work.

For instance, users can prioritize print jobs and define or enable printers. Specific pages of a document can be selected for printing, as well as the number of copies. CA-Unicenter also provides the status of the print job, and allows the printed file to be viewed online. Jobs in queue can be cancelled and resubmitted at any time.

Report Management: This level of spool control aids the distribution of reports, especially large ones that are produced on a regular basis. Report Management extends traditional report/print processes by allowing rules to be established whereby selected pages of a report can be repackaged into bundles and redistributed to multiple users through print or mail facilities.

For each report, a recipient profile can be created (Figure 9-4), which describes how it will be handled. A report can go to the accounting department's printer, for example, or be delivered to a specific user through electronic mail (e-mail). E-mail is useful when the report requires further manipulation or integration into another file. Because various recipients may need only a few pages of a large report, the specific pages or portions of pages can be selected for print or electronic delivery through page selection profiles (Figure 9-5).

CA-Unicenter tracks report delivery and maintains an audit trail of all reports. End users can even review the progress of their requested reports through the delivery process.

PERFORMANCE MANAGEMENT AND ACCOUNTING

CA-Unicenter provides the tools to evaluate the use of UNIX computing resources, enabling the operator to determine trends in computer usage and identify the excessive use (or non-use) of resources. It also provides a billing capability to place accountability for system usage with the end user.

The two primary components of the Performance Management and Accounting (PMA) facility are the online System Performance Monitor and the Resource Accounting and Chargeback system.

System Performance Monitoring: While UNIX accumulates a variety of information on resource usage and system activity, this information is stored in several separate files, and must be merged and customized through shell scripts to get a true picture of system performance. While this is adequate for basic resource accounting needs and may well satisfy the needs of UNIX environments where there are infrequent changes in system resources or the user community, most UNIX environments today are growing and evolving rapidly.

CA-Unicenter improves performance monitoring by providing a window into the real-time performance of the system, displaying critical information such as memory usage, paging rates and I/O load. By itself, this

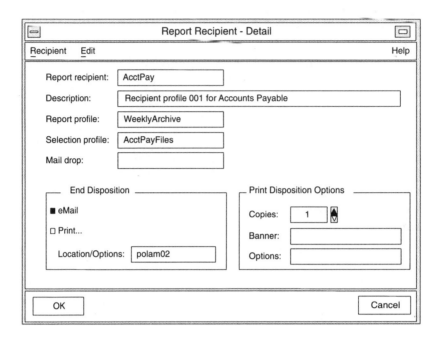

Source: Computer Associates International, Inc.

Figure 9-4: *Recipient Profile*

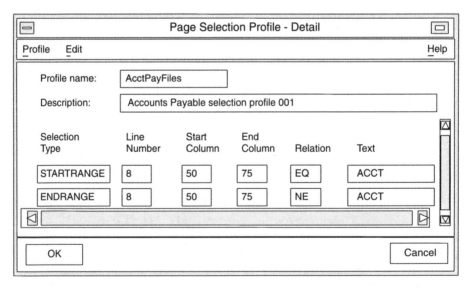

Source: Computer Associates International, Inc.

Figure 9-5: *Page Selection Profile*

capability is not extraordinary; in fact, performance monitoring is the weakest aspect of CA-Unicenter. But the CA-Unicenter GUI can launch other performance management applications, such as PerfView and PerfRX, which run under HP's OpenView OperationsCenter or HP's Network Node Manager.

PerfView provides UNIX users with the means to monitor heterogeneous networked environments. It consolidates performance information from software data-collection agents sitting on network nodes. The agents look for conditions that fail to meet IS-specified performance thresholds. PerfRX, which runs in conjunction with PerfView, is a performance analysis tool that tracks performance data including CPU, disk and memory transaction rates and response time for better network planning and improved resource use.

Resource Accounting and Chargeback: CA-Unicenter offers a flexible facility for charging users for UNIX resources. User-friendly aliases can be defined to replace the often cryptic accounting data structures found in UNIX. This makes chargeback administration more intuitive and helps to reduce implementation time and associated costs.

With the overhead allocation feature, systems overhead costs can be identified. These costs can be expressed in different terms and automatically be distributed proportionately to users of the system. The rates for various resource usage can be dynamically adjusted, with the results of each adjustment viewable immediately. The costs associated with a particular resource's consumption by a single consumer can even be split across a larger user community. Up to five nested levels of chargeback may be defined, such as division, department, team, group and member (Figure 9-6). Nesting permits the use of a common data source to report on logical groupings appropriate to organizational needs.

The resulting reports not only lend precision to resource accounting, but the information can be made available in multiple formats as required by auditors, system programmers, operations managers, applications development personnel and IS management. The accumulated information also can be used for detailed trend analysis of resource use. Statistics on system, file, memory, terminal connect, program use and other activities can be summarized to determine growth rates and to project (or justify) system upgrades and additions in a timely manner, before resource shortages become critical.

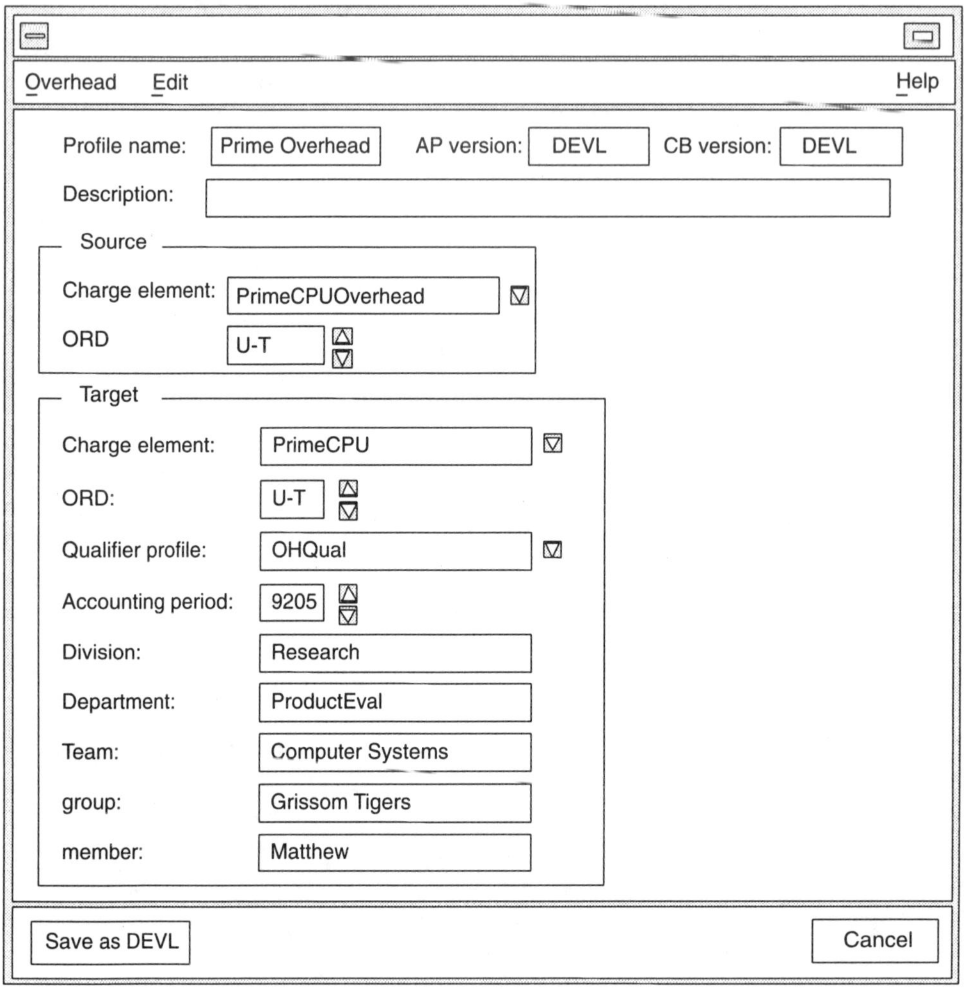

| Overhead | Edit | | | | Help |

Profile name:	Prime Overhead	AP version: DEVL	CB version: DEVL
Description:			

Source

Charge element: PrimeCPUOverhead ▽

ORD U-T △▽

Target

Charge element: PrimeCPU ▽

ORD: U-T △▽

Qualifier profile: OHQual ▽

Accounting period: 9205 △▽

Division: Research

Department: ProductEval

Team: Computer Systems

group: Grissom Tigers

member: Matthew

Save as DEVL   Cancel

Source: Computer Associates International, Inc.

Figure 9-6: *Chargeback Profile*

To make this and other kinds of information more useful, Computer Associates has bundled its Motif-based CA-20/20 spreadsheet software with CA-Unicenter. CA-20/20 provides direct access into CA-Unicenter's resource accounting database, allowing the spreadsheet's forecasting, graphing and analysis tools to be applied to raw data stored in industry-standard Structured Query Language (SQL) format, even if the user does not know SQL.

DATA CENTER ADMINISTRATION

Data center administration provides a framework for managing daily problems encountered by the system administrator. By accurately identifying the cause of a problem, and relating it to specific hardware, software, or procedural errors, the reliability of the computing environment can be improved continuously. By assigning ownership of problems and tracking progress toward their resolution, the time needed to correct problems can be reduced significantly.

Problem Management: CA-Unicenter's problem manager provides basic helpdesk functions through a problem tracking and reporting system. Problems can be entered manually (Figure 9-7) by entering the information on a terminal, automatically when abnormal events occur based on user-defined thresholds or conditions, or programmatically through policies controlled by the machine-generated problem tracking (MGPT) feature. The facility monitors progress in resolving problems, escalating them to a higher priority or shifting responsibility to another area if necessary.

Each problem area is defined by status codes, responsibility area, category and priority, as follows:

Status Code: defines the current state of a problem with as few or as many states as deemed necessary by the organization.

Responsibility Area: defines those individuals, groups, departments, or other areas that are assigned to provide attention to a problem.

Category: defines the type of problem.

Priority: defines the level of importance of each problem in relation to other problems in the system.

Machine Assisted Tracking: With machine-generated problem tracking (MGPT), the basic helpdesk functions can be extended to track other problem categories, such as applications and security. To have the system identify problems automatically, a policy can be developed that is associated with each type of problem. In this way, CA-Unicenter can detect literally hundreds of possible problems including: unusual security conditions, failed batch processing, excessive CPU usage, or unusual file activity, to name a few. When problems are resolved, the records are retained in the problem management database for reporting and future reference.

The Problem Management component of CA-Unicenter can communicate with the software that manages and monitors many of the areas where problems typically originate. For example, the Console Management function of Automated Production Control can detect many types of hardware related errors, and the Process Scheduling function is aware of failures in offline processing.

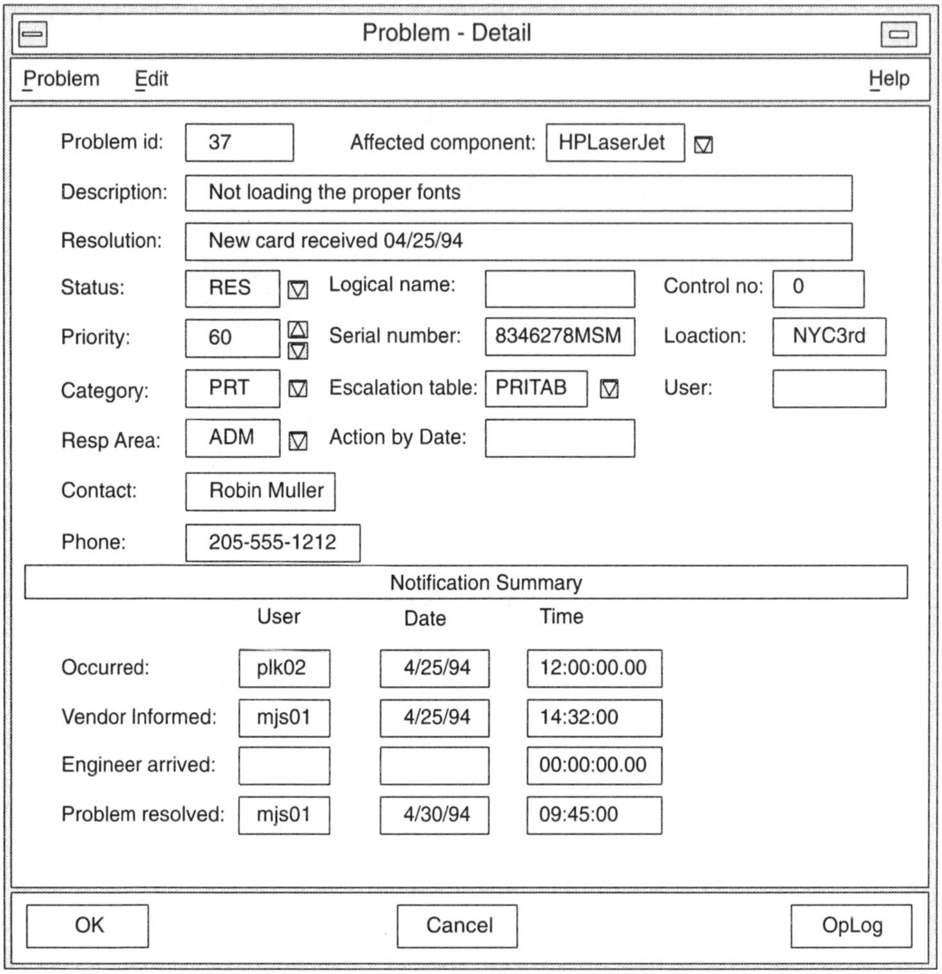

⊟	Problem - Detail	⊡

Problem	Edit		Help

Problem id: `37` Affected component: `HPLaserJet` ☑

Description: `Not loading the proper fonts`

Resolution: `New card received 04/25/94`

Status: `RES` ☑ Logical name: `` Control no: `0`

Priority: `60` ☒ Serial number: `8346278MSM` Loaction: `NYC3rd`

Category: `PRT` ☑ Escalation table: `PRITAB` ☑ User: ``

Resp Area: `ADM` ☑ Action by Date: ``

Contact: `Robin Muller`

Phone: `205-555-1212`

Notification Summary			
	User	Date	Time
Occurred:	plk02	4/25/94	12:00:00.00
Vendor Informed:	mjs01	4/25/94	14:32:00
Engineer arrived:			00:00:00.00
Problem resolved:	mjs01	4/30/94	09:45:00

OK	Cancel	OpLog

Source: Computer Associates International, Inc.

Figure 9-7: Manual Problem Entry

Problem Escalation: Escalation policies may be optionally associated with problems when they are created. Escalation helps prevent problems from becoming lost or unattended by ensuring that they are brought into focus if left unaddressed for too long. Problem management policies also can be defined to automatically reassign a problem's priority and/or area of responsibility based on such factors as: problem age, level of activity applied to the problem and manual or programmatic updating of the problem.

Eventually, all problems are resolved. The results are retained in the Problem Management database for reporting and reference. To reduce the amount of disk space used for problem information, policies can be set up for the archival and eventual deletion of information concerning resolved problems. Such policies ensure that the storage requirement is kept reasonable, while information on recent problem activity remains available.

ORIGINALLY, CA-UNICENTER WAS HEAVILY WEIGHTED TOWARD SYSTEMS MANAGEment. It lacked SNMP support, forcing users to integrate systems and network management in other ways, such as by accessing specific network monitoring and diagnostic applications that run under HP's OpenView OperationsCenter (i.e., PerfView and PerfRX) or using Unicenter in conjunction with HP's Network Node Manager, which supports SNMP. Now, with the addition of SNMP support, Unicenter more efficiently and effectively spans the systems and network management domains, providing a balanced platform suited to the needs of both.

Having the ability to integrate network and systems management into one coherent environment becomes extremely critical, especially as companies increasingly rely on client-server technology. With SNMP support, Unicenter offers single-point network, systems and database management. Streamlining these operations results in higher productivity and systems availability. Single-point management also is one of the few methods available to control skyrocketing management costs.

Integrating network and systems management provides numerous operational benefits. Security is one of the best examples. If an attempted security violation is detected by Unicenter, notification is passed to the network management system. The network management display immediately changes the color of the attacked system on the network map and/ or makes it flash. The administrator, who is watching both the network and systems, could then double-click on the attacked system's icon to launch Unicenter's security function. Unicenter shows the administrator what security violation was attempted and by whom. The administrator would then be in a position to take immediate action.

Registering as a manageable application with the OpenView platform, Unicenter sends and receives SNMP traps. In being able to receive SNMP traps, Unicenter can use its decision rule facility to move quickly in reponse to various SNMP events in the network. For example, if a printer sent an SNMP trap indicating that it was inoperable, Unicenter could pick an alternative printer for report distribution, notify the user where to find the report, and open a trouble ticket — all automatically. In addition,

Unicenter translates SNMP jargon into plain language. Instead of "device 141.201.23.46 not responding", Unicenter will issue the message, "printer in room 459 is down".

In addition to security violations and printer malfunctions, a trap can be sent by Unicenter to notify the OpenView platform about other events it detects. For example, if it notices that a job has failed, Unicenter can forward that message to the network management system, which changes the color and/or flashes the system icon to show what has happened. Following notification, the HP OpenView platform may invoke the Unicenter GUI on the client platform in the precise Unicenter application which sent the trap. This allows the network manager to immediately investigate, analyze and respond.

In these and many other ways, a single Unicenter management console can thus monitor and manage a widely distributed heterogeneous environment. Network managers benefit by having access to a much richer, critical set of systems events and from the ability to respond to events through Unicenter applications. Systems administrators benefit from the availability of network events and by being able to respond to them through integration with Unicenter.

CHAPTER
10

Managing the NetWare Environment

PEREGRINE SYSTEMS' STATIONVIEW HELPS MANAGE NOVELL NETWARE LANS. StationView also is interoperable with HP OpenView. It provides menu bar integration with HP OpenView Network Node Manager and HP OperationsCenter. Data is shared between the StationView and OpenView platforms.

From OpenView, the Novell file server icon can be selected to perform NetWare administration tasks that range from adding new users and changing print jobs to rebooting a server and editing a workstation's autoexec.bat file.

STATIONVIEW PRODUCT FAMILY

The StationView product family provide tools for each aspect of the PC workstation management process. The StationView family consists of StationView/OV, Stationview/Agent and StationView/DOS.

Stationview/OV is a management application running under the OpenView platform. It provides a centralized approach to NetWare station management. This level of management is accomplished through a seamlessly integrated connection between the IP map provided by StationView/OV's IPX client-server map.

StationView/OV offers a way to monitor and control clients distributed throughout the enterprise and to show a detailed view of PC workstations, their connections to the network, and the status of network resources such as servers and printers available to each PC workstation. StationView/OV also provides the ability to edit a PC workstation's configuration files and save them back to the PC workstation.

StationView/Agent has two components that work together to allow the client PC to be managed from StationView/OV.

- Proxy agent is a NetWare Loadable Module (NLM) that is installed on the NetWare server. It is responsible for making PC workstation information gathered by the collection software available to StationView/OV on the OpenView platform.

- Collection software is a standard DOS program that is installed on the PC workstation. The collection software runs at login time and uploads the PC client information to the NetWare server where it is stored in a compressed file.

StationView/DOS is an optional management application that runs under DOS/Windows. It is designed for the end user or local administrator and is compatible with StationView/OV.

STATIONVIEW OPERATION

StationView automatically discovers servers and workstations on NetWare LANs, eliminating the need to build graphical maps and manually enter hardware and software information whenever changes occur. StationView monitors network status, reports changes and helps the operator analyze and take inventory of each PC client's hardware and software assets. This information can be integrated into an SQL database and output to spreadsheets or reports for inventory tracking. It also provides the tools necessary to isolate and diagnose LAN problems. Collected data is consolidated and presented through a consistent graphical user interface (GUI).

StationView focuses on the PC workstation's view of the network. By examining individual workstations and the network itself, StationView determines the possible source of problems — whether it is the network, workstation, cable, adapter or the server.

Every client PC and server on the Novell network is displayed as a colored icon (Figure 10-1), providing the operator with instant notification of which clients and servers have problems, or will have them. Problems can be diagnosed by such categories as hardware, software, network or printer (Figure 10-2). Status buttons reflect the PC's health in color — green, yellow or red. The operator only has to point and click on an individual icon to view category status, or select the category button to obtain more detail.

StationView automatically scans PC hardware, software and configurations. It provides the operator with an accurate picture of workstation components and configuration. The information can assist the operator in managing:

- Local and network disk usage.

- Workstation component or configuration file changes.

- Loaded drivers and versions.

- Environment variables.

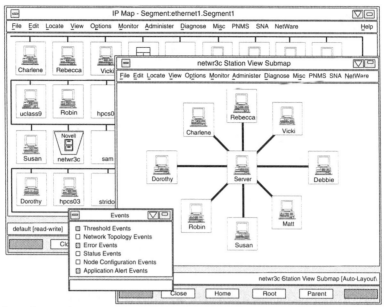

Source: Peregrine Systems, Inc.

Figure 10-1: *Client-Server Status*

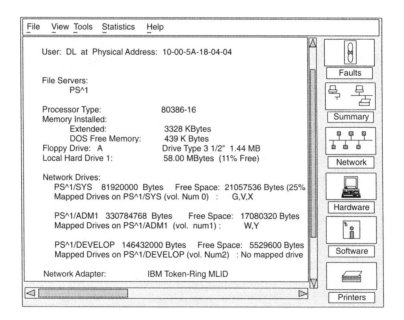

Source: Peregrine Systems, Inc.

Figure 10-2: *Category Views*

- Memory and interrupt mapping.

- Terminal stay resident (TSR) programs.

- Autoexec.bat, config.sys, win.ini, system.ini, login and other configuration files.

The operator can make configuration changes from a central location. Collected information can be used as an aid for software installation and troubleshooting.

StationView displays connections between PCs and the network, including available network and server resources. It also provides data about the hardware and software required for network connectivity, such as adapter cards, disk drives on the server and NetWare drivers. Other facilities include:

- **Network status:** provides end users with a work-around if a primary network connection is unavailable.

- **Adapter and connection statistics:** provides IPX/SPX and shell information.

- **Connectivity test, network number and adaptor information:** provides the means to troubleshoot problems.

The operator also can view available network resources such as servers for information with which to diagnose and solve connectivity problems.

StationView automatically checks printer availability and displays: DOS print command status, PC CAPTURE configuration, and Status and configuration of print servers and queues for the PC user.

Following the industry convention of using agents to monitor and control devices distributed throughout the network, the StationView product family uses agents that reside on NetWare servers throughout the enterprise. The StationView Proxy Agent is a NetWare Loadable Module (NLM) that provides a Simple Network Management Protocol interface to PC workstation data stored on the server. This agent requires the Novell TCP/IP NLM, which is standard with the NetWare 3.X operating system.

These agents gather information from the PC workstations attached to the servers. This architecture allows remote management by an authorized support staff individual, as well as local management directly by the end user.

Running on an HP-UX OpenView console, StationView provides centralized PC workstation management. StationView gets PC information through the StationView Proxy Agent on the NetWare server and makes it available to the operator (Figure 10-3).

The StationView Collector gathers data about the client and detects problems or changes with that data. It runs at regular intervals (e.g., boot or login) on all managed workstations. If the StationView Collector detects a problem with a workstation, the StationView/DOS application can be run to provide help directly at the client location. StationView/DOS, which runs on each client PC, displays the client status, giving end users the information they need to solve the problem themselves or to relay accurate information to the helpdesk or LAN administrator. The StationView/DOS application also can be used by a workgroup administrator to view other workstations on a LAN segment.

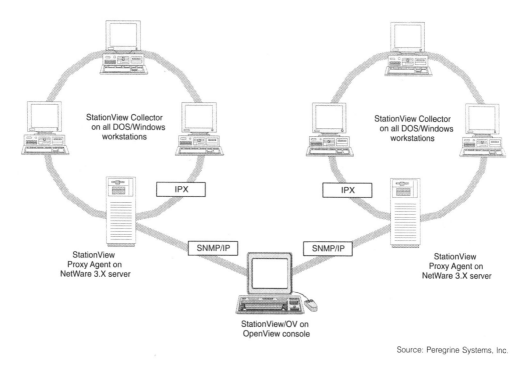

Source: Peregrine Systems, Inc.

Figure 10-3: Centralized Control via StationView

PROCESSES AND PROTOCOLS

StationView uses the following processes and protocols to gather and retrieve information:

svget: the program used to gather the information to be stored on the server.

IPX: the protocol used to transfer information between the collection software and the proxy agent NLM.

SNMP: the protocol used by StationView/OV to retrieve information from the NetWare server. StationView/OV uses proprietary SNMP port numbers to enhance security.

Figure 10-4 shows the components of the StationView product family and how they work together.

COLLECTION SOFTWARE OPERATION

The collection software collects PC workstation information in four main categories: network, hardware, software and printers.

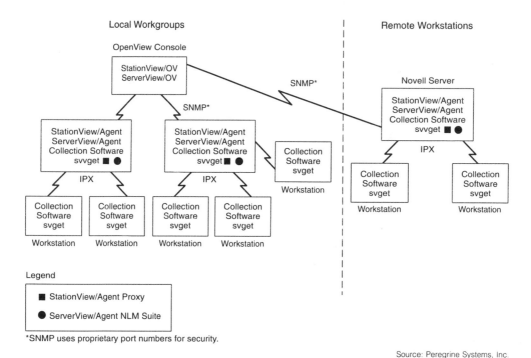

*SNMP uses proprietary port numbers for security.

Source: Peregrine Systems, Inc.

Figure 10-4: Components of StationView Product Family

The information is analyzed and any warnings or errors are saved, as is the actual workstation data that is collected. While the software is collecting the workstation data, the progress of the collection process is indicated in a separate window. The overall status of each area, as well as the first error or warning message, is displayed as that area is tested. Three levels of status are defined and indicated by the color of the messages for each area. There is a separate status indication for each of the four areas of information collected.

The status colors are as follows:

- **Green:** indicates that no problems were found.

- **Yellow:** indicates that problems or changes were detected that generated a warning message.

- **Red:** indicates that error messages were generated.

If problems are found in a particular area, the status line for that section indicates how many errors and/or warnings were generated, and lists the first warning or error found. The complete list of errors and/or warnings can be viewed using either StationView/OV or StationView/DOS.

After the final data is gathered, a message is displayed indicating that the PC workstation data is being saved. A copy of the data collected from the workstation is stored on the local hard drive of the workstation and on the NetWare file server.

When the PC workstation data is saved, there is normally a brief pause if no errors are displayed. The window disappears and the DOS prompt returns. However, if new workstation configuration files are on the file server or if errors are displayed for any of the data categories, the program pauses and a message appears informing the operator of what to do next.

LOCATING NETWARE CLIENTS

When HP OpenView is re-started after installing StationView/OV, StationView/OV automatically discovers all of the NetWare servers on which Novell's TCP/IP NLM is running. StationView/OV also locates the servers that have the proxy agent loaded.

There are two methods used to locate NetWare clients under HP OpenView: from the OpenView menu bar or from the StationView/OV IP Map.

OpenView Menu Bar: The HP OpenView menu items provide access to information about NetWare client PCs. The operator may locate clients by symbol type or name.

Through a series of menu selections, clients can be located by symbol. In the window that appears (Figure 10-5), the operator selects a symbol from the symbol class area. Selecting the server displays all of the types of servers on the network. With the selection of a particular type of server, such as a Novell File Server, a list of located objects and their descriptions is displayed. The operator selects the appropriate item from the list, in this case, the one that includes the IPX Client-Server Map.

If the operator knows the name of the NetWare server on which the TCP/IP NLM resides, the StationView/OV application can be opened by specifying the server name. This is completed through a series of menu selections. In the window that appears (Figure 10-6), the operator enters the name of the NetWare server. For all servers with that name, a list of located objects and their descriptions is displayed. The operator selects the appropriate item from the list, in this case, the one that includes the IPX Client-Server Map (nws311.pub.hp3.com IPX Client-Server Map:nws311).

StationView/OV IP Map: If the operator knows the network segment on which the NetWare server is located, and the server name, the StationView/OV application can be accessed by travelling down the IP map.

This is accomplished by double-clicking on the IP map symbol to open the IP map and then double-clicking on the segment name on which the Novell server is located. The operator continues down the IP map until the StationView/OV icon is reached. Double-clicking on the StationView/OV icon brings up the StationView/OV IPX Client-Server Map (Figure 10-7). The map is arranged in a star configuration, with the server in the center and the managed clients surrounding it. Each client has a default name based on its media access control (MAC) address.

Client status is indicated by color. The severity levels displayed for servers in the StationView/OV IPX Client-Server Map are downgraded by one level for display on the OpenView maps. For example, a server status of red on the StationView/OV window becomes yellow when displayed at the OpenView IP map level. The rationale is that a problem that causes a red error message to be displayed in StationView/OV may be critical information for an end user or workgroup manager, but is probably not critical to an enterprise manager using OpenView.

The StationView/OV application for a client shows a detailed view of that client, including the fault status, the hardware and software inventories, the network connection and network resources.

CLIENT STATUS

There are six status views to a PC workstation, which correspond to the status buttons on the right side of the StationView/OV Window (Figure 10-8). The status buttons have two functions. The first is to provide easy access to the StationView/OV main status windows. A different main window can be displayed by pressing the appropriate button or icon.

The second function of the status buttons is to indicate the overall status of the associated workstation category. The color of the button's icon indicates the severity of any problems found (green, yellow or red). The color of the icon reflects the severity of the worst problem found for that particular area.

The Fault button icon's color indicates the overall status of the entire workstation and is an **OR** function of the status of the network, hardware, software and printer areas. The most severe problem detected in the entire

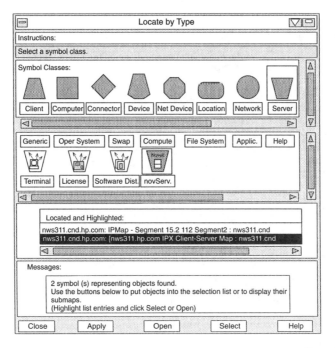

Source: Peregrine Systems, Inc.

Figure 10-5: *Locating Clients by Symbol Type*

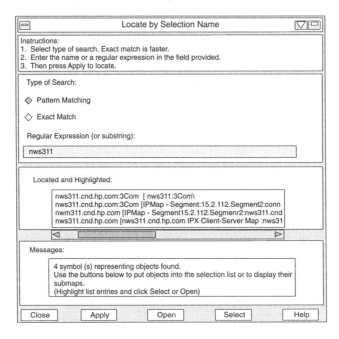

Source: Peregrine Systems, Inc.

Figure 10-6: *Locating Clients by Name*

workstation or its associated network connection determines the color of the Fault button icon.

The color of the Summary button icon does not change to reflect any status information. Any summary status would be redundant, with the overall workstation status indicated by the Fault button icon.

STATUS WINDOWS

StationView/OV contains six status windows that provide a detailed view into the PC workstation. They include: Fault window, Summary window, Network window, Hardware window, Software window and Printer window.

Typically, if a serious network connectivity problem exists, the PC workstation cannot write its current status to the NetWare server for query by StationView/OV. In this case, the operator will have access only to information from the last time there was an active connection.

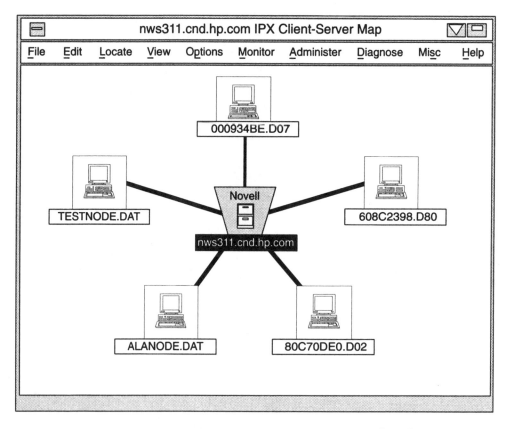

Source: Peregrine Systems, Inc.

Figure 10-7: StationView/OV IPX Client-Server Map

The *Fault window* displays a summary of all of the warnings and errors detected in the workstation or its attached network. The warning and error messages are grouped in the four main sections for which data is collected: network, hardware, software and printer. The Fault window is the default window that appears when the operator clicks on a specific PC workstation to examine through the IPX Client-Server Map.

The warning and error messages displayed here also appear in the status window with which they are associated. For example, if there is a warning message indicating that the amount of memory in a PC workstation has changed, this message appears in the Fault window under the Hardware section, as well as in the Hardware window.

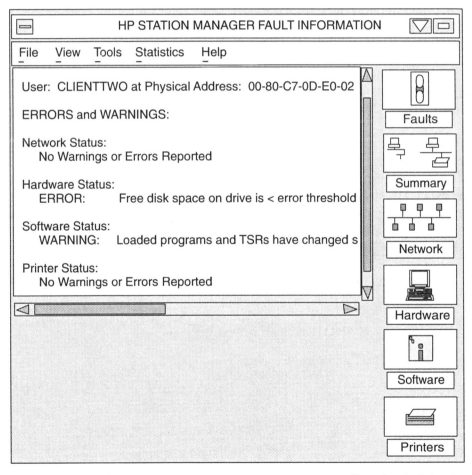

Source: Peregrine Systems, Inc.

Figure 10-8: Station Manager Fault Window

The **Summary window** displays an overview of the network, hardware, software and printer information collected. This window provides access to the most frequently requested workstation information. Summarized information includes:

- Currently attached servers.

- Processor type.

- Installed extended memory.

- DOS free memory.

- Local and network hard drives.

- Network adapter, if one is installed.

- DOS version.

- autoexec.bat and config.sys dates.

- Current PATH specification.

- Available local and network printers.

The **Network window** displays information related to the workstation's connection to the NetWare network. Information is included on the network hardware and software required for network connectivity, such as the adapter card and the NetWare drivers. In addition, disk drive information is provided for the server onto which the user is logged. The following information is displayed:

- Network status.

- Local network number.

- Network adapter.

- Workstation physical (node) address (hardware or MAC address)

- NetWare shell version.

- IPX version.

- SPX version.

- Maximum configured IPX connections.

- Server logged on to.

- User login name.

- Network hard drive size and free space.

- Attached NetWare servers.

If a problem with the network is discovered, none of the network information can be collected. In this case, only the network status information is displayed.

The **Hardware window** displays the PC workstation hardware components, such as microprocessor type and amount of installed memory. The Hardware window includes the following information:

- Processor type.

- Math coprocessor, if available.

- BIOS manufacturer and date.

- Current display mode.

- Installed memory.

- DOS free memory.

- Installed floppy drives.

- Local hard drive size and free space.

- Network server drive size and free space.

- Local printer port status.

- Local communication port status.

- Mouse information.

If any problems exist with the connection to the network, some of the network information, such as network server drive size, may not be shown.

The **Software window** displays information relating to the software components of the PC workstation, including any software-configurable parameters. The Software window displays the following information:

- DOS version.

- Loadable device drivers.

- Currently loaded programs and TSRs.

- autoexec.bat and config.sys dates.

- Login file date, if network is functional.

- NetWare shell configuration file dates.

- Microsoft Windows win.ini and system.ini dates.

- Amount of environment space used.

- Current PATH specification.

- Date of last software inventory.

The ***Printer window*** displays information about the selected workstation's local and network printers. The printer data is analyzed to determine if there are any potential printer problems. For example, a warning message occurs if a NetWare print queue is set up, but no printers are configured to service that queue. If a workstation is not configured to use a particular print queue, the warning message only applies to that workstation. However, if a workstation is configured to use that print queue because of redirection of a local printer port by the NetWare Capture command, there would be problems printing. In this case, an error message rather than a warning is displayed.

If any problems are detected in the connection to the network, the network printer information cannot be collected and thus will not be displayed.

MENUS
The main status windows also can be selected through the View menu item. More detailed information is displayed by using the submenus from the View menu, such as Network, then Network Adapter.

TROUBLESHOOTING WORKSTATIONS

StationView/OV can be used in several different ways to troubleshoot workstations throughout the enterprise.

StationView/Agents constantly are monitoring workstation information. When errors or warnings are detected on a workstation during the collection cycle, those messages are sent to the OpenView console. When the operator views the IPX Client-Server Map, the status of the workstation is indicated by green, yellow or red. The color scheme guides the operator to workstations that are either having trouble now, or are experiencing levels of performance that may result in problems later.

When a specific workstation has been selected for examination, the operator can use the colors of the status buttons on the right side of each of the status views to identify other problem areas. This status information also is summarized in the Fault status window of the StationView/OV window for that workstation.

For example, assume that a user named Robin is almost out of disk space. When StationView/OV collects information about Robin's workstation, it sends that information to OpenView, and the icon for Robin's workstation turns red on the IPX Client-Server Map. Selecting Robin's workstation brings up the Fault window for that workstation, which shows the error message *Available Disk Space* < 2% under the Hardware category. The Hardware status button on the side of the window is also red.

Following the convention of OpenView's propagation of status information up through the hierarchy of the map, the status of the server changes because of an event on an attached workstation. The server status color changes to the next lowest severity compared to the workstation.

REMOTE TROUBLESHOOTING

If an end user at a remote site reports a problem, the operator can locate the workstation easily by double-clicking on the server to which it is attached. This brings up the IPX Client-Server Map, where the workstation of interest can be selected.

Alternatively, the operator can locate the object by name from the OpenView menu bar. The default name will be a concatenation of the Novell user name and MAC address. This brings up the IPX Client-Server Map with the selected PC workstation highlighted. The operator can then double-click on the workstation to display the Fault window for that client.

Because StationView/OV allows the operator to bring up workstation configuration files directly, often problems can be fixed by making changes to the autoexec.bat, config.sys, user login script, or other file.

MONITORING WORKSTATIONS

Monitoring workstations is achieved in a similar manner as monitoring other devices under OpenView — by viewing the color of the symbols on the IP map. Because most workstations do not appear directly on the IP map, they are monitored by watching the NetWare servers to which they are attached.

When an error event occurs on a workstation that turns the symbol red, the NetWare server symbol turns yellow, consistent with the event propagation rules under OpenView. To use StationView/OV to view the status of workstations attached to that server, the operator double-clicks on the Novell server on the IP map and then double-clicks on the StationView/OV application to view the IPX Client-Server Map, including the state of each workstation.

If the server symbol is yellow, and one or more of the workstations is red, this indicates a serious condition. The operator clicks on the workstation to view the errors and warnings associated with that workstation.

CONFIGURING WORKSTATIONS

Workstations can be configured directly from the OpenView console using the Boot File Editor. This editor allows the operator to view or change the following workstation configuration files: autoexec.bat, config.sys, net.cfg, shell.cfg, win.ini, system.ini and login script.

Because the configuration files are obtained from the database on the NetWare server, these files can be edited even if the end user has turned off the workstation or has a broken connection to the network. The next time the user logs in, the new files are downloaded to the user's workstation and the workstation automatically reboots.

The next time the collection software (**svget**) is run on a workstation with an updated configuration file, the new file is copied to the workstation and the workstation reboots, allowing the new configuration to take effect.

There are four tasks the operator can perform with the Boot File Editor:

- View the file, without making changes.

- Save the file for future work. The file can then be edited with a text editor, and the cut-and-paste method used to update the workstation file.

- Change the file for the user's workstation by saving it to that workstation. However, the file will not be saved to the server until the Boot File Editor window is closed.

- Print the file by selecting Print (to **lp**). This performs an **lp** of the file. If **lp** is configured, the file is printed.

TAKING INVENTORY

The operator can perform a hardware inventory on any workstation, collecting such information as CPU type and speed, BIOS, co-processor, memory and disk storage. The collected information then can be analyzed to detect changes in workstation configuration that could affect workstation functionality. To initiate a workstation inventory, the **svcomma** NLM must be loaded.

When the **svcomma** NLM loads, it collects a subset of the data that is available through the status windows, saves it to a file, and unloads. It can be run as frequently as needed.

The resulting file, svcomma.txt, is stored on the NetWare server. This file can be imported into any database or spreadsheet program for analysis, or moved onto a UNIX console NFS or other file transfer program.

The operator can collect a software inventory manually from the workstation, or configure **svget** to collect an inventory on a regular basis. When

svget is run, either manually or automatically, the StationView/OV menu item, File: Software Inventory, displays a list of all files on the workstation's local drive, including executable files and loaded NLMs.

Data collected from each workstation can be stored on the managed NetWare server. These files are printed using standard UNIX print functions.

The operator can perform a network inventory from each server, collecting information about adapters, configured users, other known servers, network number and NetWare serial number.

Printer inventory includes information on print queues and servers as well as configured users and operators.

PERIGINE SYSTEMS OFFERS ANOTHER MANAGEMENT APPLICATION THAT RUNS ON HP's OpenView platform in conjunction with StationView/OV. ServerView/OV provides a centralized approach to NetWare server management by showing managed servers, their connections to the network, and the status of both servers and attached printers. This level of management is accomplished through a seamless integrated connection between the IP Map provided by OpenView and the IPX Client-Server Map provided by ServerView/OV.

ServerView/OV performs real-time monitoring of key server parameters such as disk space and CPU load, as well as providing alerts (traps) when conditions exist that are cause for concern. More than 100 server operating system events and ServerView agent traps indicating failure modes or abnormal operations can be sent automatically to specified management stations.

ServerView/OV also provides detailed administration capabilities such as the ability to add or delete users, change passwords, load NLMs, or edit server configuration files such as autoexec.ncf. ServerView/OV also provides the means to view server security violations, accounting information and performance graphs. NetWare information also can be viewed, such as versions, other servers, traffic statistics and adapter information.

ServerView/Agent exists as NLMs that are loaded on the managed server. The agent responds to requests made by ServerView/OV on the OpenView console. It also sends alerts to the management station(s) when an important event occurs.

ServerView/Agent includes a collector that gathers a portion of the information presented through ServerView/OV. Communication between the ServerView Agent and ServerView/OV uses SNMP and requires that the NetWare TCP/IP NLM be installed on the servers.

CHAPTER

11

Managing the SNA Environment

IN THE PAST, DATA COMMUNICATIONS WAS A RELATIVELY SIMPLE TASK, conducted within in the orderly, hierarchical confines of the Systems Network Architecture (SNA) devised by IBM. Within the last decade, there has been a marked shift in focus from the centralized information processing of the mainframe toward information sharing through distributed computing over local area networks (LANs). However, LANs have not replaced legacy systems entirely because they have strengths that many organizations continue to value.

Among the key advantages of SNA are levels of network accounting, diagnostics, security and cost control that are still unmatched by LANs. Furthermore, there are billions of dollars invested in SNA-based systems[1] and application software that cannot be thrown out without causing major disruptions to mission-critical business operations. During the past 20 years, SNA has indeed proven itself to be a stable and highly reliable architecture.

However, there is still the need to share tremendous quantities of information from one location to another over LANs and WANs in peer-to-peer fashion. Users value LANs for their connectivity to a variety of corporate resources, and TCP/IP-based WANs for their ability to access remote resources, reliably. To avoid the expense of duplicate networks, users are finding ways to integrate incompatible SNA and LAN architectures over the same facilities or services. Multiprotocol routers make this fairly easy to do over high-speed leased lines such as T1 and carrier services such as frame relay. The consolidation of such diverse resources over a single internetwork meets the special needs of SNA users by:

- Eliminating the need to provision, operate and maintain duplicate networks: one for SNA, one for token ring, and another for non-IBM environments.

---

[1]Despite the popularity of LANs, there are still more than 50,000 SNA networks and 500,000 IBM cluster controllers in use worldwide. Rather than abandon these assets, companies are looking for ways to leverage them by tying them into their LANs.

- Allowing slow leased-line SNA networks to take advantage of the higher speeds offered by LAN/WAN links.

- Consolidating network traffic and minimizing potential points of failure, saving on network usage costs and increasing network reliability.

- Offering the opportunity to consolidate management tasks using an open management platform capable of viewing and controlling diverse networks from the same console.

Peregrine Systems meets the latter need of SNA users. Its SNMP-based OpenSNA provides complete graphical management of IBM SNA networks from the HP OpenView platform. From a management perspective, the use of the OpenView platform permits greater interoperability between legacy networks and open, standards-based systems. OpenSNA conforms to the DME network management framework, which is based largely on OpenView technology. It may be used as a companion to, or a replacement for host-based NetView.

LEVEL OF INTEGRATION

OpenSNA provides menu bar integration with HP OpenView Windows and may be integrated with other OpenView enterprise management applications. In addition, OpenSNA is interoperable with OpenView Network Node Manager and shares data with OpenView software. This level of integration not only increases operator flexibility in the use of network management tools, it also leverages the expertise of existing staff and reduces training costs.

OpenSNA works with current releases of IBM's MVS/XA and MVS/ESA host operating systems that support the Virtual Telecommunications Access Method (VTAM).[2] OpenSNA uses intelligent interfacing between legacy systems and newer open systems, which means that no changes are required to existing hardware or software.

OpenSNA's major features include:

- Complete auto-discovery of the SNA network, including VTAM applications and end user devices.

- Automatic creation of OpenView maps depicting the SNA network.

- Real-time SNA system status reporting without polling, thus conserving network bandwidth.

---

[2]VTAM is an IBM mainframe software platform that allows communications between a host and outside systems such as terminals and workstations.

- VTAM command and control access through menus or command prompt.

- Optional NetView command and control access through menus or command prompt.

OpenSNA provides object display and manipulation functions by using the OpenView platform. Applications designed to work with the OpenView platform have full access to the SNA network. Network operators working from an OpenView console can issue VTAM commands to reset a device, check its status, or reboot a terminal server. Additional functionality is provided through extensions to the OpenView Windows interface and menu bars for control of the SNA network.

OpenSNA contains a manager application and an agent application. The SNA Manager and the SNA Agent use the OpenView communications infrastructure, TCP/IP, and SNA APPC to communicate.[3] The manager application (SNA Manager) maintains the user view of SNA objects and provides a graphical user interface for those objects. Most of the functionality is derived from native OpenView features. The SNA Manager runs on HP-UX, SunOS and IBM AIX systems and provides access to the user through the OpenView interface.

The SNA Agent runs as a background task on each managed SNA host. Management of all VTAM SNA elements is available through OpenSNA. The SNA network is discovered and updated automatically by the SNA Agent. All SNA control functions are available through the SNA Agent and can be accessed from OpenView menus using generic commands. Network diagnosis and automation capabilities are available through optional support for NetView.

OPENSNA ARCHITECTURE

Peregrine's OpenSNA applies an agent/manager style interface to SNA networks in keeping with the object-oriented approach endorsed by the Network Management Forum, specifically:

Object: a device or logical entity to be managed.

Manager: the application that exercises control over objects.

Agent: the application that provides the control.

---

[3]IBM's Advanced Program-to-Program Communications (APPC) protocol provides peer-to-peer communications between computers in an SNA network. It allows programs on one system to communicate with programs on another system, provided that those systems are running compatible communications applications.

The SNA Agent is host-based software that interfaces with VTAM to collect information and control the network. Separate agents are in place for each host in a multidomain SNA network.[4] A central agent, called the SNA Proxy, coordinates these separate functions. The SNA Proxy runs on the UNIX workstation running OpenSNA.

The SNA Manager runs under the OpenView platform, and collects the information from the SNA Agent routed to the SNA Manager by the SNA Proxy. The SNA Manager displays the information in the OpenView maps and sends commands to the SNA Agent.

The SNA Agent and SNA Manager use a common definition of an SNA device in the network. That definition is entered as an object in the SNA database.

OBJECTS

OpenSNA uses objects to represent physical or logical entities within the network. The following objects contain information and some control capability:

- All Logical Units (LUs), including application LUs. LUs are the points through which end-users gain access to the SNA network. They serve as the go-between for the end users and the network by managing data flow.

- All Physical Units (PUs), including PU5 (SSCP) and PU4 (NCP).[5] A PU consists of hardware and software that together manage the resources of the device, as well as represent that device.

- Cross Domain managers and resources. A cross domain resource manager (CDRM) allows network resources to communicate between multiple domains. It locates and requests a session with a target resource in another domain. Cross Domain Resources (CDRSC) are resources that are available to another domain through the second domain's CDRM.

- Lines, line groups and link stations.

- Major nodes, which are a set of resources that are grouped so they can be activated and deactivated together.

---

[4]A *domain* consists of the resources controlled by one SSCP, which is the controller within a host. It consists of the communications links, along with Network Addressable Units (NAUs), and components that perform boundary functions, gateway functions, and intermediate session routing.

[5]NCP refers to IBM's Network Control Program, which provides control of a communications controller. SSCP is the System Service Control Point, which activates, deactivates and monitors SNA network resources from within a host processor.

All objects have a standard interface composed of a graphical symbol and accompanying menus. Each unique type of object (e.g., 3278 model 3 terminals) is an object class. All objects in a class have the same set of data available and each data item (e.g., SNANetworkName) is an object attribute. A particular object in an object class, with a unique identifying object attribute (e.g., 3278 terminal with network name L06CA108), is an object instance.

SNA AGENT

The SNA Agent runs on the SNA host (currently MVS only), and communicates with VTAM to obtain the actual network status. The SNA Agent also processes generic action requests from the SNA Manager and issues VTAM commands to carry out the action. The SNA Agent actually interfaces with several VTAM facilities other system facilities. The SNA Agent can interface with NetView to allow NetView-specific commands to be issued. The SNA Agent also receives NMVT[6] alerts from NetView and sends those alerts to the SNA Manager.

The three major tasks of the SNA Agent and their functions are summarized as follows:

- Agent (main) task:
  - Handles communications via TCP/IP and APPC.
  - Processes OpenSNA commands.
  - Controls other tasks.

- Watcher task:
  - Obtains SNA topology changes from VTAM.
  - Obtains SNA status changes from VTAM.

- Listener task:
  - Receives SNA messages from VTAM.
  - Issues VTAM commands to VTAM.
  - Interfaces with NetView for NetView messages and commands.

SNA MANAGER

The SNA Manager handles both the user interface and the auto-discovery of the SNA network. The auto-discovery process works through event messages from the SNA Agents. The SNA Manager uses that information to build or update the OpenView map dynamically.

---

[6]NMVT (Network Management Vector Transport) is the request unit used in the SNA management services data flow. In addition to returning information about objects, and performing actions on them, the SNA Agent forwards event messages from the objects. An event indicates status or topology changes within the network.

The SNA Manager application runs in the background on the OpenView platform. Real time status and topology changes are made immediately as long as OpenView is running. If OpenView is not running, changes to the SNA network are updated the next time OpenView is started.

The five major components of SNA Manager and their functions are summarized as follows:

snamap :
- Builds and maintains SNA submaps in OpenView maps.
- Maintains real-time status on SNA objects.

snamapdb :
- Creates and maintains SNA objects in the OpenView database.

snacmd :
- Issues VTAM or NetView commands, or both, to the correct host.

snalog :
- Logs or filters messages and alerts.

snaoper :
- Motif dialog for SNA messages and commands.

SNA PROXY

The SNA Proxy is an OpenView background process that runs on the UNIX system. The SNA Proxy serves as a catalyst to facilitate communication between the SNA Agent and the SNA Manager. The SNA Proxy is the OpenView registered address for all SNA objects. The SNA Proxy only directly manages information about the interconnected SNA subareas. All other information is routed to the appropriate SNA Agent for the associated network address. SNA Agents register with the SNA Proxy when communications are first established.

The two major components of SNA Proxy and their functions are summarized as follows:

snaproxy :
- Coordinates communications between OpenSNA management tasks and SNA Agents.
- Directly supports TCP/IP communications with agents.

snaappc :
- Supports optional APPC communication with agents using the HP SNAplusLink software[7]

---

[7]HP SNAplusLink provides communications between an HP 9000 Series 700 or 800 and an IBM mainframe or an IBM peer system such as the AS/400.

CONNECTIVITY

The SNA Proxy communicates with the SNA Agent via TCP/IP or APPC. APPC also may be used to connect multiple SNA Agents to one SNA routing agent which is connected to the SNA Proxy. Figure 11-1 shows an example of SNA connectivity.

VISUAL ORGANIZATION OF THE SNA NETWORK

OpenView uses maps and submaps to represent the SNA environment (Figure 11-2). A map is a collection of symbols or objects for all resources that are managed, specifically: networks, PUs, LUs and connections. A submap corresponds to a group of symbols that are directly related. A submap is displayed within a Motif window. The default submap that is displayed on start-up is the Root submap.

ROOT WINDOW

After OpenSNA discovers the network, a top-level SNA network is displayed, which the starting point for the entire SNA network, much like the Internet symbol represents the TCP/IP network. The operator double-clicks on the SNA symbol in the Root Window to access the SNA Network submaps.

SUBMAPS

The next submap contains all of the subareas of the network. If the network consists of multiple SNA Network Interconnect (SNI) networks[8], then each SNA network can be viewed in separate submaps when a new map is created. By default, all the subarea symbols first appear as beige — indicating that they are unmanaged — until the operator chooses to manage them.

SUBAREAS

A subarea is the part of the SNA network that includes a subarea node and the resources associated with that node. Subarea nodes use network addresses for routing and maintain routing tables that provide the network configuration. Thus, they are affected by network address changes. Subarea nodes can be used to provide gateways for connecting multiple subarea networks, intermediate routing, and protocol support for peripheral nodes.

Clicking on a subarea symbol selects that object. When an object is selected, the operator can choose from among various menu options that can be performed on that object.

The lines between subareas represent links in the network. Generally, at least two lines are defined between any two subareas — one in each

---

[8]SNI is an SNA facility for interconnecting networks through gateways, such that end users can communicate across networks without being aware that more than one network is involved.

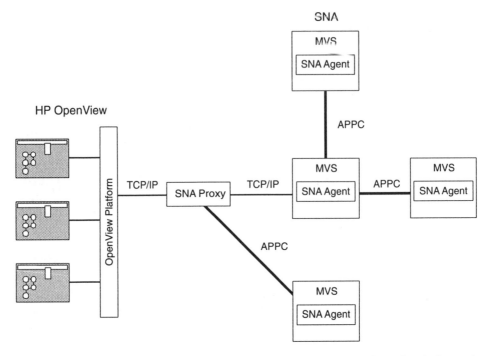

Figure 11-1: *Overview of SNA Connectivity*

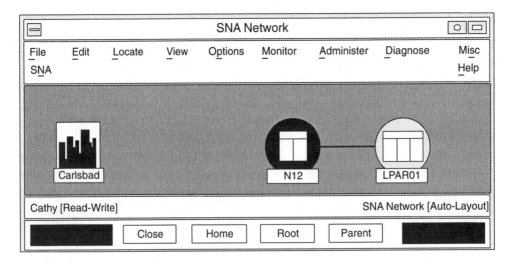

Figure 11-2: *SNA Network Map*

direction. An exception is that the host subareas may not have a line defined from the NCP back to the host. When more than one line is defined, the lines will be placed on a meta connection submap by OpenView. This special submap is used to display multiple lines between symbols. By default, the lines have their name displayed as a label. Meta connections do not have a label by default.

Double-clicking on a subarea symbol opens the submap for that subarea. Under each subarea symbol (either a host or NCP), a submap exists representing the devices that are attached to that host or NCP. The symbols on the subarea submap basically represent physical units (PUs) and link stations that are connected to the NCP or host with lines that represent the SNA links.

By double-clicking, the PU symbols and the meta connections can be exploded to show the devices attached to the PUs or the lines. Figure 11-3 illustrates the available OpenSNA symbols.

STATUS PRESENTATION

OpenSNA uses the same status colors for symbols and lines as defined by OpenView. These colors inform the operator of the status of a line or device, according to what OpenSNA has discovered. The status colors can be set to propagate to the higher submap levels.

STATUS TYPES

OpenSNA supports two types of status: object and compound. Some symbols obtain their status directly from the SNA status of the device or application (object status). Other symbols have a compound status that is propagated from lower-level symbols.

Group symbols such as networks, subareas, line groups or major nodes have compound (propagated) status. Actual device symbols, such as PUs, applications/LUs and lines, have object status.

The SNA status is mapped into the OpenView status colors so that active devices are green, inactive devices are red, and devices in any one of several pending states[9] are yellow. The operator can find the actual SNA status of a device by using the menu bar commands.

OpenSNA allows the operator to change the status source of an object; that is, how the color is obtained for a device. To obtain a status color, a compound status source applies propagation rules to the symbols on the selected object's submap. The object status source causes the color to be mapped directly from the SNA status for the object.

Status propagation determines how the symbol's status is propagated from a lower level (child) submap to a higher level (parent) symbol. Con-

---

[9]A pending state is one in which the status of the network object is in the process of activation or deactivation.

figuring status propagation is done from within OpenView and is carried out by OpenSNA.

SUBMAP CUSTOMIZATION

OpenView allows the operator to add custom background graphics to the OpenSNA submap windows. A bitmap graphic is placed in the background plane and can be different for each submap. For example, the operator may want to add a background map to a higher level submap to show locations of a different network, and add a floor plan to a submap to show the location of devices within a building. For a graphic to be displayed, the file must be in either Graphics Interchange Format (GIF) or X11 bitmap format (XBM). OpenView comes with a series of bitmapped graphics that can be used for this purpose.

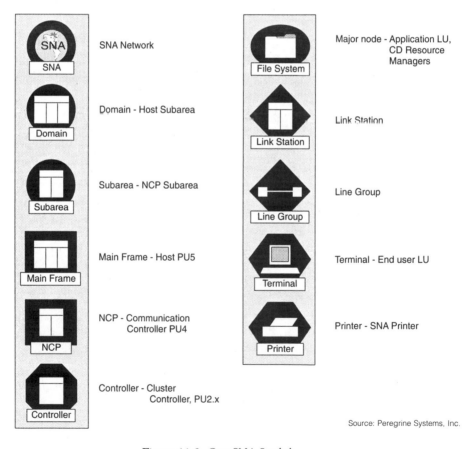

SNA	SNA Network
Domain	Domain - Host Subarea
Subarea	Subarea - NCP Subarea
Main Frame	Main Frame - Host PU5
NCP	NCP - Communication Controller PU4
Controller	Controller - Cluster Controller, PU2.x
File System	Major node - Application LU, CD Resource Managers
Link Station	Link Station
Line Group	Line Group
Terminal	Terminal - End user LU
Printer	Printer - SNA Printer

Source: Peregrine Systems, Inc.

Figure 11-3: OpenSNA Symbols

MANUAL SUBMAP CREATION

The operator can create a new submap that contains the same function as a submap automatically created by OpenSNA. Symbols and background graphics can be added to the new submap. A new submap is useful in situations where the operator wants to display an alternate version of a submap without rearranging the original submap. For example, the original submap might show a group of PUs arranged in a spiral layout. The operator could create a new submap, paste appropriate symbols into it, and arrange them in a row/column format.

SNA COMMANDS

OpenSNA command and control functions are provided through the OpenView menu bar. Any command normally entered in the MVS system through VTAM can be incorporated into the graphical OpenView's menu structure. The operator can execute commands available on the MVS host without knowing the command syntax and without knowing the environment in which the command is executed. The commands are issued through pull-down menus and the results are displayed in a separate pop-up dialog box. The SNA commands available through the OpenView menu bars are defined in the registration files provided with the product.

VTAM and NetView commands also can be directly entered at the command line at the bottom of the SNA Operator dialog box (Figure 11-4). The results of VTAM commands also are displayed in the SNA Operator dialog box, if it is active, and by status color changes within the submap.

EXECUTING COMMANDS AGAINST SNA NETWORK RESOURCES

OpenSNA uses a series of menu options to provide resource control and gather data from the SNA network. OpenSNA includes a default set of commands that are most commonly executed by the SNA systems engineer.

The following scenario provides an example of executing commands against the SNA network:

1. The operator enters OpenView and double-clicks on the SNA network symbol in the Root submap.

2. The SNA Network submap appears. If the SNI network view for multinetwork environments appears, the operator double-clicks on a Network symbol to view the subarea symbols. The SNA Network submap shows all the SNA subareas, such as NCPs and hosts.

3. The operator double-clicks on an NCP subarea symbol. The subarea submap appears.

4. The operator selects a PU symbol.

5. In the Monitor menu, the operator selects Device Configuration, then SNA, then Device Summary... This sends a display command to the appropriate MVS system and returns the results in a dialog box.

Additional commands can be executed on any of the SNA resources in any of the submaps.

DATABASE

OpenSNA does not have a user addressable database of its own. Instead, it updates the OpenView database using an application programming interface (API) available in OpenView. The next version of OpenView, version 4.0, will replace the OpenView database with an SQL interface to support popular databases and a data integration schema. OpenSNA will support this integration in OpenView 4.0.

SECURITY

OpenSNA offers two security mechanisms, both having advantages and disadvantages.

Commands from all users can be validated with a common security profile under a single NetView auto task. This is easy to configure and does not tie up NetView operator tasks. However, there is only one level of security available and auditing requires that the operator use CLIST[10] to implement modifications.

Also, commands can be excluded from some or all users within the OpenView user interface. This is done by removing the read attribute from the command registration file for the type of commands to be secured (control or display). The disabled commands are removed from users' menus, preventing their use. Authorized users are placed in a group that has read access to the file. This security is implemented by the **sna_cmd** process and cannot be bypassed by a non-root user.

SESSION RECAP

Session ReCap is an OpenSNA add-on product that gives the operator the ability to analyze 3270 terminal data in real time using both screen snapshot and trace formats. Session ReCap's approach to network data capture

---

[10]CLIST is short for Command List. It is the interactive TSO/MVS production control language underlying NetView. Its complexity makes it difficult for network operators to use advantageously. To make CLIST easier to use, IBM offers a Solution Pack consisting of a large collection of command procedures that enhance and extend NetView's functionality.

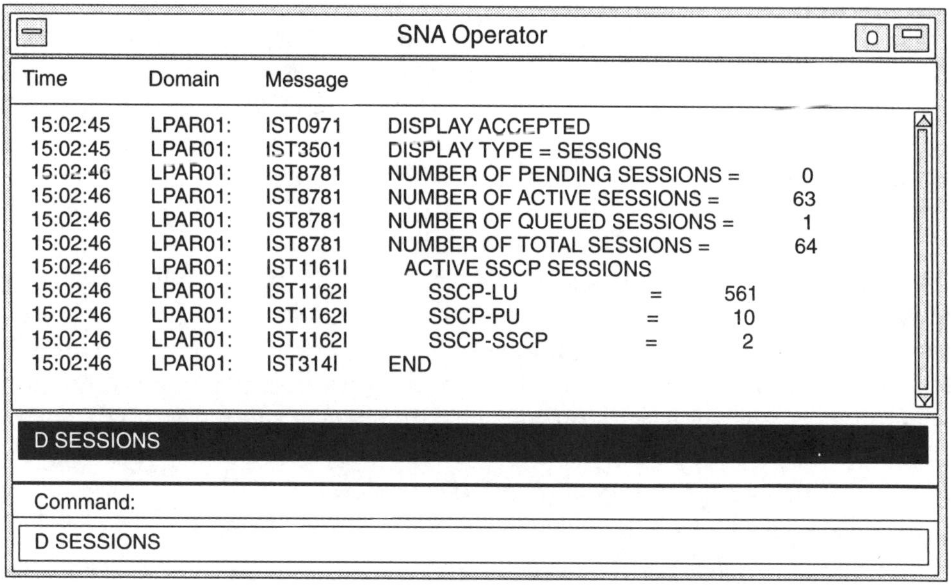

SNA Operator
Time
Domain
Message
15:02:45 LPAR01: IST0971 DISPLAY ACCEPTED
15:02:45 LPAR01: IST3501 DISPLAY TYPE = SESSIONS
15:02:46 LPAR01: IST8781 NUMBER OF PENDING SESSIONS = 0
15:02:46 LPAR01: IST8781 NUMBER OF ACTIVE SESSIONS = 63
15:02:46 LPAR01: IST8781 NUMBER OF QUEUED SESSIONS = 1
15:02:46 LPAR01: IST8781 NUMBER OF TOTAL SESSIONS = 64
15:02:46 LPAR01: IST1161I ACTIVE SSCP SESSIONS
15:02:46 LPAR01: IST1162I SSCP-LU = 561
15:02:46 LPAR01: IST1162I SSCP-PU = 10
15:02:46 LPAR01: IST1162I SSCP-SSCP = 2
15:02:46 LPAR01: IST314I END
D SESSIONS
Command:
D SESSIONS

Source: Peregrine Systems, Inc.

Figure 11-4: *SNA Operator Dialog Box*

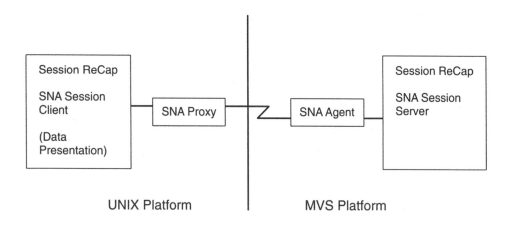

Session ReCap
SNA Session Client
(Data Presentation)
SNA Proxy
SNA Agent
Session ReCap
SNA Session Server
UNIX Platform
MVS Platform

Source: Peregrine Systems, Inc.

Figure 11-5: *Components of Session ReCap*

allows terminal data to be displayed, even though it was transmitted several hours prior to the time a problem is reported.

The application is used as a troubleshooting aid in conjunction with OpenSNA. The operator can collect and analyze real-time 3270 terminal snapshots and track data flow sessions that occur between the host and the terminal. Session ReCap continuously gathers and stores data on error messages, time-outs and keystrokes. Combining this data with HP's OpenView graphical user interface, network managers can monitor users' sessions in real time, improving the accuracy of troubleshooting.

Session ReCap is composed of two basic components. The first is the client component, referred to as the SNA Session Client, which runs as an application under OpenView and uses the SNA Proxy to communicate with the second component of Session ReCap: the server. The server component, referred to as the SNA Session Server, runs under the SNA Agent started task. It maintains a data repository containing session information. Figure 11-5 illustrates the two components of Session ReCap.

FUNCTIONS

There are two basic functions provided by Session ReCap: Screens and Trace. Both functions are available from the Session History List window (Figure 11-6), which is the root window for Session ReCap. This window displays a chronologically sorted list of sessions that the terminal has conducted. The operator can analyze one of these sessions by selecting it and clicking on either the Trace or Screens button in the bottom of the window. Session ReCap also provides an archive facility that allows sessions to be saved for later use.

Screens Function: When the Screens function is invoked, the data for the actual session is retrieved from the host repository. The data is summarized as a list of screen images (or snapshots) in the Screen Summary List window (Figure 11-7).

From the Screen List, the operator can view the actual 3270 screen for the selected item. The first screen of the session — the SNA Screen Detail window — is initially displayed (Figure 11-8). To display another screen, the operator simply clicks on another item in the Screen Summary List, causing the screen detail (snapshot) to display the terminal data associated with the newly selected summary line. The previously opened screen display window does not have to be closed before selecting and displaying another screen.

The Auto button on the Screen List allows continuous forward scrolling of the Screen List, pausing one second on each screen, until the end of the list is reached. The Auto button also will show new screens each time the 3270 user presses the Enter (or a function) key.

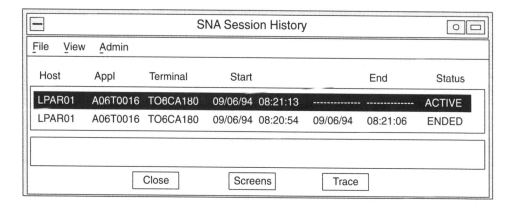

Figure 11-6: *Session History List Window*

SNA Screen Summary

Scrn	Time		Description
135	09/06/94	13:28:58.63	PF3 key^pressed
136	09/06/94	13:28:58.75	Output screen
137	09/06/94	13:28:59.75	PF9 key^pressed
138	09/06/94	13:28:59.88	Output screen
139	09/06/94	13:29:10.28	PF9 key^pressed
140	09/06/94	13:29:10.34	Output screen
141	09/06/94	13:29:13.39	Enter key^pressed (data included)
142	09/06/94	13:29:13.91	Output screen
143	09/06/94	13:29:27.29	Enter key^pressed (data included)
144	09/06/94	13:29:38.20	Output screen
145	09/06/94	13:29:39.88	Enter key^pressed (data included)
146	09/06/94	13:29:40.43	Output screen

Close   Auto

Figure 11-7: *Screen Summary List Window*

If session data does not appear in the Session History window, then the SNA Session Server data repository does not contain session history information for the named LU. This may be because of the following conditions:

- The LU is participating in a session that began prior to the start of the SNA Session Server.

- The LU has not participated yet in any sessions.

- The LU participated in sessions that were wrapped off of the SNA Session Server data repository to make room for newer session data.

Trace Function: When the Trace function is invoked, the data for the actual session is retrieved from the host repository. This data is summarized as a list of formatted Path Information Units (PIUs) in the Trace Summary window (Figure 11-9).

If session data is not displayed in the Trace Summary window, then the SNA Session Server no longer has detailed data for this session. The data probably is not available because the data repository wrapped over this data to make room for more recent data.

To display the data for a PIU, the operator selects one of the PIUs listed in the Trace Summary window and clicks on the Detail button on the bottom of the screen. The data for the selected PIU is displayed in the Trace Detail window (Figure 11-10). This data is displayed in hexidecimal form by clicking the Raw Data button at the bottom of the window.

Session Archive: Session ReCap data is transitory in nature; after some period of time, data is wrapped off in order to make room for more recent session data. If the operator wants to keep a session for later analysis, Session ReCap's archive facility is invoked, which saves it in the local UNIX file system.

SNAPRO

SNApro is an add-on product that provides integrated performance data for the SNA network. Response time and congestion can be viewed and graphed for the entire SNA hierarchy. Also, OpenView traps are generated based on user modifiable performance thresholds.

OPENSNA IS LICENSED BY HEWLETT-PACKARD AS SNA NODE MANAGER. IT IS functionally identical to OpenSNA. Both fill the holes left open by host-based NetView, providing network operators with easier-to-use tools and an all-important graphical view of the SNA network.

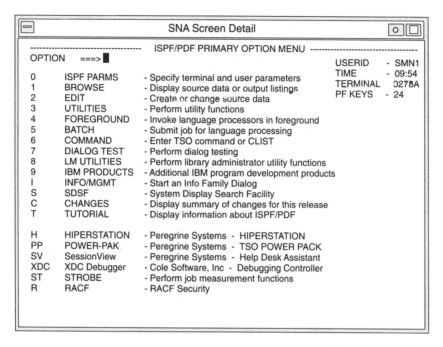

Source: Peregrine Systems, Inc.

Figure 11-8: SNA Screen Detail Window

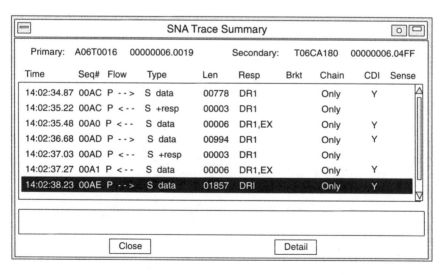

Source: Peregrine Systems, Inc.

Figure 11-9: Trace Summary Window

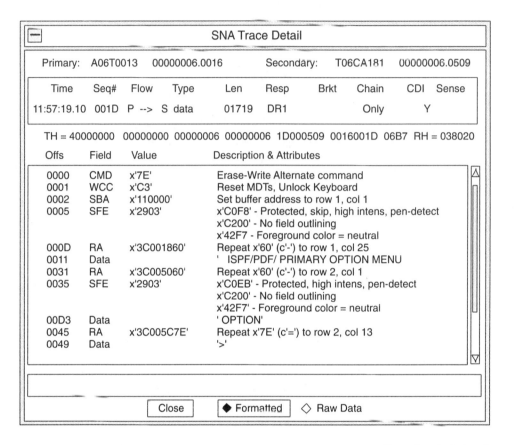

Figure 11-10: *Trace Detail Window (formatted)*

CHAPTER
12

Enterprise Hub Management

Today's sprawling networks present many challenges to managers. The proliferation of local area networks (LANs) and associated management systems has inserted additional layers of complexity into the computing environment that must be effectively controlled. In addition, individual computer systems that have been procured outside of the information system (IS) department's jurisdiction must now be integrated into an enterprise-wide network. While IS seeks to centralize control over corporate LANs and remote resources, it must still be able to detect and administer faults right down to the desktop. An efficient and economical solution is to use intelligent hubs.

The idea behind the intelligent hub is simple: instead of running cable all over the building, collapse the LAN topology and put it in a box. First, terminate all the devices on the network at the box using separate wires for each device. Then put the box in a convenient location, like a wiring closet. Equip the box with boards for local connections to Ethernet and token ring networks, and routers and bridges for connections to remote locations. Add some central processing units and management software to automate fault isolation, network reconfiguration and statistics gathering, and it is no longer just a box, but a highly intelligent device capable of supporting a range of distributed applications and transmission media efficiently and economically.

Depending on organizational needs, there are hubs for workgroups, departments and the enterprise. There are approximately 140 hub vendors offering innovative solutions that span these administrative domains. Among them is ADC Fibermux, which offers the Crossbow family of multiLAN intelligent hubs in support of Ethernet, token ring, AppleTalk and Apollo Domain networks over twisted-pair, coaxial or fiber-optic media. The company also offers the Extend and SnapLAN family of hubs for Ethernet and token ring networks.

LEVEL OF INTEGRATION

Fibermux is an HP OpenView Premier Partner and was the first hub vendor to integrate its network management system — LightWatch/Open — with HP OpenView. This integration was the first step toward making LightWatch compliant with the emerging Distributed Management Environment (DME) standard to which Hewlett-Packard has been a key contributor.

The UNIX-based LightWatch/Open network management application offers the highest level of integration with the HP OpenView platform. LightWatch/Open is a fully functional network management system capable of operating independently or as a software module within the HP OpenView Network Node Manager. LightWatch/Open adds value to OpenView by providing powerful element managers that offer detailed control of the Crossbow hubs within OpenView. Together, LightWatch/Open and HP OpenView enable an operator to manage a worldwide, multivendor SNMP network from a single network map, using the comprehensive feature set of LightWatch/Open when needed.

Fibermux supplies a disk of integration files that establishes connections between the two applications. When the integration files are installed, the operator starts HP OpenView, which automatically discovers all Crossbow hubs and displays them as icons. Additional Crossbow hubs are added to the LightWatch/Open topology window from within HP OpenView. This provides a link between the two applications. LightWatch/Open can be launched from HP OpenView by double-clicking on a Crossbow icon from within HP OpenView.

LIGHTWATCH/OPEN

LightWatch/Open features a graphical Motif user interface and offers complete remote control of the Crossbow hubs' unique features, such as any-port-to-any-port redundancy. It interoperates with OpenView to provide a single network map from which various LightWatch modules can be launched. This lowers installation and training costs and allows for a faster response to problems on the network.

LightWatch/Open is a graphics-based system that creates a map of the actual network topology. A map may provide access to one or more submaps, with each submap depicting ever increasing details of the network all the way down to individual hubs, modules and ports. The network manager can monitor, control and diagnose problems anywhere on the network using the mouse, pull-down menus and other graphical tools available with LightWatch.

MANAGEMENT FUNCTIONS

With LightWatch, the network manager can do the following:

- Manage a network of up to 100 hubs.

- Manage Ethernet and token ring networks from a single management station.

- Create and view a network map, showing the network topology including its hubs, computers, routers, bridges and other networking equipment.

- View graphic representations of the hubs and the current state of their indicators.

- Manage and control each module and each port in the networks, enabling, disabling, or toggling any port or I/O module. In the case of token ring I/O modules, the left, center or right termination also can be set.

- Collect, view and reset statistics for Ethernet hubs and for individual Ethernet ports. Token ring statistics also may be collected, viewed and reset. These statistics enable real-time network analysis to be performed to determine the network's traffic load, error rates and other critical data.

- Set alarms for hubs in Ethernet or token ring networks. LightWatch can be configured to alert the operator visually and audibly if any hub fails, loses power, or exceeds defined operating thresholds.

- Download firmware from the management station to Ethernet and token ring SmartLink control modules in the network.

- Configure LightWatch to split a token ring automatically if beaconing occurs, thus walling off the beaconing area from the rest of the ring. Automatic beacon isolation also can be performed.

- Configure any optical fiber or twisted-pair (shielded or unshielded) port as a redundant link for any other port, regardless of media type or port location. Automatic link switchover occurs with the loss of integrity. For Ethernet links, the error threshold level that triggers link switchover can be defined.

- Collect and view a log of all alarm messages generated in the network and search it for specific alarm events. Wildcard characters can be used in the search.

- Manage Ethernet bridge modules, control bridge ports, configure the operation of the Spanning Tree Protocol (STP) and filter tables, and view and reset bridge statistics.

CONTROL LOGIC

To use LightWatch, each hub must be equipped with at least one SmartLink module installed in one or more Crossbow hubs. One SmartLink module provides control for all ports in the hub that are configured for the same bus controller time slot. To completely monitor traffic and control ports, including port redundancy, one SmartLink module is required per Ethernet segment or token ring. With the Extend line of hubs, which do not have plug-in modules, LightWatch works in conjunction with resident SmartLink control logic.

An SNMP in-band or RS-232C serial connection from the management station to the Crossbow network gives LightWatch access to information from the SmartLink control modules and SmartLink control logic throughout the network. Either type of connection can be used to manage Ethernet networks, but only the SNMP in-band connection can be used to manage token ring networks.

OPERATING MODES

LightWatch supports two operating modes: supervisor mode and user mode. Each mode has an appropriate password that must be entered upon log in. Supervisors can monitor and modify the network, as well as add operators and assign passwords. Operators can monitor the network, or their assigned portion of the network, but cannot modify it.

LIGHTWATCH DATABASE

The LightWatch database stores the information an operator creates while managing the network, as well as the information the system automatically generates as it operates. The database is built on the Paradox engine from Borland International Inc., which facilitates data extraction and manipulation. With this database, the operator can analyze many alarm messages, for example, or generate a report listing all hub communication addresses.

The LightWatch database stores the following types of information:

- Redundancy definitions.

- Comments about hubs, cards and ports.

- Bridge structure data.

- Bridge filter data.

- Communication data for each hub, including hub name, IP address, Ethernet MAC address and status.

- Hub contents.

- Alarm definitions.

LightWatch stores alarm messages for the period of time specified by the network manager. After that, the alarm messages are purged from the database automatically.

NETWORK MAPS

LightWatch displays the logical map and physical map of the hub network. The logical map uses simple rectangular icons to represent logical hubs in the network (Figure 12-1). Through assigned ports, a logical hub connects various devices over the same segment and bus controller time slot. The physical map depicts each hub with a unique icon (Figure 12-2), even if its chassis is partitioned into multiple logical hubs.

When the physical network map is displayed, each chassis icon is labelled with an appropriate name. However, when the logical map is displayed the View menu allows a variety of hub labels to be displayed:

Hub name: displays the names of the logical hubs.

MAC Address: displays the media access control (MAC) addresses of the local hubs; specifically, the MAC addresses of the SmartLink modules or Extend hubs.

IP Address: displays the internet protocol (IP) addresses of the logical hubs; specifically, the IP addresses of the SmartLink modules or Extend hubs.

Firmware Version: displays the firmware versions of the logical hubs; specifically, the firmware version of the SmartLink modules or Extend hubs.

Chassis: displays the names of the physical chassis in which the logical hubs reside.

CONTROLLING HUBS

LightWatch controls hubs in the network by configuring redundancy, viewing hub or ring statistics, mapping MAC addresses to comments, listing bridges and downloading firmware. LightWatch also configures a token ring network and display its status, as well as retrieve and display a list of nearest active upstream neighbors (NAUN).

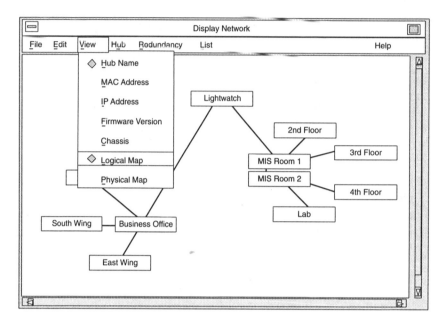

Source: ADC Fibermux

Figure 12-1: *Logical Map with View Menu Selected*

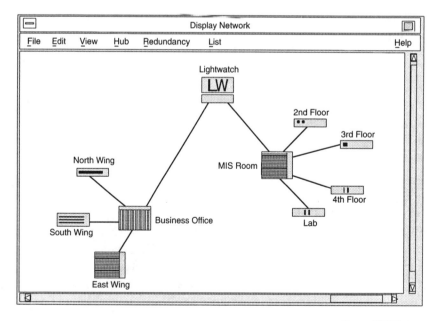

Source: ADC Fibermux

Figure 12-2: *Physical Map*

REDUNDANCY

The network manager can define redundancy: that is, redundant connections — for any logical hub. Redundant hub-to-hub connections and redundant hub-to-device connections can be defined. Each redundancy definition specifies a primary connection and a secondary connection. Switchover occurs automatically upon loss of link integrity. In addition, for Ethernet connections, the network manager can specify an error threshold that triggers link switchover.

Redundant connections are defined through the Redundancy window, which is displayed from the logical network map (Figure 12-3). When redundancy is defined in LightWatch, switchover between redundant links is controlled by the SmartLink module (or the SmartLink logic resident in Extend hubs). This means that automatic link switchover will occur even when LightWatch is not running.

With the logical network map displayed, the network manager selects two hubs for which redundant connections are defined.

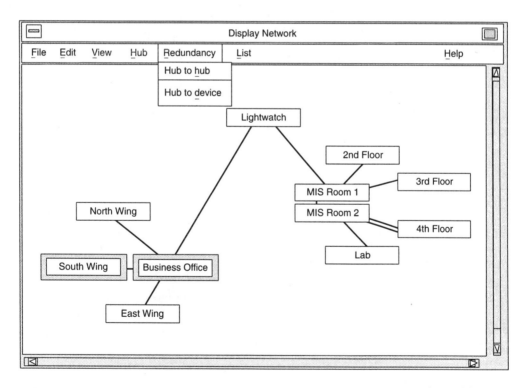

Source: ADC Fibermux

Figure 12-3: Redundancy Window

Hub-to-Hub Redundancy: Each hub-to-hub redundancy definition specifies two physical connections between the same two hubs. One connection
is the primary link between the two hubs and the other connection is the
secondary link. Only one of these connections can be active at one time.

For both Ethernet and token ring redundancy definitions, automatic
switchover to the secondary link occurs when primary link integrity is lost,
such as a physical disconnection. An error threshold, defined by the network manager, triggers link switchover for Ethernet redundancy
definitions — if they are controlled by an Ethernet SmartLink module.
Link switchover occurs as follows:

- If both logical hubs contain Ethernet SmartLinks and the redundancy
  definition is Ethernet, link switchover occurs upon a loss of link integrity or when the defined error threshold is exceeded.

- If both logical hubs contain Ethernet SmartLinks and the redundancy
  definition is token ring, or if both logical hubs contain token ring
  SmartLinks and the redundancy definition is either Ethernet or token
  ring, switchover occurs upon loss of link integrity only.

- If one logical hub contains a token ring SmartLink and the other
  logical hub contains an Ethernet SmartLink and the redundancy
  definition is Ethernet, switchover occurs upon loss of link integrity
  only from the token ring SmartLink side. From the Ethernet
  SmartLink side, switchover occurs upon loss of link integrity or an
  exceeded error threshold.

The primary and secondary connections in a redundancy definition are
redundant to each other; that is, if a secondary connection is active and
experiences a loss of link integrity or an exceeded error threshold, the
secondary connection is disabled and the primary connection is re-enabled.

Hub-to-Device Redundancy: Hub-to-device redundancy definitions
function in the same manner as hub-to-hub redundancy definitions, with
the exception that only one hub is involved.

Each hub-to-device redundancy definition lists two physical connections
between the same hub and the same device. For example, two ports on a
hub could be connected to two network interface cards (NICs) in the same
file server or to two media converters that connect to the same ThickNet
(10Base-5) or ThinNet (10Base-2) segment.

All redundancy definitions must be valid for the particular network
configuration, because LightWatch does not check that the connections in
a redundancy definition provide real physical redundancy.

A list of all redundancy definitions — both hub-to-hub and hub-to-device — is displayed in the List Redundant Links window (Figure 12-4).

STATISTICS

LightWatch displays performance statistics for a logical Ethernet hub or for a token ring. These statistics can be used to monitor network operation and diagnose problems.

Ethernet Hub Statistics: The Ethernet Hub Statistics Window (Figure 12-5) provides information about the data transmitted on a logical hub. As noted, a logical hub consists of one SmartLink module and any other modules set for the same segment and bus controller time slot. All statistics are updated at the interval specified — in seconds — as the Sampling Rate. The types of statistics displayed for an Ethernet hub are:

Peak Traffic: the highest percent of traffic on the segment since the time displayed in the Start Time box.

Average Traffic: the average percent of traffic on the segment since the time displayed in the Start Time box.

Current Traffic: the current percent of traffic on the segment at the time of the last sample.

The graph at the bottom of the window displays the current flow of activity on the network, as measured by the type of statistics selected in the transmission data box. When the sample rate is set at 10 seconds, the graph can display up to 24 hours of statistics.

Total Packets Received: the total number of valid packets received on the segment since the time displayed in the Start Time box. This number can be used to compare the values listed for CRC errors, frame alignment errors, and missed packets to evaluate the seriousness of these conditions. If the number of errors is not unusually high compared to the total packet count, there may not be any serious problems with the network. Each manager must determine what values suggest serious problems on their network.

Average Bytes/Packet: the average packet size in bytes received on the segment since the time displayed in the Start Time box.

CRC Errors: the number of cyclic redundancy check errors on the segment. CRC is the last 32 bits of information contained in a packet/frame[1] and is

---

[1] A packet/frame transmitted on the network contains up to 1526 bytes of information and consists of seven fields: preamble, start frame delimiter (SFD), destination address (DA), source address (SA), length, data, and frame check sequence (FCS). The FCS is the CRC value — a four-octet (32-bit) value.

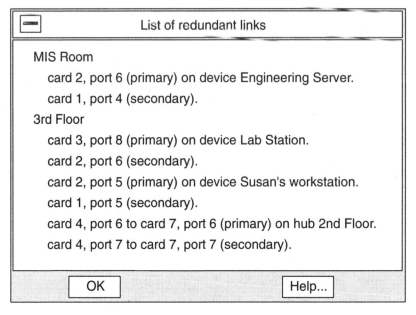

Source: ADC Fibermux

Figure 12-4: *List Redundant Links Window*

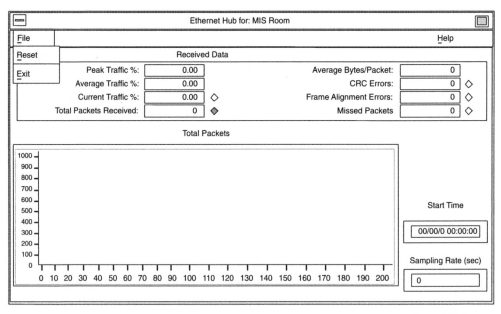

Source: ADC Fibermux

Figure 12-5: *Ethernet Hub Statistics Window*

used for detecting transmission errors. When the CRC value of an incoming frame is not identical to the CRC value of an outgoing frame, a bit flop is said to occur, which generates a CRC error. This is usually caused by faulty cable, as when an impedance mismatch occurs, causing a reflection on the cable, which in turn causes the bit flop.

Frame Alignment Errors: the number of frame alignment errors on the segment. When a frame is not an integral number of octets in length, a frame alignment error is detected. This number represents data that was destroyed. This type of error usually is caused by a frame collision on the network, although a loose or noisy cable also can be the cause. To determine if there are serious problems, a network manager should establish an acceptable ratio of frame alignment errors to total packets received. When the ratio is exceeded, the cause should be investigated.

Missed Packets: the number of packets on the segment for which the SmartLink control module was unable to provide statistics. This occurs when the SmartLink's buffer fills during heavy network traffic. If the missed packet count is high compared to total packets received, the network traffic may be too high or the SmartLink may be engaged in too many tasks, such as providing statistics for too many ports. A high missed-packet count also would indicate that the Peak Traffic figure is not accurate.

Token Ring Statistics: For token rings, statistics for both hard and soft errors are displayed (Figure 12-6), as well as general performance statistics.

Token Ring Hard Error Statistics include:

Ring Purges: indicates the number of ring purges. Ring purges are initiated by the active monitor to normalize the ring and create a new token on the ring. The active monitor initiates a ring purge when it is first selected as the active monitor[2]. It also initiates a ring purge when a token error occurs.

Loss of Signal: indicates the number of times that a total loss of input signal is reported.

---

[2]The active monitor is selected by contention between the nodes. The node serving as the active monitor ensures normal token operation on the ring by providing master clocking, starting the ring poll process, executing the ring purge process, and periodically checking for the presence of a good token, among other tasks.

Beacons: indicates the number of times temporary or permanent beaconing has occurred on the ring.

Token Ring Soft Error Statistics include:

Line Errors: indicates the number of line errors reported by all nodes on the ring. A line error occurs when a node receives a corrupted frame or token. Line errors only should occur as nodes join and leave the ring, because the ring is broken briefly at these times. Line errors that occur at other times or occur continuously indicate a problem with the ring. Bad cable connections or excessively long cables can cause line errors.

Burst Errors: indicates the number of burst errors reported by all nodes on the ring. A burst error occurs when a node experiences an absence of signal transitions for four or five half-bit times. Like line errors, burst errors should only occur as nodes join and leave the ring. Burst errors that occur at other times or occur continuously indicate a problem with the ring.

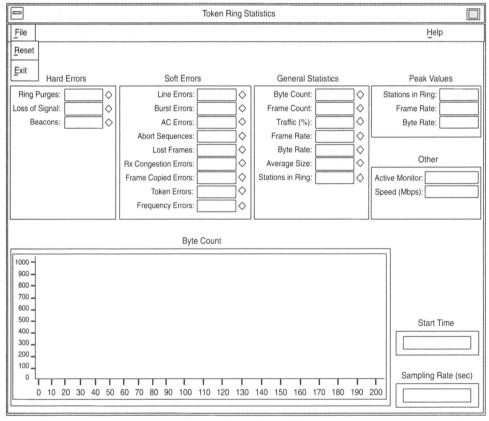

Source: ADC Fibermux

Figure 12-6: Token Ring Statistics Window

Bad cable connections or excessively long cables can cause burst errors.

AC Errors: indicates the number of AC errors reported by all nodes on the ring. An AC error occurs when an upstream node is unable to indicate to its downstream neighboring node that it received a frame. This is detected during the neighbor notification process. AC errors are uncommon and should not normally occur, except infrequently when a node joins or leaves the ring. AC errors that occur at other times or occur frequently indicate a problem.

Abort Sequences: indicates the number of abort sequences transmitted by all nodes on the ring. When a node transmits an abort sequence it interrupts a frame during transmission because a brief or permanent internal error occurred on the node, or because the end of the token that the node transformed into a frame was invalid. Transmission of an abort sequence is uncommon and should not normally occur, except perhaps when a node joins or leaves the ring. Abort sequences transmitted at other times or transmitted frequently indicate a problem. The cause of this error usually can be isolated to the reporting node, its NAUN, or the cabling, connectors, or equipment between them.

Lost Frames: indicates the number of lost frames reported by all nodes on the ring. A lost frame occurs when a node transmits a frame but does not receive it in return, indicating that the frame was lost somewhere along the ring. Lost frames only should occur as nodes join and leave the ring. Lost frames that occur at other times or occur continuously indicate a problem with the ring or with a node on the ring. Bad cable connections, excessively long cables, or faulty equipment connected between nodes can cause lost frames. This is a non-isolating error, the cause of which, although detected and reported by an individual node, can be isolated only to the ring on which it occurred.

Rx Congestion Errors: indicates the number of receive data congestion errors reported by all nodes on the ring. A receive data congestion error occurs when a node recognizes that it has received a frame, but is unable to copy the frame into memory because its adapter memory is already full. Although receive data congestion errors would appear to be isolating errors, they can be caused by a streaming node on the ring (i.e., continuously transmitting frames in quick succession), although this is not very common.

Receive data congestion errors occasionally may occur when a workstation on the ring is rebooted, because the network adapter resets itself shortly after a workstation starts rebooting and so cannot process received frames during its brief reset process. More frequently, congestion errors are caused by a workstation (typically a file server) simply being unable to process the data it receives fast enough. If this is the case, a higher performance workstation or network adapter may be required.

However, when a file server experiences congestion errors because it cannot process fast enough, the network software detects that the server is not receiving all frames transmitted to it and retransmits the frames. This slows down the workstations and causes even more network traffic. In extreme cases, workstations using the server may time-out, assume the server is no longer functioning, and issue a message or prompt to this effect.

Frame Copied Errors: indicates the number of frame copied errors reported by all nodes on the ring. A frame copied error occurs when a node receives a frame that is addressed to it, but notices that another node on the ring also received the same frame. Frame copied errors occur if two nodes on the ring have the same node address, or they can be caused by a line hit (wire fault).

Token Errors: indicates the number of token errors reported by all nodes on the ring. A token error is reported when either of the following occurs:

- A node detects that a token has been lost, as can happen when nodes join and leave the ring, breaking it briefly.

- A node detects that a frame is continuously circulating around the ring, as happens when a node that transmits a frame does not subsequently strip the frame from the ring, and thus does not release the token.

These events can only be detected by the active monitor, so any node that reports token errors should be the current active monitor. The active monitor initiates a ring purge when a token error is reported. Token errors should only occur as nodes join and leave the ring. Token errors that occur at other times or occur continuously indicate a problem with the ring or with a node. Bad cable connections or excessively long cables can cause token errors.

Frequency Errors: indicates the number of frequency errors reported by all nodes on the ring. A frequency error occurs when a node compares its internal clock to the incoming master clock provided by the active monitors and finds that the two clocks are not synchronized within the permitted tolerance. When a node reports a frequent error it also initiates the monitor contention process to select a new active monitor, because the clock problem could reside in the current active monitor. Frequent errors of this type are uncommon and should not occur. If they do occur, there is probably a problem with either the node reporting the errors or with the active monitor.

Token Ring General Statistics include:

Byte Count: indicates the cumulative number of bytes on the ring since the displayed Start Time.

Frame Count: indicates the cumulative number of frames on the ring since the displayed Start Time.

Traffic (%): indicates percent of traffic currently circulating on the ring.

Frame Rate: indicates the current number of frames-per-second circulating on the ring.

Byte Rate: indicates the current number of bytes-per-second circulating on the ring.

Average Size: indicates the current average frame size (in bytes) currently on the ring.

Stations in Ring: indicates the number of active stations currently on the ring.

Token Ring Peak Values include:

Stations in Ring: indicates the highest total number of active stations on the ring since the displayed Start Time.

Frame Rate: indicates the highest number of frames-per-second circulating on the ring since the displayed Start Time.

Byte Rate: indicates the highest number of bytes-per-second circulating on the ring since the displayed Start Time.

Two other token ring values are also displayed:

Active Monitor: indicates the MAC address of the current active monitor.

Speed (Mbps): indicates the current speed of the network, either 4 Mbps or 16 Mbps.

MAPPING MAC ADDRESSES TO COMMENTS
The MAC Address Mapping window (Figure 12-7), enables the operator to map individual network MAC addresses to comments, such as usernames or equipment locations. When a MAC address is mapped to a comment, the comment displays along with the address in the Ethernet Port Statistics window or in the Token Ring NAUN List window.

LISTING BRIDGES
The Bridge List window (Figure 12-8), enables the operator to display a list of the Ethernet Bridge modules in the network. It also enables the

operator to delete configuration information for a bridge that has been removed from the network. Listings include bridge address, IP address, hub address and card ID.

DOWNLOADING FIRMWARE

The operator can download Ethernet SmartLink firmware and token ring SmartLink firmware from the management workstation running LightWatch to any SmartLink module in the network. To download firmware, all MAC addresses and all IP addresses in the various types of networks must be unique. This means that a SmartLink module cannot be part of two different networks. In addition, any gateway that may exist between the management workstation and the Crossbow hub network must broadcast the BootP[3] request packets sent by the SmartLink as well as receive BootP's reply packets.

CONFIGURING A TOKEN RING

Through the Token Ring Status window (Figure 12-9), the operator can configure a token ring network and display its status.

The following fields are available to facilitate token ring configuration:

Max Stations in Ring: a read-only field that indicates the number of stations on the ring.

Split Ring on Beacon: clicking on this field enables the token ring SmartLink in the selected logical hub to split the ring when beaconing occurs. A check mark means the ring will be split.

Auto Beacon Isolation: clicking on this field enables the token ring SmartLink in the selected logical hub to automatically isolate a beacon condition. A check mark means automatic beacon isolation will occur, as long as the Split Ring on Beacon feature is also enabled.

The following buttons provide indications of token ring status:

Rings Are (Joined, Isolated, or Locked Isolated): provide indications of the current status of the ring as joined (that is, the ring is whole) or isolated (that is, a beaconing area of the ring is split off). At this writing, locked isolated rings are not supported. Clicking on the Joined or Isolated button forces the ring into the joined or isolated state.

Beacon Isolation (Active or Inactive): when the Active button is enabled, this indicates that the auto beacon isolation feature is actively isolating a

---

[3]BootP (Boot Protocol) is an industry-standard download protocol that is used to load new versions of software or firmware from a central management station to a remote network device.

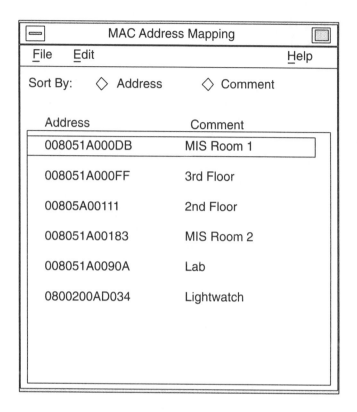

Source: ADC Fibermux

Figure 12-7: *MAC Address Mapping Window*

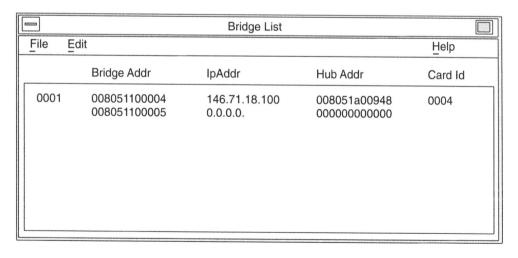

Source: ADC Fibermux

Figure 12-8: *Bridge List Window*

beacon condition. When the auto beacon isolation feature is active, the operator can click the Inactive button to disable it.

NAUN LISTS

The operator can retrieve and display a list of NAUNs (nearest active upstream neighbors) from a token ring SmartLink module. The NAUN list includes all nodes that are currently on the ring.

The NAUN List window (Figure 12-10) includes buttons that allow the operator to sort information by address, comment or NAUN order. Clicking on the Address button provides the MAC addresses of the nodes on the ring. Clicking on the Comments button provides comments associated with each node. Clicking on the NAUN Order button provides the MAC address of each node's nearest active upstream neighbor.

CONTROLLING CARDS AND PORTS

The network manager can open a Hub Detail window that displays a graphic representation of the cards, ports and power supplies in a selected physical chassis or in a selected logical hub. With a Hub Detail window open, a variety of card and port control tasks can be performed and port statistics viewed.

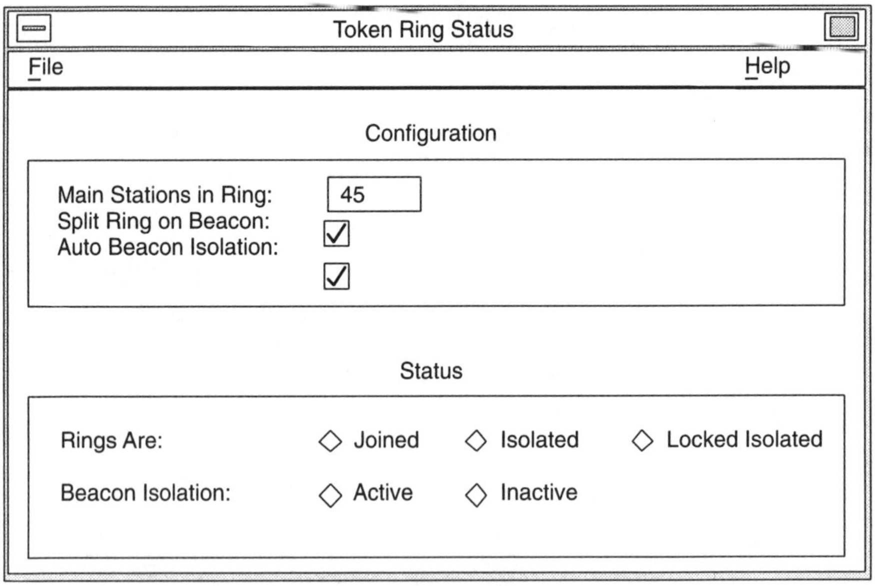

Source: ADC Fibermux

Figure 12-9: Token Ring Status Window

CARD INFORMATION

The Card Info window displays information about a selected card and its ports, or about the ports on an Extend hub. The operator can enable and disable ports from the Card Info window. Different versions of the Card Info window are displayed for Ethernet modules token ring I/O modules, token ring SmartLink modules and Extend hubs.

The Card Info window for Ethernet modules (Figure 12-11), for example, displays the following information:

Port #: indicates the number of the port. The scroll bar is used to display ports not shown.

Ena/Dis: indicates the port's enable/disable status. Clicking on the button enables or disables the port. A check mark indicates the port is enabled.

Integrity: indicates the link's integrity (a read-only field). A check mark indicates the link has integrity; that is, the link is complete and functional, and both ends could potentially transmit data.

Partition: indicates the port's partition status (a read-only file). A check mark indicates the port is partitioned; that is, the port has been disabled because it received 31 consecutive colliding packets or one colliding packet longer than 1024 bits. A partitioned port is automatically re-enabled upon receipt of the next non-colliding packet.

Comments: for each port, the operator can enter a descriptive comment containing a maximum of 49 characters. When an alarm event occurs for a port, the comment for that port is appended to the description of the alarm in the Alarm Log.

PORT STATISTICS

The Ethernet Port Statistics window[4] shows current traffic statistics on a selected port (Figure 12-12). The same statistics displayed in the Ethernet Hub Statistics window are applicable for the Ethernet Port Statistics window except, of course, they apply to the port level. While Missed Packets is not applicable to the port level, there are several additional statistics that are accessible from the Ethernet Port Statistics window:

Multicast Packets: the number of multicast packets received by the selected port. These are packets addressed to a group of specified nodes, as opposed to broadcast packets, which are addressed to all network nodes. Network bridge spanning tree protocol frames are an example of multicast packets.

---

[4]Port statistics are available only through SNMP communications, a direct in-band connection to the Ethernet. These statistics are not available for token ring ports.

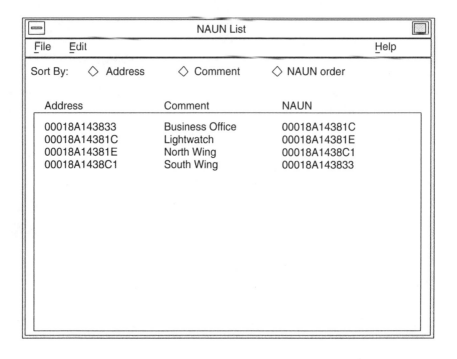

Source: ADC Fibermux

Figure 12-10: NAUN List Window

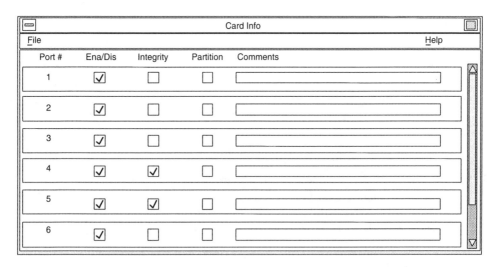

Source: ADC Fibermux

Figure 12-11: Card Info Window (for Ethernet Modules)

Broadcast Packets: the number of packets addressed to all network nodes, including the selected port. Broadcast packets usually result from the TCP/IP suite of protocols, such as ARP, RARP and RIP, which request information from every node on the network. The number of these packets will increase rapidly if a broadcast storm occurs. This is an unusually high number of broadcast packets on the network, which is usually caused by bridges that create a loop of broadcast requests across subnetworks.

Runt Packets: the number of runt packets received at the selected port. This is an Ethernet packet of less than 64 bytes, which is usually caused by a collision on the network.

Giant Packets: the number of oversized packets received at the selected port. This is an Ethernet packet that exceeds the maximum 1518 bytes, which can be caused by a node that is jabbering or streaming.

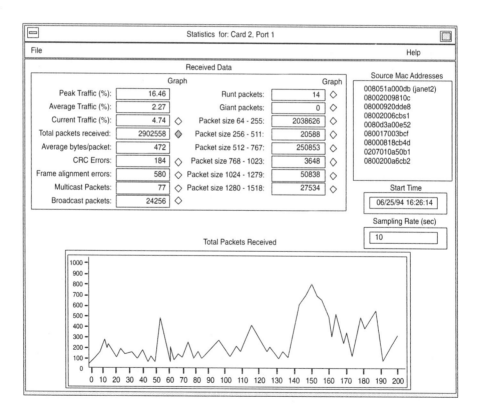

Source: ADC Fibermux

Figure 12-12: Ethernet Port Statistics Window

Packet Size: the number of packets, listed according to size, that were received at the selected port. This breakdown of packet sizes allows the network manager to fine-tune network performance by determining if the network traffic is dominated by packets of a particular size.

Source MAC Addresses: the address of the node that sent the last packet received at the selected port. The MAC address is generated by the network interface card within the node that sent the last packet. As with the Ethernet Hub Statistics window, the graph at the bottom of the Ethernet Port Statistics window displays the Current Traffic statistic as a percentage of packets received.

SETTING TOKEN RING CARDS
Through the Token menu, the operator can set the left, center or right termination of token ring cards. The current termination of each token ring card is displayed at the bottom of the Hub Detail window, as shown in Figure 12-13. Token ring cards must form an unbroken ring within the hub. Each card can be set as follows:

Left Terminated: sets all highlighted token ring cards for left termination within the token ring. This is equivalent to setting the card's left/ctr/right front panel switch to **left**.

Center Terminated: sets all highlighted token ring cards for center termination within the token ring. This is equivalent to setting the card's left/ctr/right front panel switch to **ctr**.

Right Terminated: sets all highlighted token ring cards for right termination within the token ring. This is equivalent to setting the card's left/ctr/right front panel switch to **right**.

THRESHOLD ALARMS
The Alarms window allows the network manager to set alarms for a selected logical hub (Figure 12-14). The types of network failures that generate alarms can be specified as well as the threshold values for various operating conditions. When any of these values is exceeded, an alarm is generated. When an alarm event occurs, the hub where it took place changes color on the LightWatch map: red, if the alarm event was set to major; yellow, if the alarm event was set to minor. In addition, an audible alarm may be set when an alarm event is generated.

For Ethernet hubs, the Alarms window is used to set threshold alarms for peak traffic percent, average traffic percent, average bytes/packets, CRC errors, frame alignment errors, missed packets and broadcast packets.

For token rings, threshold alarms can be set for line errors, burst errors, AC errors, abort sequences, lost frames, Rx (receive) congestion errors, frame copies errors, token errors, frequency errors, ring purges, loss of signal, stations in ring, average traffic and peak frames.

For both Ethernet and token ring, the following failure alarms can be set:

Primary Communication: detects a communications failure between LightWatch and the selected logical hub. A communications failure can occur if the network becomes overloaded or if the network connection to LightWatch is severed.

Power Fail: detects an interruption in power to the selected logical hub.

Card: detects the failure, removal or insertion of a card in the selected logical hub.

Port (Integrity): detects a failure of port integrity in the selected logical hub; that is, a link connected to the hub is no longer functional. One or both ends of the link have lost the potential for transmitting data.

Port (Partition): detects the partitioning of a port in the selected logical hub; that is, a port has been disabled because it received 31 consecutive colliding packets or one colliding packet longer than 1024 bits. A partitioned port is automatically re-enabled upon receipt of the next non-colliding packet.

Primary: detects the failure of a primary connection in a redundancy definition for the selected logical hub.

Secondary: detects the failure of a secondary connection in a redundancy definition for the selected logical hub.

Beaconing: detects temporary or permanent beaconing on a token ring. The Alarm Log message indicates the card that has detected the beaconing.

No Token: detects the absence of a token on the ring.

Temperature: detects overheating of the physical chassis that houses the selected logical hub.

Fan: detects the operational failure of a fan in the physical chassis that houses the selected logical hub.

Power Supply: detects a power supply failure in the physical chassis that houses the selected logical hub if two redundant power supplies are in use. If only one power supply is in use, this parameter is set to none.

LightWatch records all alarm events generated throughout the network, which are displayed in the Alarm Log window. Alarms can be displayed for a hub, a card, and a port. Current alarm log messages can be displayed

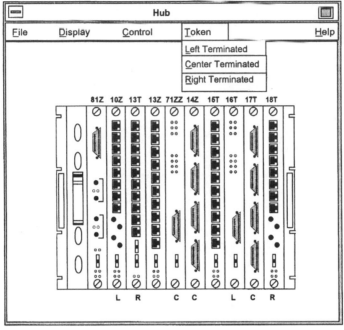

Source: ADC Fibermux

Figure 12-13: *Hub Detail Window (showing token ring modules)*

Threshold Alarms			Failure Alarms	
Peak Traffic (%):	50	Minor - Bell	Primary Communication:	Major - Bell
Average Traffic (%):	30	Minor - Bell	Power Fail:	Major - Bell
CRC Errors:	1000	Minor	Card:	Minor
Average bytes/packet:	0	None	Port (integrity):	None
Frame alignment :	1000	Minor	Partition:	None
Missed Packet:	500	Minor	Primary:	None
Broadcast packet:	500	Minor	Secondary:	None
			Beaconing:	Minor
			No Token:	Minor
			Temperature:	Major
			Fan:	Major
			Power Supply:	Major

Alarm Settings — File — Help

Source: ADC Fibermux

Figure 12-14: *Ethernet Alarm Settings Window*

as well as the alarm log's history. Hewlett-Packard has licensed this alarm log technology from Fibermux and uses it in HP OpenView for Windows.

CONTROLLING ETHERNET BRIDGES

With LightWatch, the following functions can be performed on Ethernet bridge modules: define bridge port addresses and the segments that the ports bridge, reset the bridge, configure the operation of the IEEE 802.1d spanning tree protocol and view spanning tree statistics, configure the operation of the bridge's filter and range filter tables, view bridge port statistics and set alarms.

Setting up a bridge module for management by LightWatch consists of assigning it addresses: an Ethernet address (MAC address)[5] and an Internet Protocol (IP) address for the SNMP agent. A bridge name also can be defined. For each of the two bridge ports, one of four segments is assigned.

For each port, threshold alarms can be set: CRC errors, received overflow (also known as buffer overflow) and collisions. The bridge module also has two failure alarms: primary communications, indicating that communication between the bridge and LightWatch has failed; and power fail, indicating that the bridge was removed from the hub.

Statistics for each port can be displayed in terms of packets received, packets forwarded, packets filtered, packets multicast/broadcast, runt packets, transmit/receive (Tx/Rx) overflows, packets transmitted, average packet size received, average packet size forwarded, average packet size filtered, CRC errors and collisions.

When resetting the bridge, the filter table and spanning tree parameters go back to their default values, statistics counters reset to zero and begin to accumulate anew, and port assignments are reset to the defaults defined by the switch on the module's circuit board.

When the STP Bridge Parameters window is opened, SNMP's get command is performed automatically, which retrieves current information from the bridge for display. The following parameters are displayed and may be edited by the network manager.

Bridge Identifier: a value that uniquely identifies the bridge. This value is used to select one of several redundant bridges as the LAN's active bridge. Bridge identifiers are compared, and the bridge with the lowest value is selected as the designated (active) bridge.

---

[5]This address is printed on the bridge's front panel. Installed at the factory, IEEE addresses are guaranteed to be unique in the world.

Bridge Priority: values between 0 and 65536 may be selected. Lower values give the bridge higher priority. One of several redundant bridges can be selected as the LAN's designated (active) bridge by lowering its priority value. Setting bridge priority is required to establish the spanning tree protocol (STP) root bridge.

Maximum BPDU Age: the maximum amount of time (between 6 and 40 seconds) that can occur between reception of configuration bridge protocol data units (BPDUs) by a bridge that is not the root bridge. If a BPDU is not received within this time, data defining the root bridge times out and the bridge attempts to reconfigure the active topology. By decreasing the value (in seconds), the bridge can be made more sensitive to root bridge failures.

Bridge Forward Delay: specifies the period of time (between 4 and 30 seconds) that a bridge port remains in the listening and learning states before moving to the forwarding state. Decreasing the value increases the bridge's response to topology changes or bridge failures. However, values that are too low may cause temporary loops.

Bridge Hello Time: specifies the period of time (between 1 and 10 seconds) between generation of configuration BPDUs by the root bridge. Increasing this value lessens the impact of spanning tree operation on bridge performance.

In addition, the following read-only STP bridge parameter fields are displayed:

Forward Delay: indicates the Bridge Forward Delay value of the root bridge and the currrently-used forward delay for the queried bridge.

Hello Time: indicates the Bridge Hello Time value of the root bridge and the currently-used hello time for the queried bridge.

Designated Root: is the Bridge Identifier value of the network's root bridge.

Root Cost: is the sum of the Port Path Cost values for each port on the path between this bridge and the root bridge. If this bridge is the root bridge, the Root Cost is zero.

Root Por: is the number of the port through which the root bridge can be reached. If this bridge is the root bridge, the Root Port is zero.

Maximum BPDU Age: is the value currently being used as the maximum BPDU age throughout the network.

Root Bridge: a check mark indicates the bridge is the root bridge for the network, as calculated by Spanning Tree.

Designated Bridge: a check mark indicates the bridge is a designated bridge. A designated bridge actively forwards data on the LAN.

SNMP's SET command is used to send the values currently displayed in the STP Bridge Parameters window to the bridge.

SPANNING TREE STATISTICS

For each port on a bridge, statistics for the spanning tree protocol are displayed in the STP Statistics window. When the window is opened, the get command is automatically performed so that the following current values can be displayed: port enables/disables, configuration BPDUs received and transmitted, topology change BPDUs transmitted, topology changes noticed and configuration timeouts.

FILTER TABLE PARAMETERS

Current filter table parameters for each bridge can be retrieved from the bridge, changed, and then sent back to the bridge through SNMP. The following filter table parameters can be defined by the network manager:

Maximum Age: the number of seconds before a dynamic unreferenced filter table entry is removed from the table.

Maximum Remove: the number of entries that are automatically removed when the filter table reaches its capacity.

Maximum Static Entries: the maximum number of static entries that can be entered into the filter table.

Forward Multicast/Broadcast: enables or disables the forwarding of multicast and broadcast packets.

Secure Mode: enables or disables secure mode. When in secure mode, the bridge forwards only those packets for which static entries exist in the filter table. Also, the bridge does not learn addresses from packets, nor enter them into the filter table dynamically.

RANGE FILTER TABLE

For each bridge, a Range Filter Table (Figure 12-15) defines the disposition of ranges of packets, and is usually used to filter groups of devices (using the manufacturer's ID in the first part of the address). For the fields in both the lower and upper boundaries of the range, the following information is provided:

Number: number of the entry in the range filter table.

U/L Boundary: indicates whether the entry is in the upper boundary of the range (U) or lower boundary of the range (L).

Packet Type: the type of packet, written as a hexadecimal value.

Source Address: the address of the packet's source or point of origin.

Destination Address: the address to which the packet is being sent.

The disposition of packets within the range is also given; that is, what the bridge will do with them. For the Range Filter Table entries shown in Figure 12-15, the disposition can be as follows:

Forw1: forward to port 1, if received on port 2.

Forw2: forward to port 2, if received on port 1.

Flood: forward to all ports.

Discard: discard all packets.

For both the filter table and range filter table, entries can be added, deleted, and changed. In addition, a specific entry can be searched for by complete or partial Ethernet address.

THIS CHAPTER PRESENTED AN OVERVIEW OF GENERAL LIGHTWATCH/OPEN management capabilities. Although Fibermux was chosen for this in-depth profile, there are other hub vendors that also offer a comparable level of integration with OpenView.

SynOptics Communications[6], for example, holds the largest market share for intelligent wiring hubs. Like Fibermux, SynOptics is an HP OpenView

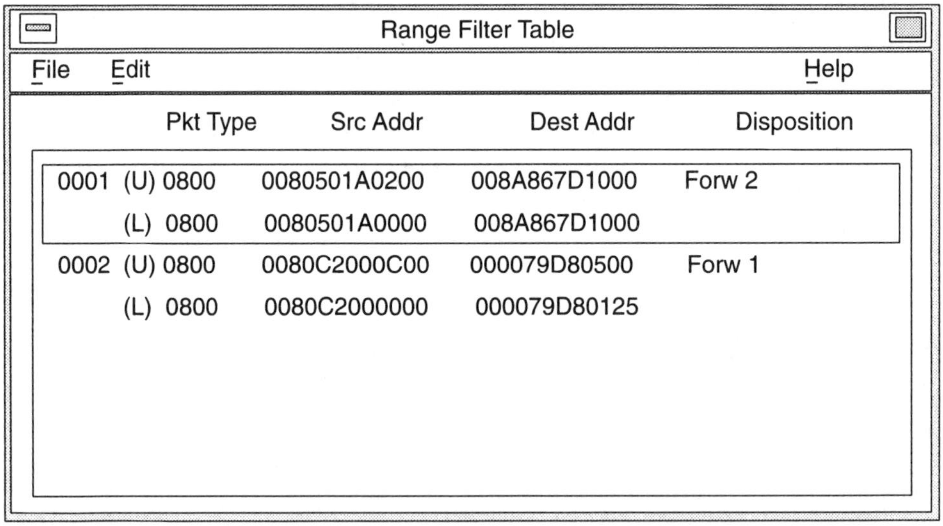

Range Filter Table			
File Edit			Help
Pkt Type	Src Addr	Dest Addr	Disposition
0001 (U) 0800	0080501A0200	008A867D1000	Forw 2
(L) 0800	0080501A0000	008A867D1000	
0002 (U) 0800	0080C2000C00	000079D80500	Forw 1
(L) 0800	0080C2000000	000079D80125	

Source: ADC Fibermux

Figure 12-15: Range Filter Table for an Ethernet Bridge

Premier Partner. Its Optivity network management system offers the highest degree of integration with OpenView and has passed OpenView Solution Certification testing by Hewlett-Packard. Optivity manages all the key building blocks of the network fabric — hubs, routers, bridges and end-systems — as one cohesive system. Combined with OpenView Network Node Manager, Optivity provides comprehensive end-to-end management capabilities for enterprise networks.

Ungermann-Bass, Inc. is another HP OpenView Premier Partner. The company's NetDirector for UNIX is a multitasking network management platform that is used to monitor, configure, inventory and control Ungermann-Bass networks. NetDirector's multitasking capabilities permit multiple network views and management applications to be accessed in a different window, allowing server and monitoring activities to continue, while necessary control actions can be taken on specific network segments or attached devices.

Other hub vendors are original equipment manufacturers (OEMs) that resell HP OpenView products bundled with their management applications. Among the most noteworthy of these are Cabletron Systems, which offers Spectrum; Chipcom, which offers the ONdemand Network Control System; and Optical Data Systems, Inc., which offers LanVision.

---

[6] In 1994, SynOptics and Wellfleet Communications merged to form Bay Networks. The two companies have developed a unified network architecture called BaySIS. The company's enterprise management view will allow rapid views across region, campus and office environments and across a wide range of resources, including: hubs, routers, switches, LANs, WANs and paths. Network managers will be able to troubleshoot and control these environments by simply dragging and dropping icons into *monitor, alarm, configure, map, trend*, or *analyze* buttons. This capability will extend to hubs and routers from all leading vendors, from a single network operations center. Automated and integrated with other Optivity applications, this new management capability complements management platforms from HP, IBM and Sun.

The Future of OpenView

DESPITE ITS SUCCESS, OPENVIEW HAS PLENTY OF ROOM FOR IMPROVEMENT. Users always are looking for enhancements that will help them manage ever larger networks in a more integrated and distributed manner. After all, networks continue to grow and expand because corporate operations increasingly are becoming decentralized. Not only is LAN growth expected to continue at a brisk pace for the rest of this decade, but LAN interconnection over WANs is becoming increasingly necessary to tie together the proliferating number of branch sites, mobile workers and telecommuters. Managing all of this requires a distributed, highly scalable network management platform.

The HP OpenView Users Forum[1] meets annually to discuss these and other issues, providing Hewlett-Packard with valuable insight into customer needs. At the 1994 meeting of the Forum, OpenView users proposed the following ways to improve the OpenView platform:

- Add distributed management capabilities to let administrators centrally manage remote sites.

- Improve the ability to manage large networks.

- Improve the correlation of trouble-ticketing among management applications.

- Provide the ability to both read and write to distributed management applications.

- Provide better integration between LAN-based management applications and UNIX-based applications, such as those used to manage routers and hubs.

---

[1]OpenView Forum is a non-profit corporation formed by Duke Power, GTE FSD, Martin Marietta Corp., and US West to represent the interests of OpenView users and application developers worldwide. The Forum is an independent corporation and is not affiliated with Hewlett-Packard Co.

- Provide distributed interfaces that allow management applications to share information.

Other improvements OpenView users want to see is a single interface, multiple-map support, and better scalability in the software. Currently, maps are available for multiple LANs, but they do not stay in synch with each other to reflect changes across networks. Although network operators can view these maps in a variety of applications, they cannot always make changes from the OpenView console.

OPENVIEW 4.0

According to HP, many of these requirements will be addressed in OpenView 4.0, which is planned for release in 1996.

HP plans to evolve OpenView from a centralized management platform dependent on a single database to a fully distributed, highly scalable platform capable of storing and accessing management information anywhere on an enterprise network. It will provide the foundation for millions of objects to be managed by hundreds of operators and meld data from multiple databases in a virtual repository.

Key to OpenView's transition will be enhancements in three areas: the user interface, data storage and data collection.

THE USER INTERFACE

HP will give network operators the ability to view an OpenView graphical map from any UNIX, Windows or Windows NT workstation. Management applications will be launchable from any of these workstations, whether the application resides locally or remotely, with management data being shared by multiple OpenView operators. Currently, OpenView operators only can launch applications resident on their own consoles.

A distributed user interface will help users establish management domains whereby an enterprise network is managed as a collection of subnetworks. Specific management functions can then be delegated to specific domains by the network administrator.

DATA STORAGE

For data storage, HP's plans hinge on defining a way to integrate multiple databases containing different information into a single logical repository (Figure 13-1). The SQL-based repository is intended to let users store management data wherever they want, while having that data immediately accessible from any OpenView console in the network. With a common repository, users can store different types of information — such as event, topology or map — in different databases or group the databases by domain, while maintaining uniform access from every OpenView console.

The data repository also will house inventory, topology, event, trend and historical attribute information on TCP/IP, SNA, NetWare and other network environments, and on users, systems and software on the enterprise network. In addition to Ingres, which is currently supported, the next version of OpenView will support the Oracle, Sybase and Informix databases. Eventually, a more advanced version of OpenView will support any database and incorporate object-oriented technology, including an object request broker based on OSF's Common Object Request Broker Architecture (CORBA). OpenView also will work with Microsoft's Object Linking and Embedding (OLE) objects. Ultimately, users and vendors will be able to write applications to the repository itself, rather than to specific databases. This paves the way for powerful new mapping, report generation, event correlation and other features.

HP has even submitted the draft schema for its common repository to the Management Integration Consortium (MIC), a group of management

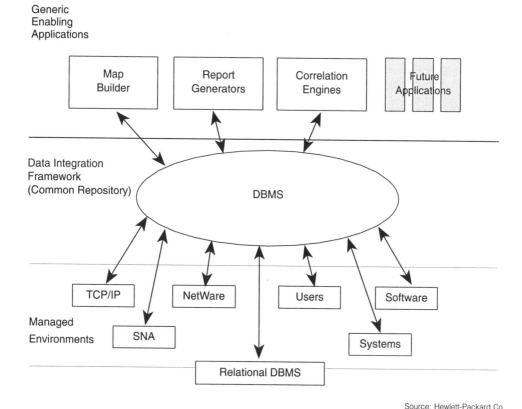

Source: Hewlett-Packard Co.

Figure 13-1: HP's Planned Common Repository

applications vendors, management platform providers and end-users defining standards for tighter integration between management applications and platforms, as well as easier applications portability. The group's mission is to support an open process for the development of management integration services and to ensure that standards are made available to users and vendors.

DATA COLLECTION

Data collection functions also will be distributed, enabling management data to be collected locally. Data collectors will perform event threshold and baseline security checking, and automatically compile data based on those examinations. With HP's eventual support of SNMP version 2 (SNMP2) in OpenView, data collectors will be able to take advantage of the manager-to-manager management information base (MIB), which allows management consoles to exchange information.

These distributed functions will go a long way toward making OpenView more scalable and improve its performance in large networks.

HP plans to make OpenView modular enough to scale from a single work-group console to several regional site managers and then up to multiple enterprise managers controlling heterogeneous environments. OpenView consoles at each level will be able to share management information and engage in cooperative, peer-to-peer management of the enterprise.

This capability will let users start with OpenView at the work group or enterprise level and then scale up or down as their nets grow and change, while maintaining consistency and ease of use throughout the management process.

NETWORKING STRATEGY

Throughout the years, HP's attention has shifted beyond providing mere connectivity solutions to industry standards and multivendor networking. HP's current networking framework encompasses several layers: networking infrastructure, applications infrastructure, network and systems management (OpenView), user-specific applications, and networking support and professional services. HP has closely aligned its networking strategy with its overall computing strategy, using integrated management as a differentiator to sell networked systems solutions.

HP's networking strategy and management platform development efforts are linked together through its HP Technology Triad, as shown in Figure 13-2. The triad addresses the needs of the emerging high-bandwidth, multimedia environment; specifically: the high-performance workgroup, with connectivity provided by 100VG-AnyLAN; remote client-server mass storage and cluster computing, supported by Fibre Channel; and the WAN/LAN backbone, with Asynchronous Transfer Mode (ATM) switching as the underlying technology for a variety of broadband services.

At the desktop, low-cost 100VG-AnyLAN will provide 100 Mbps performance that can be shared by a workgroup for data and multimedia traffic over existing voice-grade unshielded twisted-pair (UTP) cable. Designed as the natural evolution of 10Base-T — today's most widely installed LAN technology — VG will be the upgrade technology of choice for the workgroup with requirements for increased bandwidth and/or emerging multimedia applications support. Migration to VG from legacy Ethernets is accomplished using simple speed-matching bridges. VG not only offers 10 times the data performance of Ethernet, but low latency and traffic congestion control for multimedia applications at prices that are only slightly higher than Ethernet.

Fibre channel (FC) is a high-speed connection designed to support the mass storage requirements of multicomputer clusters. It offers scalable bandwidth to support data rates ranging from 266 Mbps to gigabit-per-second rates over coaxial cable for short hauls and optical fiber for distances up to 10 km. These links, coupled with FC's high speed, low-delay switching fabric — which supports simultaneous virtual circuit connections and packet switching — will

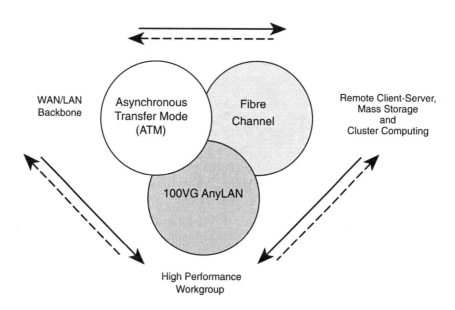

Figure 13-2: HP Technology Triad

consolidate mass storage and network traffic on flexible topologies, including support for high availability configurations.

ATM is well suited to backbone applications and will provide seamless integration of campus LAN backbones with emerging ATM-based WANs. For high-end clients, ATM will deliver data, voice and video to the desktop with dedicated bandwidth links using UTP and optical fiber. ATM transmission rates range from 25 Mbps over UTP to 155/622 Mbps over fiber optic links, providing numerous connectivity options for workstations, servers and backbones. ATM can even accommodate other high-speed services such as frame relay and switched multimegabit data services (SMDS). The switched, dedicated bandwidth of ATM scales easily as network traffic increases, making ATM a strategic investment for high-performance multimedia enterprise networks.

This triad of technologies will form the foundation of the networked computing infrastructure of the future. HP will offer solutions in each, while providing a robust integration of all three where and when they exist together. By directing its attention on the lower layers of the communications protocol stack, HP has positioned itself to meet the diverse, high-bandwidth needs of users with current and emerging network technologies, which also will be manageable by OpenView.

IN OPENVIEW, HP HAS PRODUCED A WELL-ENGINEERED MANAGEMENT platform. The company participates in a comprehensive, well-orchestrated support structure that promises to ensure the long-term success of the platform. HP's Premier Partners program is one of the most effective in the industry. Today, there are more third-party applications that work under OpenView than any other network management platform.

In addition, the company's participation in the OpenView Users Forum keeps it abreast of customer needs. (HP responds within 90 days to the Forum's recommendations for platform improvements.) HP's involvement in emerging broadband technologies, as well as legacy LANs and the internetworking environment through hubs and bridge/routers, and its leadership role in the standards process, reinforce the widespread opinion that OpenView is and will remain the management platform of choice long into the future.

APPENDIX
A

Organizations Mentioned

ADC Fibermux Corp.
21415 Plummer St.
Chatsworth, CA 91311
818-709-6000 (tel)
818-709-1556 (fax)

Cabletron Systems
35 Industrial Way
Rochester, NH 03866-5005
603-332-9400 (tel)
603-332-7386 (fax)

Chipcom Corp.
118 Turnpike Rd.
Southborough, MA 01772
508-460-8900 (tel)
508-460-8950 (fax)

Cisco Systems Inc.
170 W. Tasman Dr.
San Jose, CA 95134
800-326-1941
415-526-4000 (tel)
415-526-4100 (fax)

Computer Associates International Inc.
One Computer Associates Plaza
Islandia, NY 11788-7000
800-325-5324
516-342-5224 (tel)
516-342-6866 (fax)

Digital Equipment Corp.
Digital Dr.
Merrimack, NH 03054-9501
800-344-4825

Hewlett-Packard Co.
Network and Systems Management Division
3404 East Harmony Rd., M/S 45
Fort Collins, CO 80525
800-637-7740

IBM Corp.
Old Orchard Rd.
Armonk, NY 10504
800-426-2255
914-965-1900 (tel)

Intel Corp.
Personal Computer Enhancement Division
5200 N.E. Elam Young Pkwy.
Hillsboro, OR 97124-6497
800-538-3373
503-629-7354 (tel)
503-629-7580 (fax)

ISICAD, Inc.
1920 West Corporate Way
Anaheim, CA 92803-6122
800-634-1223
714-533-8910 (tel)
714-533-8642 (fax)

Microsoft Corp.
One Microsoft Way
Redmond, WA 98052-6399
800-426-9400
206-882-8080 (tel)

NetLabs Inc.
4920 El Camino Real
Los Altos, CA 94022
800-447-9300
415-961-9500 (tel)
415-961-9300 (fax)

Novell, Inc.
122 E. 1700 South
Provo, UT 84606
800-453-1267
801-429-7000 (tel)
801-429-5155 (fax)

OpenView Forum
P.O. Box 77046
San Francisco, CA 94107
800-538-6680 (tel)
415-512-0865 (tel outside U.S.)
415-512-1325 (fax)

Open Software Foundation Inc.
11 Cambridge Center
Cambridge, MA 02142
617-621-8700 (tel)
617-621-0799 (fax)

Peregrine Systems, Inc.
1959 Palomar Oaks Way
Carlsbad, CA 92009
619-431-2400 (tel)
619-431-0696 (fax)

Remedy Corp.
1505 Salado Dr.
Mountain View, CA 94043
415-903-5200 (tel)
415-903-9001 (fax)

SynOptics Communications Corp. (Bay Networks)
4401 Great American Pkwy.
Santa Clara, CA 95052
408-988-2400 (tel)
408-988-5525 (fax)

Ungermann-Bass, Inc.
3900 Freedom Circle
Santa Clara, CA 95054
800-777-4526
408-496-0111 (tel)
408-970-7337 (fax)

UNIX System Laboratories Inc.
190 River Rd.
Summit, NJ 07901
908-522-6000 (tel)

Wellfleet Communications Corp.
8 Federal St.
Billerica, MA 01821
508-670-8888 (tel)
508-436-3658 (fax)

Acronyms

ANSI	American National Standards Institute
API	Application Programming Interface
APPC	Advanced Program-to-Program Communications (IBM Corp.)
ARP	Address Resolution Protocol
ARS	Action Request System (Remedy Systems Inc.)
ASCII	American Standard Code for Information Interchange
ASM	Automated Storage Management
ASN.1	Abstract Syntax Notation 1
AT&T	American Telephone & Telegraph
ATM	Asynchronous Transfer Mode
BER	Bit Error Rate
BELLCORE	Bell Communications Research
BIOS	Basic Input-Output System
BOC	Bell Operating Company
BootP	Boot Protocol
BPDU	Bridge Protocol Data Unit
BPS	Bits Per Second
BSC	Binary Synchronous Communications
CA	Computer Associates International Inc.
CAD	Computer Aided Design
CAM	Computer Aided Manufacturing
CCITT	Consultative Committee for International Telegraphy and Telephony
CD-ROM	Compact Disk-Read Only Memory
CDRM	Cross Domain Resource Manager (IBM Corp.)
CDRSC	Cross Domain Resources (IBM Corp.)
CGM	Computer Graphics Metafile
CLIST	Command List (IBM Corp.)
CMIP	Common Management Information Protocol

CMIS	Common Management Information Service
CMISE	Common Management Information Service Element
CMOL	CMIP over Logical Link Control
CMOT	CMIP over TCP/IP
CPE	Customer Premises Equipment
CPU	Central Processing Unit
CRC	Cyclic Redundancy Check
DA	Destination Address
DAT	Digital Audio Tape
DBMS	Data Base Management System
DCE	Distributed Computing Environment
DDS	Digital Data System
DEC	Digital Equipment Corp.
DECmcc	DEC management control center (Digital Equipment Corp.)
DM	Distributed Management
DME	Distributed Management Environment
DOS	Disk Operating System
DS-0	Digital Signal — Level Zero
DS-1	Digital Signal — Level One
DS-3	Digital Signal — Level Three
DSI	Data Source Integration (Hewlett-Packard Co.)
DXF	Drawing Interchange File
EASE	Embedded Advanced Sampling Environment (Hewlett-Packard Co.)
EBCDIC	Extended Binary Coded Decimal Interchange Code
EGP	External Gateway Protocol
EISA	Extended Industry Standard Architecture
EMA	Enterprise Management Architecture (Digital Equipment Corp.)
EMAIL	Electronic Mail
EMS	Element Management System
4GL	Fourth-Generation Language
FC	Fibre Channel
FCS	Frame Check Sequence
FDDI	Fiber Distributed Data Interface
FEP	Front-End Processor
FT1	Fractional T1

GIF	Graphics Image File
GNMP	Government Network Management Profile
GUI	Graphical User Interface
HP	Hewlett-Packard Co.
HSM	Hierarchical Storage Management
ICMP	Internet Control Message Protocol
ID	Identification
I/O	Input/Output
IDP	Internetwork Datagram Protocol (Xerox Corp.)
IEEE	Institute of Electrical and Electronic Engineers
IETF	Internet Engineering Task Force
IGES	Initial Graphics Exchange Format
IGP	Interior Gateway Protocol
IMS	Internetwork Management System (CrossComm Corp.)
IMS/VS	Information Management System/Virtual Storage (IBM Corp.)
IP	Internet Protocol
IPD	Installed Products Database (Hewlett-Packard Co.)
IPX	Internet Packet Exchange
IS	Information System
ISO	International Organization for Standardization
IT	Information Technology
ITU-TSS	International Telecommunications Union-Telecommunications Standardization Sector (formerly, CCITT)
JFIF	JPEG File Interchange Format
JPEG	Joint Photographic Experts Group
K	(Kilo) One Thousand (e.g., kbps)
KB	Kilobyte
LAN	Local Area Network
LAT	Local Area Transport (Digital Equipment Corp.)
LU	Logical Unit (IBM Corp.)
LZW	Lempel-ZivWelch (compression algorithm)
M	(Mega) One Million (e.g., Mbps)
MAC	Media Access Control

MB	Megabyte
MGPT	Machine Generated Problem Tracking (Computer Associates International, Inc.)
MIB	Management Information Base
MIC	Management Integration Consortium
MIT	Massachusetts Institute of Technology
MUX	Multiplexer
NAU	Network Addressable Unit (IBM Corp.)
NCP	Network Control Program (IBM Corp.)
NFS	Network File System
NIC	Network Interface Card
NICE	Network Information and Control Exchange (Digital Equipment Corp.)
NIST	National Institute of Standards and Technology
NLM	NetWare Loadable Module (Novell Inc.)
NMO	Network Management Option
NMS	NetWare Management System (Novell, Inc.)
NMS	Network Management System
NMVT	Network Management Vector Transport (IBM Corp.)
NNM	Network Node Manager (Hewlett-Packard Co.)
NOS	Network Operating System
NAUN	Nearest Active Upstream Neighbor
ODBC	Open Data Base Connectivity (Microsoft Corp.)
ODI	Open Datalink Interface (Novell, Inc.)
OEM	Original Equipment Manufacturer
OMA	Object Management Architecture
OMF	Object Management Framework
OMG	Object Management Group
OMT	Object Modeling Technology (Ungermann-Bass, Inc.)
ORB	Object Request Broker
OS	Operating System
OS/2	Operating System/2 (IBM)
OSF	Open Software Foundation
OSI	Open Systems Interconnection
OTS	OSI Transport Services (Hewlett-Packard Co.)
OVw	OpenView Windows
PAD	Packet Assembler-Disassembler
PBX	Private Branch Exchange

PC	Personal Computer
PCL	Printer Control Language
PIU	Path Information Unit (Peregrine Systems, Inc.)
PMA	Performance Management and Accounting (Computer Associates International, Inc.)
PRM	Process Resource Manager (Hewlett-Packard Co.)
PU	Physical Unit (IBM Corp.)
RAM	Random Access Memory
RARP	Reverse Address Resolution Protocol
RDBMS	Relational Data Base Management System
RFC	Request for Comment
RFI	Radio Frequency Interference
RIP	Routing Information Protocol
RISC	Reduced Instruction Set Computing
RMON	Remote Monitoring
ROM	Read Only Memory
RPC	Remote Procedure Call
RX	Receive
SA	Source Address
SAM	System Administration Manager (Hewlett-Packard Co.)
SDS	Software Distribution Services (Hewlett-Packard Co.)
SFD	Start Frame Delimiter
SMDS	Switched Multimegabit Data Services
SMT	Station Management
SNMP	Simple Network Management Protocol
SNA	Systems Network Architecture
SNI	SNA Network Interconnect (IBM Corp.)
SPARC	Scalable Processing Architecture (Sun Microsystems, Inc.)
SPX	Synchronous Packet Exchange (Novell, Inc.)
SQL	Structured Query Language
SSCP	System Services Control Point (IBM Corp.)
SSCP/PU	System Services Control Point/Physical Unit (IBM Corp.)
STP	Spanning Tree Protocol
T1	Transmission service at the DS-1 rate of 1.544 Mbps
T3	Transmission service at the DS-3 rate of 44.736 Mbps
TCP	Transmission Control Protocol

TIFF	Tagged Image File Format
TME	Tivoli Management Environment (Tivoli Systems, Inc.)
TSO	Time Sharing Option (IBM Corp.)
TSR	Terminal Stay Resident
TX	Transmit
UDP	User Datagram Protocol
UDP/IP	User Datagram Protocol/Internet Protocol
U/L	Upper/Lower
UNMA	Unified Network Management Architecture (AT&T)
UTP	Unshield Twisted-Pair
VAP	Value Added Process (Novell Inc.)
VG	Voice Grade
VMS	Virtual Machine System (Digital Equipment Corp.)
VT	Virtual Terminal
VTAM	Virtual Telecommunications Access Method (IBM Corp.)
WAN	Wide Area Network
XBM	X11 Bitmap
XMP	X/Open Management Protocol
XNS	Xerox Network System (Xerox Corp.)
XOM	X/Open Object Manipulation
XWD	X11 Window Dump

Index

Benefit from these other CBM Books!

Multimedia Exploration: Working with Tools, Tips, Products and Sources

Jamie Showrank
$39, Softcover, 270 pages
ISBN 1-878956-42-6

Multimedia Exploration shows readers how to get started in creating multimedia applications and sharing multimedia files over a network. It explains how to use multimedia resources and develop CD-ROM titles. The text also includes a CD-ROM for hands-on training.

Client/Server Programming in PC LANs

Ed Barfield and Brian Walters
$45, Softcover, 450 pages
ISBN 1-878956-44-2

Designed as a tutorial for beginning-to-intermediate level developers of sockets and named pipes programs in a PC LAN environment, this book teaches how to program TCP and IPX sockets, NT named pipes and the NetBIOS API in a client/server network. This book also demonstrates how to apply a Visual C++ class model to Windows sockets programming using Microsoft's Visual C++ application.

PATHWORKS V5 Network Administration Guide

Ed Barfield
$39, Softcover, 360 pages
ISBN 1-878956-49-3

This book highlights the fundamentals of managing, tuning and troubleshooting a PATHWORKS V5 LAN Manager Domain. Topics include PC, DOS/Windows client configuration, domain security, network tuning and troubleshooting, license management and domain management with ManageWorks, Netadmin and Digital's Admin/PATHWORKS menu and the NET command-line interfaces.

Ethernet Tips and Techniques: For Designing, Installing, and Troubleshooting Your Ethernet Network, 2nd Edition

Byron Spinney
$15, Softcover, 120 pages
ISBN 1-878956-43-4.

Installing an Ethernet network begins with *Ethernet Tips and Techniques, 2nd Edition*. This how-to guide is the starting point for anyone who needs to install an Ethernet network. With clear, concise definitions, this book covers: an introduction to Ethernet, an introduction to transceivers, repeaters, bridges, hubs, routers and gateways, the three basic rules of design, methods of installation, and how to maintain an Ethernet network once it's completed.

Total SNMP: Exploring the Simple Network Management Protocol

Sean Harnedy
$45, Softcover, 656 pages
ISBN 1-878956-33-7

This book provides useful information and practice on mastering the dynamics of SNMP. It is intended for anyone interested in the use of the SNMP framework as a Network Management Solution.

Introduction To UNIX by Philip E. Bourne

VHS Video, Length: 4 1/2 Hours
$299

Invite Dr. Philip E. Bourne into you home or office. Understand the principles behind the UNIX philosophy with this 4 1/2 hour VHS video and an easy-to-follow workbook

Your CBM Books Order Form

For fast, easy ordering. . .
- Toll Free 1-800-285-1755 ■ FAX (215) 643-8099
- Through CompuServe Mail — User ID 76702,1564

Title		Quantity	Subtotal
Focus on OpenView: A Guide to Hewlett-Packard's Network and Systems Management Platform 1-5 books $40 each			
6-15 books SAVE 15%! $34 each			
16-49 books SAVE 30%! $28 each			
50 + books SAVE 40%! $24 each			
Multimedia Exploration: Working with Tools, Tips, Products and Sources $39			
Client/Server Programming in PC LANs $45			
Pathworks V5 Network Administration Guide $39			
Ethernet Tips and Techniques: For Designing, Installing and Troubleshooting Your Ethernet Network, 2nd Edition $15			
Total SNMP: Exploring the Simple Network Management Protocol $45			
Introduction to UNIX (VHS video) $299			
PA residents add 6% sales tax.			
Handling Charge			$1.50
UPS shipping: In the U.S., $4 for the first book, $2 for each additional book. Outside the U.S., please call (215) 643-8105 for shipping information.			
TOTAL ORDER			

Name _____

Title _____

Company _____

Street Address (required) _____

City _____ State _____ Zip _____

Country _____

Telephone (_____) _____ FAX (_____) _____

☐ Payment enclosed $_____ (payable to Cardinal Business Media Inc.)

Charge to: ☐ [MasterCard] MasterCard ☐ [VISA] VISA ☐ [AMERICAN EXPRESS] American Express

Account #: _____ Exp. Date _____

Signature _____ Date _____

☐ **Please send me a FREE catalog.**

Mail to: **CBM Books**
1300 Virginia Drive, Suite 400
Fort Washington, PA 19034

Satisfaction Guaranteed!

CBM Books Money Back Guarantee: CBM Books guarantees all books. If you are not completely satisfied with your selection, for any reason, return it within 30 days for a refund.

FOBI0495